'This is a provocative book in the best sense of the word. The exploitation of nature and the exploitation of labour are two sides of the same capitalist dynamic; effective resistance to both requires a common struggle in which green activists and trade unionists combine as equal partners.'

Richard Hyman, London School of Economics and Political Science, UK

'Environmental Labour studies is a young and burgeoning research field. This book is a landmark publication offering the first theoretically and empirically brilliant analysis of trade union's actions for climate change in the UK, suggesting that the workers' movement can become an environmental innovator in the struggle for climate justice.'

Nora Räthzel, Umeå University, Sweden

'Paul Hampton's analysis is built on a thorough review of mainstream and radical literature on the politics of climate change, together with an in depth narrative of worker and trade union attempts to grapple with climate change and the various forms of 'green capitalism' thinking in the UK context.'

Paul Burkett, Indiana State University, USA

'Who has the interest and power to confront the apocalyptic dangers of global warming, and the vested interests blocking mitigation? This book tackles the largely ignored question of agency. Theoretically sophisticated and empirically thorough, it explores the potential of the working class and its organisations to lead an effective response.'

Constance Lever-Tracy, University of South Australia, Australia

'Paul Hampton has assembled a wealth of evidence to demonstrate that trade unions are not only becoming increasingly important participants in climate change debates, but important actors in contributing to a more sustainable planet. This book deserves to be read by all those who profess to be interested not only in climate change and the environment, but also labour studies.'

David Uzzell, University of Surrey, UK

'A ground-breaking book on the most timely of topics: how workers and their trade unions are organising in order to fuse struggles for social justice and against climate change. Highly recommended to anyone interested in environmental politics, industrial relations, social movements and sustainable development.'

Romain Felli, University of Geneva and Swiss National Science Foundation, Switzerland

'At last a book arguing that presents convincing evidence of climate-conscious trade unionism, whether through environmental representatives or bargaining for a just transition, inspiring us all to become strategic climate actors.'

˄ inda Clarke, University of Westminster, UK

T0300525

Workers and Trade Unions for Climate Solidarity

This book is a theoretically rich and empirically grounded account of UK trade union engagement with climate change over the last three decades. It offers a rigorous critique of the mainstream neoliberal and ecological modernisation approaches, extending the concepts of Marxist social and employment relations theory to the climate realm. The book applies insights from employment relations to the political economy of climate change, developing a model for understanding trade union behaviour over climate matters. The strong interdisciplinary approach draws together lessons from both physical and social science, providing an original empirical investigation into the climate politics of the UK trade union movement from high-level officials down to workplace climate representatives, from issues of climate jobs to workers' climate action.

Workers and Trade Unions for Climate Solidarity will be of great interest to students and researchers in environmental politics, climate change and environmental sociology.

Paul Hampton received his PhD in climate change and employment relations from London Metropolitan University. He is head of research and policy at the Fire Brigades Union in the UK.

Routledge Studies in Climate, Work and Society

In *The Routledge Studies in Climate, Work and Society* series, scholars and other thinkers at the forefront of constructing a strategic link between work and climate change contribute to identifying the issues, evaluating policies and silences, tracking change, and stimulating international exchange of ideas and experience. Collectively, the books in this series will emphasise fresh thinking, strategic creativity, international and inter-sectoral comparisons and contribute to the further development of the role of work in societal responses to global warming.

Series Editor: Dr. Carla Lipsig-Mummé, Professor of Work and Labour Studies, York University, Canada.

Editorial Board:

Professor Elaine Bernard, Executive Director, Labor and Worklife Program Harvard Law School, Harvard University, US

Professor Emeritus Richard Hyman, Industrial Relations, London School of Economics and Political Science UK

Dr. Kenneth Odero, Climate XL-Africa, Kenya

Workers and Trade Unions for Climate Solidarity
Tackling climate change in a neoliberal world
Paul Hampton

Workers and Trade Unions for Climate Solidarity

Tackling climate change in a neoliberal world

Paul Hampton

LONDON AND NEW YORK

First published 2015 by Routledge

2 Park Square, Milton Park, Abingdon, Oxon OX14 4RN
711 Third Avenue, New York, NY 10017, USA

Routledge is an imprint of the Taylor & Francis Group, an informa business

First issued in paperback 2016

British Library Cataloguing-in-Publication Data
A catalogue record for this book is available from the British Library

Library of Congress Cataloging-in-Publication Data
Hampton, Paul Stephen.
Workers and trade unions for climate solidarity : tackling climate change
in a neoliberal world / Paul Hampton.
pages cm
1. Climatic changes--Political aspects--Great Britain.
2. Climatic changes--Economic aspects--Great Britain. 3. Environmental
policy--Great Britain. 4. Labor unions--Political activity--Great Britain. I. Title.
QC903.2.G7H36 2015
363.738'740941--dc23
2014047322

ISBN: 978-1-138-84142-0 (hbk)
ISBN: 978-1-138-28363-3 (pbk)

Typeset in Goudy
by Taylor & Francis Books

For Elliott, whose future depends on solidarity

Contents

Foreword

"If the questions of employment and human resources are not more closely integrated into climate policies, we may expect them to become a major barrier to the transformations demanded".

Sylvie Dupressoir *et al.* 2007

"While there has been considerable research on the role of employers as climate actors, the actual and potential role for workers has been largely overlooked. Yet workers, organised in trade unions generally represent the largest voluntary organisations within states and historically have been great forces for progress.... Unions offer a potential pole around which a revived climate movement might coalesce."

Paul Hampton 2015

Climate change has already shaken up the nature of work and the distribution of employment within and between countries, regions and communities. It is changing how we work, what we produce, and where we can produce it. It disrupts the lives of workers and the global supply chains of transnational corporations, undermines governments and creates a new class of precarity—climate migrants. But at the same time as global warming destroys livelihoods and communities, it is forcing the emergence of new alliances: between labour and youth movements, labour and environmental groups, labour and professional associations, and in some countries, labour and first nations. These new labour-environmental alliances, although volatile, are revitalizing the much abused idea of a just transition for labour. Originally a visionary statement of labour's autonomy in crafting its struggle to slow global warming, over the past 15 years just transition has shrunk to mean no more than fair remuneration for job loss because of climate change, and adaptive training for "greener" jobs.

Now, however, as just transition emerges from its defensive slide, it is broadening again to include root-and-branch transformation of the labour process, the social relations of work, and the relation between work, workers, unions and the environment.

However, although much writing, scholarly and otherwise, has been devoted to the role of corporate leaders in 'going green', the silence about the capacity of workers and their unions to actually make the changes that will slow global warming, is frankly astonishing.

It is here that Paul Hampton's book makes its pathbreaking contribution. Focusing squarely on "bringing labour back into climate politics" his analysis is multi-scalar: broad, deep, and focused. It ranges from the political economy of climate change to a sociology of strikes, bringing out what labour environmentalism shares with community unionism and social movement unionism. But as convincing as his analysis of the Vestas occupation is on the necessity of autonomy for unions in climate action and the value of organizational merging in certain strikes, Hampton also leaves us with what seems to be a universal caveat in the union world: climate action yes, but keep your distance from how we unions operate internally.

In sum, Paul Hampton's pioneering book argues for the necessity of linking greening work with democratizing its control, with organized labour as key actor and driver. The breadth of his vision and the elegance with which he melds methodologies opens the doors for the next generation of labour environmentalist research.

Carla Lipsig-Mummé
Toronto, Canada

Preface and acknowledgements

The fear is that Hegel was right about knowledge and collective action. If the Owl of Minerva takes flight only as dusk begins to fall, then human society may have already missed the opportunity to avoid dangerous climate change. This book is written in the hope that it is not too late – and with the conviction that organised labour can play a central role in global political efforts to reduce greenhouse gas emissions.

Authors are often lucky to experience a stimulating intellectual panorama and I have been fortunate to stand on some lofty shoulders. This book is based on research for a PhD awarded by London Metropolitan University. I would like to thank my supervisors Steve Jefferys, Sian Moore, Allan Williams, Nigel Morter and Mary Davis, who guided me through the arduous process. David Uzzell and Sonia McKay conducted an exacting viva, providing valuable critical comments. I am grateful to the librarians at the TUC Library and at the London School of Economics, who assisted with obtaining important texts.

I thank the scores of socialists, trade unionists, climate activists and scholars who have kindly shared their expertise, criticism and solidarity with me. I must register the political, moral and financial support provided by the Labour Research Department and the Fire Brigades Union, where I was employed during the research. I am grateful to Philip Pearson at the TUC for his advice and comments on the manuscript and to the TUC for access to source materials. At Routledge, Louisa Earls, Beth Wright, Annabelle Harris, Susan Dunsmore and Siobhán Greaney contributed vital editorial guidance. Diane and Peter Hampton have given unflagging backing throughout my life, while Mark Hampton understood ecology long before I did. Claire Standring and Elliott Hampton sustained my research and deserve special thanks. Errors or omissions are my responsibility.

Tackling climate change requires Gramsci's 'permanently active persuaders', intellectuals of a new type, rooted in powerful social movements. An effective climate movement must be underlaboured by physical science evidence, but its strategies and political conclusions should follow from grounded social-scientific assessments. I hope this book will provoke debate, particularly in the labour movement and between climate scholars and campaigners. Liberty is above all for dissenters who think differently. We should cherish the right to tell people what they do not want to hear and the 'concrete utopianism' of those who conceive of hitherto unactualised possibilities. If workers and their organisations make climate change a core concern, then this work will have served its purpose.

London, December 2014

Abbreviations

Unions and Union Federations

AEEU   Amalgamated Engineering and Electrical Union. Merged with MSF to form Amicus in 2001

AFL-CIO   American Federation of Labor and Congress of Industrial Organizations

Amicus Union formed in 2001 from AEEU and MSF. Merged with TGWU to form Unite in 2007

ASLEF   Associated Society of Locomotive Engineers and Firemen

ASTMS   Association of Scientific, Technical and Managerial Staffs. Merged with TASS to form MSF in 1988

AUT   Association of University Teachers. Merged with NATFHE to form UCU in 2006

BACM-TEAM   British Association of Colliery Management – Technical, Energy and Administrative Management

BALPA   British Air Line Pilots Association

BECTU   Broadcasting, Entertainment, Cinematograph and Theatre Union

Community formed in 2004 through the merger of the ISTC and KFAT

Connect Communications professionals union. Joined Prospect in 2010

CPSA   Civil and Public Services Association – merged with PTC to form PCS in 1998

CWU   Communication Workers Union formed in 1995

EMA   Engineers and Managers Association. Merged with IPMS to form Prospect in 2001

ETUC   European Trade Union Confederation

FBU   Fire Brigades Union

GMB   General, Municipal, Boilermakers and Allied Trades Union

ICEM   International Federation of Chemical, Energy, Mine and General Workers' Unions, now IndustriALL

ICFTU   International Confederation of Free Trade Unions. Merged with WCL to form ITUC in 2006

IPMS   Institution of Professionals Managers and Specialists. Merged with EMA to form Prospect in 2001

ISTC	Iron and Steel Trades Confederation. Merged with KFAT to form Community in 2004
ITUC	International Trade Union Confederation. Formed in 2006 through the merger of ICFTU and WCL
KFAT	National Union of Knitwear, Footwear and Apparel Trades. Merged with ISTC to form Community in 2004
MSF	Manufacturing, Science and Finance union. Merged with AEEU to form Amicus in 2001
MU	Musicians' Union
NATFHE	National Association of Teachers in Further and Higher Education. Merged with AUT to form UCU in 2006
NUM	National Union of Mineworkers
NUR	National Union of Railwaymen. Merged with NUS to form RMT in 1990
NUS	National Union of Seamen. Merged with NUR to form RMT in 1990
NUT	National Union of Teachers
PCS	Public and Commercial Services Union. Formed in 1998 through the merger of CPSA and PTC

Prospect formed in 2001 through the merger of IPMS and EMA

PTC	Public Services, Tax and Commerce union. Merged with CPSA to form PCS in 1998
RMT	National Union of Rail, Maritime and Transport Workers. Formed in 1990 through the merger of NUR and NUS
TASS	Technical, Administrative and Supervisory Section. Merged with ASTMS to form MSF in 1988
TGWU	Transport and General Workers' Union. Merged with Amicus to form Unite in 2007
TSSA	Transport Salaried Staffs' Association
TUC	Trades Union Congress
UCATT	Union of Construction, Allied Trades and Technicians
UCU	University and College Union. Formed in 2006 through the merger of AUT and NATFHE

Unison Public services union formed in 1993
Unite formed in 2007 through the merger of Amicus and TGWU

| USDAW | Union of Shop, Distributive and Allied Workers |
| WCL | World Confederation of Labour. Merged with ICFTU to form ITUC in 2006 |

Other abbreviations

| ACAS | Advisory, Conciliatory and Arbitration Service |
| AWL | Alliance for Workers' Liberty |

BERR	Department for Business, Enterprise and Regulatory Reform
BIS	Department for Business, Innovation and Skills
BWEA	British Wind Energy Association
CBI	Confederation of British Industry
CCC	Committee on Climate Change
CCL	Climate Change Levy
CCS	carbon capture and storage
CCSA	Carbon Capture and Storage Association
CO_2	carbon dioxide
COP	Conference of the Parties
CRC	Carbon Reduction Commitment
DECC	Department for Energy and Climate Change
Defra	Department for the Environment, Farming and Rural Affairs
DETR	Department of the Environment, Transport and the Regions
DfT	Department for Transport
EAC	Environmental Audit Committee
ETS	Emissions Trading Scheme
EU	European Union
IEA	International Energy Agency
ILO	International Labour Organisation
IPCC	Intergovernmental Panel on Climate Change
LRD	Labour Research Department
MECW	*Marx/Engels Collected Works*
NGO	non-governmental organisation
OECD	Organisation for Economic Cooperation and Development
RO	Renewables Obligation
SWP	Socialist Workers Party
TUSDAC	Trade Union Sustainable Development Advisory Committee
UK	United Kingdom
UMF	Union Modernisation Fund
UNEP	United Nations Environment Programme
UNFCCC	United Nations Framework Convention on Climate Change

1   Introduction

The early decades of the twenty-first century are the best of times and the worst of times for climate change politics. It is the age of climate science, but also the age of stupidity. It is the era of inconvenient truths, but nonetheless one of climate denial. It should be the springtime of hope, yet often resembles the winter of despair. The failure is not principally due to the physical science evidence for climate change, which as a scientific hypothesis is increasingly robust, though still evolving and variously contested. Reports by the Intergovernmental Panel on Climate Change (IPCC) articulate the widely held but conservative consensus on the physical science of climate change: the climate system is now warming significantly and is likely to continue, human activities are the major cause of it and potentially serious impacts are likely (Barker 2008; Dietz *et al.* 2007).

The fifth IPCC report predicts significant increases in surface warming and sea temperatures by the end of this century. It identifies 'severe, widespread and irreversible' impacts on natural systems, water resources, species, crop yields, human health, social processes (including gender, class, ethnicity, age and disability), extreme weather, poverty and violent conflicts at the global, regional, national and local scales (IPCC 2013; 2014a; 2014b; 2014c: 33). The IPCC suggests a range of technologies and measures to mitigate greenhouse gas emissions, along with steps to adapt to extreme weather and other current effects. The United Nations Framework Convention on Climate Change (UNFCCC) identifies a 2°C increase as constituting 'dangerous climate change' and is orchestrating annual Conferences of the Parties (COPs). While the UNFCCC heralds the need for a paradigm shift towards a low-carbon society, such a transition is presently a long way from reality.

The impasse of contemporary climate politics

The current political response to climate change is not commensurate with the identified risks. Global greenhouse gas emissions have risen rapidly in recent decades, and more than half the carbon budget has already been burned, if global warming is to be limited to 2°C (McKibben 2012). Leading climate scientists warn that there is now little or no chance of maintaining the global mean surface temperature at or below this tipping point. They argue that 2°C 'now more appropriately represents the threshold between "dangerous" and "extremely dangerous" climate change' (Anderson and Bows 2011: 20). After more than a quarter of a century of international conferences, virtually nothing of substance has been achieved to tackle climate change. Instead, a potential era of energy abundance has emerged, where fossil fuels from conventional and unconventional sources remain dominant (Helm 2013). If global society embarks on another golden age of fossil fuels and no significant action is taken soon, then much of the energy infrastructure will be locked in for decades and mitigation targets will not be met (IEA 2012). This extreme energy scenario threatens to derail global efforts to prevent dangerous climate change.

Bringing society and politics back into climate change

Over three decades ago, Stephen Schneider (1983: 9, 17) proposed a multidisciplinary approach to climate change, because 'at the very base of the pyramid of CO_2 issues is neither physics nor chemistry nor biology, but rather social science'. He argued that it is 'society that is the subject of research – not climate'. Subsequently, scholars across a range of disciplines have made passionate demands for social science expertise to become the focus of climate research, including radical proposals for a 'new science of deliberate transformation' to supplement current research on climate mitigation and adaptation (Rayner and Malone 1998; Lever-Tracy 2010; O'Brien 2012: 668).

Some social theorists recognise the contemporary stalemate. Climate change politics proceeds on the basis of 'an extraordinarily limited understanding of the social world' and is for the most part 'untouched by theoretical debate of any kind at all' (Shove 2010: 278). The dominant climate frames are 'an expert and elitist discourse in which peoples, societies, citizens, workers, voters and their interests, views and voices are very much neglected'. Climate change politics often concentrates on the post-hoc consequences and 'ignores the conditions and causes which produce and reproduce the climatic (and other) problems' (Beck 2010: 254–5, 260). The Stern Review contains 'no analysis of power or of the tense nature of international relations'. In short, 'we have no politics of climate change' (Giddens 2009: 201, 4).

The roots of this predicament are deep. Erik Swyngedouw (2010: 219) is scathing about the hegemonic framings of climate change, which invoke 'a common condition or predicament, the need for common humanity-wide action [and] mutual collaboration'. There are no social tensions or internal generative conflicts: global humanity is called into being as political subject, thereby 'disavowing the radical heterogeneity and antagonisms that cut through "the people"'. Climate change discourse does not currently have a 'positively embodied name or signifier; it does not call a political subject into being that stands in for the universality of egalitarian democratic demands' (ibid.: 223). Climate change challenges the dominant political economy all the way down, hence the demand for a radical reframing by many climate activists.

Climate change has been conceptualised in positivist, constructivist and post-modernist terms (Bolin 2007; Demeritt 2001; Glover 2006). Even those who see climate change as an urgent issue for the most part lack a framework to coherently incorporate the findings of physical sciences and to integrate those findings into political discourse and action. Critical realists propose a philosophical framework to support climate change, which encompasses 'an ontology that ranges from the metatheory of so-called hard sciences through biology and evolutionary theory, to social sciences, to a critical engagement with the "cultural turn" and the importance of discourse to human action and identity and action' (Bhaskar and Parker 2010: viii). This approach emphasises the interdependence of natural and social worlds, the stratified depth of reality, the importance of generative mechanisms and critical engagement with different theories. The critical realist interpretation is highly applicable to climate change, because it promulgates an ontology centred on the reality of the material dimension of the problem, together with an epistemology that recognises the social dimensions of knowledge. Such a theory can coherently combine the capacities of natural systems with the power of human beings to take transformative action.

Climate change is in its infancy so far as critical social and political theory is concerned. Most orthodox epistemologies (including ecological theory[1]) suffer from an apparent dualism between nature and politics, an anthropocentric estrangement that hampers engagement with the significance of climate change (Latour 2004). Many economists proceed as if 'society is almost independent of nature' (Schneider 1997: 134). Monetary values tend to understate the urgency of the climate problem. Some of the most important benefits of mitigation have no meaningful prices, while most economic models minimise costs by suggesting that a little bit of global warming would be good for us. Compressing the potential damage wrought by climate change into a single price of carbon fails to capture the manifold effects (Ackerman 2009). If climate change is perceived as a failure of markets, this implies that 'it is market entrepreneurs, economists and businesses that need to take the lead in "correcting" this failure'. But if it is framed as a challenge to individual and corporate behaviour, then this suggests 'very different cohorts of actors should be mobilised' (Hulme 2009: 226–7).

Mature political science requires a mode of analysis and a corresponding social ontology 'capable of reconciling structural and agential factors within a single explanation'. Structure and agency are not so much a problem as 'a language by which ontological differences between contending accounts might be registered'. Structure includes context and refers to the setting within which social, political and economic events occur and acquire meaning, while agency refers to action, specifically political conduct. Agency can be defined as 'the ability or capacity of an actor to act consciously and, in so doing, to attempt to realise his or her intentions' (Hay 2002: 113, 91–4). The relevance of structure and agency to climate politics has been recognised by some scholars (Berkhout and Hertin 2000; McLaughlin and Dietz 2008; Okereke *et al.* 2009). However, this has not resulted in greater clarity about the structures that might constrain or enable action, nor which agents might constitute the privileged subject of change. Jessop (2007: 41) proposes a promising reconciliation of structure and agency known as the strategic-relational approach, which involves identifying strategic actors within a 'strategically selective context'. In this book, I magnify the potential of workers and their organisations as strategic climate actors.

Bringing labour back into climate change

Marxism: class, emancipation, democracy

This book proposes a Marxist interpretation of climate change politics. This conception is best summed up in the rules of the First International, that 'the emancipation of the working classes must be conquered by the working classes themselves' (Marx 1985: 14). Working-class self-liberation is at the heart of Marxism (Draper 1978). In his early work, Marx evoked the idea that 'the emancipation of the workers contains universal human emancipation', while shortly before his death, he argued that 'the emancipation of the producing class is that of all human beings without distinction of sex or race' (Marx 1975: 280; 1989: 340). Emancipation means freedom from exploitation, oppression and all forms of domination. It also denotes freedom for human flourishing, where the labour movement plays a hegemonic role leading all kinds of liberation struggles. The conception takes cognisance of the ecological context and can be extended to climate change – much to the chagrin of mainstream politicians.[2]

This vision of working-class self-emancipation also offers a strategic reconciliation of structure and agency, bringing theoretical depth to climate change politics. Marxism identifies class societies – and in the contemporary world, global capitalism – as the ultimate structural cause of all forms of exploitation, oppression and ecological degradation. Further, the common experience of waged labour, together with the interdependence of global circuits of capital, provides workers collectively with the attribute of solidarity, the potential to become a global social agent with interests and powers to effect the desired emancipation. An additional claim is the required commitment of the working-class movement to consistent democracy. The democratic element is integral to the alternative mechanisms for governance that Marxists juxtapose to the dominance of private corporations and existing states. In this vision, conscious control of the political economy through collective, democratic planning replaces the imperatives of the market.

Similarly, the goals of meeting social needs, understood not just as material necessities but also greater free time for leisure and cultural activities, replaces the drive for profit. By extension, these needs can include the requirements for a sustainable biosphere. The argument for consistent democracy also applies to workers' own organisations. The collective strength of organised labour is expressed through definite forms, such as political parties, trade unions, workplace councils or committees. But so that these organisations avoid bureaucratic degeneration, they require the light and air of democratic freedom to determine collective objectives, formulate strategies and decide on tactics to achieve agreed goals.[3] Marxism offers an intellectually coherent alternative explanation of evolving global realities, together with a political approach that can shape movements for immediate improvements while seeking much deeper social transformation. Such a vision is notably absent from mainstream contemporary climate discourse.

An 'outrageous proposal': labour and climate change

The Marxist geographer Neil Smith recognised the dualisms within hegemonic discourses on nature and society, while pioneering efforts to supersede them. Smith (1984: 2, 31) highlighted the first dualism, which treats nature as *external*, pristine and ripe for anthropocentric mastery, where society is separate. A second dualism treats nature as *universal*, dissolving everything into it and thereby naturalising social relations and rendering them immutable. His solution was to posit a quixotic notion of the 'production of nature', which begins with 'the relation with nature as a unity and derives as a simultaneously historical and logical result whatever separation between them exists'. In this way 'the social priority of nature is not something that must be infused from the outside, but something that already exists in the social relation with nature'. The production of nature implies a historical future still to be determined by political events and forces, not technical necessity (Castree 1995).

The production of nature approach draws into sharp relief the impact of modern global capitalism in reshaping, remaking and reworking nature all the way down. Writing before climate change became widely discussed in the social sciences, Smith (1984: 56) argued that, 'No part of the earth's surface, the atmosphere, the oceans, the geological substratum or the biological superstratum are immune from transformation by capital' and that 'the alteration of climate by human activity' was an expression of this phenomenon of the social production of nature. The dominant approaches to climate change generally focus on the technical and geographically selective curtailment of emissions, without questioning the specific social relations that organise prevailing production and consumption, or even the global social restructuring implied by emission-abatement policies.

Smith advanced the apparently scandalous proposal that 'labour is the ontological key to understanding how nature is produced' (Smith 2011: 262). This focus on productive activity was a 'politically inspired move' aimed at placing labour at the centre of ecological politics (Ekers and Loftus 2013: 235).[4]

Ecological problems are best theorised as the outcome of a specific natural/ social articulation (Benton 1989: 77). A rich knowledge of the interaction between nature and society can be produced by employing social relations as an entry point of the analysis. This is because 'the interaction between society and nature is mediated by social labour, which is performed within class relations in class societies' (Vlachou 1994: 124). Therefore, the search for the structures that give rise to climate change, its differentiated impacts and the social agents most able and willing to tackle it are sought in the realm of work.[5]

The foremost metaphor in contemporary Marxist framings of nature–society relations mediated by labour is the notion of metabolism (Schmidt 1971; Foster 2000). Metabolism suggests a dialectical interdependence between nature and society, and is used in three senses: (1) to define how labour mediates the relationship between society and nature; (2) to describe how class societies generate metabolic rifts in the ecology of the Earth; and (3) to outline the systemic conditions necessary for metabolic restoration (Burkett 1999). This *Capital*-centric Marxism contributes insight into the political economy of climate change.

First, in Marx's *Capital* (1976: 283), the concept of metabolism expressed the prominence of labour in mediating the social relations of nature. Labour is a process by which humanity, through its own actions, 'mediates, regulates and controls' the metabolism between society and nature. Through the appropriation of the materials of nature and by adapting them to its needs, humans 'act upon external nature and change it, and … simultaneously change their own nature'. By extension, climate is a condition of human existence, but the labour process in contemporary society modifies the climate.

Second, metabolism is used to conceptualise the breakdown in humanity's relationship with nature. Marx (1981: 949) explained in *Capital* that capitalism 'produces conditions that provoke an irreparable rift in the interdependent process of social metabolism, a metabolism prescribed by the natural laws of life itself'. Marx discussed in some depth the drives that led to agricultural degradation under capitalism. Climate change can be understood as an even greater rift between humanity and the biosphere, a state of crisis brought about by particular social relations with nature.

Third, metabolism captures the need to restore the relationship between humanity and nature. Marx (ibid.: 911, 959) wrote of the absurdity of the private ownership of the Earth, instead suggesting that humans are 'simply its possessors, its beneficiaries, and have to bequeath it in an improved state to succeeding generations'. Under a socialist system of democratic control over production, 'the associated producers govern the human metabolism with nature in a rational way, bringing it under their collective control, instead of being dominated by it as a blind power'. Society would be reorganised to accomplish this 'with the least expenditure of energy and in conditions most worthy and appropriate for their human nature'. In short, a different set of social relations with nature is necessary to tackle climate change, centred on democratic control over labour time, where communism becomes 'a form of sustainable human development' (Burkett 2006: 320).

Climate change and the pertinence of employment relations

Climate politics has largely ignored employment relations and other social divisions, despite the importance of work to both the changing climate and to human society in general (Perry 2013). IPCC reports attribute the causes of global increases in greenhouse gas concentrations to general types of human activity, such as fossil fuel use in transport, heating and cooling buildings, from manufacturing and deforestation, agriculture, natural gas distribution, landfills and fertiliser use. British government figures indicate that work-related greenhouse gas emissions from electricity generation, manufacturing and construction, work-related road transport, other business and commercial activities and agriculture account for at least a half of total greenhouse gas emissions by end user and around one-fifth by source in the UK (DECC 2014). These figures are revealing, if rather shallow. The dominant discourses do not explain the particular social relations of production that give rise to greenhouse gas emissions or the social agents that are responsible. Nor do they delve beneath the superficial level of analysis to probe issues of ownership and control.

Employment relations investigate production, industrial and related work relations. Clarke *et al.* (2011: 242–3) argue that the discipline focuses on 'the regulation, control, and – in the currently fashionable term – governance of work and the employment relationship'. It is an interdisciplinary field of study drawing on economics, law, sociology, psychology, political science and history. The discipline provides a multi-level understanding of relationships at work, analysing the interconnections between different actors, scales and locations, as well as conflicts between multiple and competing goals, such as 'efficiency, equity, voice, productivity and workplace justice'. Employment relations theories offer many insights for climate change politics.

This book contributes to an exciting synthesis proposed by Nora Räthzel and David Uzzell (Uzzell and Räthzel 2013: 3, 10), who ask provocatively: Where is the environment in labour studies? Where is the labour in environmental studies? They propose a new field of research – 'environmental labour studies' – to envisage the necessary synthesis for emerging themes, tasks and issues that are 'multiple, urgent and unsolved'. Scholars have noted the virtual absence of explicit discussion of organised labour within mainstream climate social science. This book attempts to address that hiatus. The importance of climate change for working lives and the possibilities of workers' action on climate change animate this study. While there has been considerable research on the role of employers as climate actors, the actual and potential role for workers has been largely overlooked. Yet workers, organised in trade unions, generally represent the largest voluntary organisations in states and historically have been great forces for progress.

Workers as climate agents organised in trade unions can offer what might be called 'climate solidarity': distinctive framings of climate questions, together with specific forms of representation and mobilisation on climate matters. The climate promises made by trade unions could become more than rhetorical pledges. Unions offer a potential pole around which a revived climate movement might coalesce.

Organisation

Aims and scope

The main aim of the book is to articulate the valence of organised workers for climate politics. The first objective is to critically assess the dominant social science framings of climate change and to extend a Marxist theoretical approach to climate politics. I propose that the interlocking processes of exploitation and ecological degradation provide workers with good material reasons to make climate change their own particular interest. Second, the book aims to investigate workers' climate interests and capacities, and the potential for workers' climate agency. It offers a conception of workers and trade unions as strategic climate actors. I also argue that workers' location within capitalist relations of production and their organisation in trade unions give them a unique social power to affect climate mitigation and adaptation action.

Third, the book aims to extend Hyman's (2001) model of trade unions operating between the market, society and class to understand their role in climate change politics. I offer an original, theoretically informed and empirically grounded investigation of trade union policy and practice on climate change (particularly in the UK) at the beginning of the twenty-first century. The book assesses how far trade unions, as representatives of organised labour, articulate working-class interests in their formulations of climate change policy. I examine whether trade unionists have developed distinctive conceptualisations, forms of representation and mobilisation strategies that can contribute towards preventing dangerous climate change. I further ask whether trade unions can lead a social movement to tackle climate change.

The book's time frame straddles the past three decades, an appropriate time span often cited for climatic purposes. In the climate context, it covers the period when climate change first appeared in the public domain, especially after 1988 and with the founding of the IPCC. It includes the establishment of the United Nations Framework Convention on Climate Change (UNFCCC) and the annual Conferences of the Parties (COPs), with the Kyoto Protocol enacted in 1997 at its third gathering. The period has also seen a significant increase in emissions and the failure to agree a way forward in Copenhagen at COP15. The book was completed before the Paris COP21 in 2015, the deadline for a new global agreement.

The global political economy context of these three decades has seen tumultuous changes, including the fall of the Stalinist states in Russia and Eastern Europe, the apparent triumph of neoliberal globalisation and the economic downturn that began in 2007. In the UK, the period spans the last years of the Thatcher era, the period of New Labour under Tony Blair and Gordon Brown (1997–2010), followed by the Conservative–Liberal Democrat Coalition government. In trade union terms, it encompasses the period following the defeat of the 1984–85 miners' strike, a pivotal turning point in modern employment relations, after which trade union membership halved. Yet trade unions in Britain still constitute the largest voluntary organisation in the country, representing seven million workers, and negotiating on behalf of one-third of all employees.

Methods

After several decades of investigation, the central research question remains whether, as a global society, we can avoid the most dangerous aspects of climate change. What sorts of structures of power and political responses are consistent with ecology? A focus on structure and agency for tackling climate change informs the choice of questions tackled in the book (Newell and Paterson 2010; Paterson 2000; Lever-Tracy 2008). I ask whether workers organised in trade unions have the interest and capacity to tackle dangerous climate change, and specifically, whether unionised workers can become strategic climate actors. The term 'strategic' spotlights the structural constraints and enabling conditions, which may privilege waged labour as a plausible alternative social agency for leading a movement to tackle climate change. Further, I ask whether trade unionism in the twenty-first century can succeed by re-inventing itself as a virtual social movement, including around climate change. This turns on whose interests unions represent, which issues they embrace as relevant for the task of representation, and which methods and procedures they adopt in undertaking this task (Hyman 2004). The book therefore examines not only the potential of organised workers for climate action, but also the actual practices of trade unions in climate politics.

Scholars have long recognised the virtues of an interdisciplinary approach to the study of climate change. Explanations of climate change and possible response strategies require contributions from the natural and social sciences, from scholars and from activists. Events and processes influencing climate change must be understood through physical, biological, socio-economic, cultural and ethical mechanisms. This book draws on a wide literature across a range of disciplines and fields, including politics, economics, geography, sociology, employment relations, environmental studies and international relations.

The primary research data consists of published and unpublished documents produced by trade unions on climate change. The critical analysis of those materials was chosen as the main methodology because the field has hardly been explored in the UK, and it made sense to begin with public and semi-public texts. The TUC Library collection at London Metropolitan University contains rich and previously neglected sources of documents accessible to researchers. Individual unions and the Trade Union Congress (TUC) made materials available from their own collections. Documents include: trade union and TUC Congress resolutions; magazines, pamphlets, guides and campaign materials; contributions to government consultations; climate conference speeches and notes; internal position papers; press releases; minutes of union, TUC and the Trade Union Sustainable Development Advisory Committee (TUSDAC) meetings; and newspaper cuttings reporting union views and actions. The critical interrogation of union blogs supplements this method of research.

There are both strengths and limitations in these research methods. Documents alone do not capture many of the perceptions and attitudes of organisations or social agents. Data derived from official sources may be inadequate to some extent. They may be subject to bias or distortion, or bureaucracies' practical concerns may mean that data are not formulated in accordance with scholars' interests. However, rather than viewing official documents as more or less biased sources of data, they 'should be treated as social products: they must be examined, not relied on uncritically as a research resource' (Hammersley and Atkinson 2007: 130–3). The book takes a critical stance towards trade union efforts to engage with climate change throughout.

The account of the Vestas occupation also forms a bottom-up, in-depth case study (Yin 2003). Chapter 6 draws upon an array of media reporting on the Vestas occupation in print and online, with the accompanying strengths and weaknesses of utilising those sources. The empirical data were generated through primary and secondary documentary analysis, particularly a reliance on quality mainstream media, union publications and activist reportage. These sources provide immediate and contemporaneous evidence of the occupation, particularly the workers' behaviour and their immediate reflections on the events as they happened. The use of documentary material also offered access to data that otherwise would be difficult to collect. The use of a range of different media sources and reportage perspectives provides some rudimentary triangulation of the accuracy of events (Cullinane and Dundon 2011).[6]

I have been able to draw on the experiences and opportunities available through involvement in trade union discussions, meetings and events on climate change. A wide range of documents were collected, which provide a comprehensive record of trade union discourse and activity on climate change over the period. Other work during this time involved self-initiated and commissioned research, including obtaining survey and other data from union representatives. Although these data came from self-selected union reps and were not an objective sample, they were nevertheless indicative of qualitative attitudes, behaviours and activities. Professional involvement in the labour movement also afforded opportunities to access key individual actors, attend internal union meetings and make extensive field notes. This experience has been brought to bear on the study.

It is reasonable to ask whether this professional involvement introduces unavoidable bias or prejudices the noble pursuit of objectivity. No doubt it is impossible to research untainted by personal and political sympathies, or by what Hobsbawm (1998) called partisanship, of taking sides. There is no privileged vantage point or ivory watchtower. But objectivity can be attained (or at least aspired to) through transparency about theoretical assumptions, methods, data sources, funding, interests as well as the self-critical analysis of interpretations. Participant observers gain valuable insights that are not otherwise available to an academic witnessing events from the side lines.

Structure of the book

Chapter 1 introduces the current impasse in tackling climate change, which is related to theoretical failures to engage with fundamental political, economic, social and geographical processes. The limited engagement with the employment relations aspects of climate change is a particularly glaring hiatus. This chapter establishes the theoretical approach, main research questions and methods utilised in the research. Chapter 2 discusses how the dominant climate politics is framed in the literature, notably in neoliberal and ecological modernisation approaches. It proffers an alternative, Marxist approach to the mechanisms that generate climate change and outlines the limits of climate capitalism. This chapter examines challenges to working-class-based politics and introduces insights from the employment relations literature. It suggests that workers may become ecological agents with the power and interest to tackle climate change. Trade unions as workers' organisations are conceptualised, following Hyman (2001), as buffeted between market, society and class, but with the potential to embrace climate concerns as a core interest. The argument is made that trade unions could become strategic climate actors.

Chapter 3 assesses how some trade unions internationally have framed the employment impacts of climate change and whether they inevitably face a trade-off between jobs and climate. Through a discussion of climate jobs and the concept of just transition, the chapter aims to show how some trade unionists have begun to integrate the employment impacts of climate change into climate politics in class terms. Chapter 4 provides an overview of the climate politics articulated by UK trade unions over three decades within the context of global debates. Through the prism of TUC policy, the chapter focuses on specific policy areas such as the Climate Change Act, carbon capture and aviation, examining inter-union debates over how to articulate trade union climate concerns. It investigates how trade union representatives have framed climate change politics and how much they have expressed working-class interests.

Chapter 5 evaluates the perceived successes of some trade unions and unions reps with respect to climate change in particular UK workplaces. It addresses the extent to which some trade union representatives have become independent climate actors and whether workplace climate politics involves conflict or partnership. This chapter and the following one discuss trade union power with regard to climate change. Chapter 6 examines the mobilising capacity of trade unions on climate issues, investigating the workers' occupation of the Vestas factory in 2009. The chapter examines the significance of the occupation for climate politics and for particular climate actors, including the trade unionists involved. Finally, Chapter 7 combines and integrates the results of the research with the theoretical analysis to assess the implications of the book for climate politics and for employment relations. It concludes by critically examining the extent to which trade unions are becoming effective climate actors and the potential role unions might play in tackling climate change.

Notes

1 Ecology refers to a wide range of natural relations and interdependencies, including human relations with nature. The difference between ecologism and environmentalism is that 'ecologism argues that care for the environment … presupposes radical changes in our relationship with it, and thus in our mode of social and political life', whereas environmentalism is a managerial approach, 'the belief that [environmental problems] can be solved without fundamental changes in present values or patterns of production and consumption' (Dobson 1990: 13).

2 Lord Deben, chair of the Committee on Climate Change, warned mainstream environmentalists to disassociate themselves from 'people who have extremist views' and who promote 'sort of Trotskyite politics', which he said were not green (Mason 2014).

3 It should be clear that this interpretation of Marxism has nothing in common with the official ideology of former Stalinist states of the USSR and Eastern Europe, or indeed other 'Communist' states, such as China, North Korea, Cuba or Vietnam.

4 Gramsci (1971: 352) argued that humanity 'does not enter into relations with the natural world just by being himself [sic] part of the natural world, but actively, by means of work and technique'.

5 An emphasis on workers and organisations such as trade unions should not assume a generic 'worker' who turns out to be white and male. Nor does it assume that the structure of work is simply filling empty places. Class relations do not preclude other relations of domination, such as ethnicity, gender, nationality and sexuality. These forms of oppression intersect and interpolate with class relations, just as they are fractured along class lines. Working-class movements striving for social transformation cannot ignore the intersections of multiple, cross-cutting institutionalised power relations defined by race, class, gender, sexuality and other axes of domination, particularly as the labour market is a key location where racial and gender differences are transformed into class inequalities (Acker 2006; Moore 2010; Brenner 2000).

6 Web and blog posts are referenced in the same way as printed material throughout the book. This was a conscious decision. Books filled with web links can appear somewhat gratuitous, dated and arbitrary. Adding specific links would add hugely to the length of the references at the end of each chapter – particularly when so much material is now available online. Adding these links does not

necessarily make the process of tracing the original sources easier – search engines can locate them from name, title and/or key words. Links also change – as I found frequently with union, government and media websites during this research – so they may be out of date soon after the book is published. Some newspaper articles are now subscription only, while others are currently free. Better to be consistent with full references, but no specific links.

References

Acker, J. (2006) *Class Questions: Feminist Answers*. Lanham, MD: Rowman & Littlefield.

Ackerman, F. (2009) *Can We Afford the Future? The Economics of a Warming World*. London: Zed Books.

Anderson, K. and Bows, A. (2011) 'Beyond "Dangerous" Climate Change: Emission Scenarios for a New World', *Philosophical Transactions of the Royal Society a-Mathematical Physical and Engineering Sciences*, 369: 20–44.

Barker, T. (2008) 'Climate Policy: Issues and Opportunities'. In H. Compston and I. Bailey (eds) *Turning Down the Heat: The Politics of Climate Policy in Affluent Democracies*. Basingstoke: Palgrave Macmillan.

Beck, U. (2010) 'Climate for Change, or How to Create a Green Modernity?' *Theory, Culture & Society*, 27(2–3): 254–66.

Benton, T. (1989) 'Marxism and Natural Limits', *New Left Review*, I(178): 51–86.

Berkhout, F. and Hertin, J. (2000) 'Socio-Economic Scenarios for Climate Impact Assessment', *Global Environmental Change*, 10(3): 165–8.

Bhaskar, R. and Parker, J. (2010) 'Introduction'. In R. Bhaskar, C. Frank, K. Høyer, P. Naess and J. Parker (eds) *Interdisciplinarity and Climate Change: Transforming Knowledge and Practice for Our Global Future*. London: Routledge.

Bolin, B. (2007) *A History of the Science and Politics of Climate Change: The Role of the Intergovernmental Panel on Climate Change*. Cambridge: Cambridge University Press.

Brenner, J. (2000) *Women and the Politics of Class*. New York: Monthly Review Press.

Burkett, P. (1999) *Marx and Nature: A Red and Green Perspective*. Basingstoke: Palgrave Macmillan.

——(2006) *Marxism and Ecological Economics: Toward a Red and Green Political Economy*. Leiden: Brill Academic Publishers.

Castree, N. (1995) 'The Nature of Produced Nature: Materiality and Knowledge Construction in Marxism', *Antipode*, 27(1): 12–47.

Clarke, L., Donnelly, E., Hyman, R., Kelly, J., McKay, S. and Moore, S. (2011) 'What's the Point of Industrial Relations?', *International Journal of Comparative Labour Law and Industrial Relations*, 27(3): 239–53.

Cullinane, N. and Dundon, T. (2011) 'Redundancy and Workplace Occupation: The Case of the Republic of Ireland', *Employee Relations*, 33(6): 624–41.

DECC (2014) '2013 UK Greenhouse Gas Emissions, Provisional Figures and 2012 UK Greenhouse Gas Emissions: Final Figures by Fuel Type and End-User', London: DECC.

Demeritt, D. (2001) 'The Construction of Global Warming and the Politics of Science', *Annals of the Association of American Geographers*, 91(2): 307–37.

Dietz, S., Anderson, D., Stern, N., Taylor, C. and Zenghelis, D. (2007) 'Right for the Right Reasons: A Final Rejoinder on the Stern Review', *World Economics*, 8(2): 229–58.

Dobson, A. (1990) *Green Political Thought*. London: Unwin Hyman.

Draper, H. (1978) *Karl Marx's Theory of Revolution, Volume II: The Politics of Social Classes*. New York: Monthly Review Press.

Ekers, M. and Loftus, A. (2013) 'Revitalizing the Production of Nature Thesis: A Gramscian Turn?' *Progress in Human Geography*, 37(2): 234–52.

Foster, J. (2000) *Marx's Ecology: Materialism and Nature*. New York: Monthly Review Press.

Giddens, A. (2009) *The Politics of Climate Change*. Cambridge: Polity Press.

Glover, L. (2006) *Postmodern Climate Change*. London: Routledge.

Gramsci, A. (1971) *Selections from the Prison Notebooks*. London: Lawrence and Wishart.

Hammersley, M. and Atkinson, P. (2007) *Ethnography: Principles in Practice*, 3rd edn. London: Routledge.

Hay, C. (2002) *Political Analysis*. Basingstoke: Palgrave.

Helm, D. (2013) *The Carbon Crunch: How We're Getting Climate Change Wrong – and How to Fix It*. New Haven, CT: Yale University Press.

Hobsbawm, E. (1998) *On History*. London: Abacus.

Hulme, M. (2009) *Why We Disagree About Climate Change: Understanding Controversy, Inaction and Opportunity*. Cambridge: Cambridge University Press.

Hyman, R. (2001) *Understanding European Trade Unionism: Between Market, Class and Society*. London: Sage.

——(2004) 'The Future of Trade Unions'. In A. Verma and T. Kochan (eds) *Unions in the 21st Century: An International Perspective*. Basingstoke: Palgrave Macmillan.

IEA (2012) *World Energy Outlook 2012*. Paris: OECD/International Energy Agency.

IPCC (2013) *Climate Change 2013: The Physical Science Basis*. Cambridge: Cambridge University Press.

——(2014a) *Climate Change 2014: Impacts, Adaptation and Vulnerability*. Cambridge: Cambridge University Press.

——(2014b) *Climate Change 2014: Mitigation of Climate Change*. Cambridge: Cambridge University Press.

——(2014c) *Climate Change 2014: Synthesis Report*. Cambridge: Cambridge University Press.

Jessop, B. (2007) *State Power: A Strategic-Relational Approach*. Cambridge: Polity.

Latour, B. (2004) *Politics of Nature: How to Bring the Sciences into Democracy*. Cambridge, MA: Harvard University Press.

Lever-Tracy, C. (2008) 'Global Warming and Sociology', *Current Sociology*, 56(3): 445–66.

——(ed.) (2010) *Routledge Handbook of Climate Change and Society*. London: Routledge.

Marx, K. (1975) 'Economic and Philosophical Manuscripts of 1844: Estranged Labour'. *MECW*, vol. 3. London: Lawrence and Wishart.

——(1976) *Capital*. vol. I. Harmondsworth: Penguin.

——(1981) *Capital*. vol. III. Harmondsworth: Penguin.

——(1985) 'Provisional Rules of the Association, October 1864', *MECW*, vol. 20. London: Lawrence and Wishart.

——(1989) 'The Programme of the Workers Party Preamble, 10 May 1880', *MECW*, vol. 24. London: Lawrence and Wishart.

Mason, R. (2014) 'Some Green Extremists "Close to Trotskyites", Says Lord Deben', *The Guardian*, 20 January.

McKibben, B. (2012) 'Global Warming's Terrible New Math'. In M. Berners-Lee and D. Clark (eds) *The Burning Question*. London: Profile Books.

McLaughlin, P. and Dietz, T. (2008) 'Structure, Agency and Environment: Toward an Integrated Perspective on Vulnerability', *Global Environmental Change*, 18(1): 99–111.

Moore, S. (2010) *New Trade Union Activism: Class Consciousness or Social Identity?* Basingstoke: Palgrave.

Newell, P. and Paterson, M. (2010) *Climate Capitalism: Global Warming and the Transformation of the Global Economy*. Cambridge: Cambridge University Press.

O'Brien, K. (2012) 'Global Environmental Change II: From Adaptation to Deliberate Transformation', *Progress in Human Geography*, 36(5): 667–76.

Okereke, C., Bulkeley, H. and Schroeder, H. (2009) 'Conceptualizing Climate Governance Beyond the International Regime', *Global Environmental Politics*, 9(1): 58–78.

Paterson, M. (2000) *Understanding Global Environmental Politics: Domination, Accumulation, Resistance*. Basingstoke: Palgrave Macmillan.

Perry, E. (2013) 'The Research of Academics, Government and Social Actors'. In C. Lipsig-Mummé (ed.) *Climate@Work*. Black Point, Nova Scotia: Fernwood Publishing.

Rayner, S and Malone, E. (eds) (1998) *Human Choice and Climate Change*. 4 vols. Columbus, OH: Battelle Press.

Schmidt, A. (1971) *The Concept of Nature in Marx*. London: New Left Books.

Schneider, S. (1983) 'CO$_2$, Climate and Society: A Brief Overview'. In R. Chen, E. Boulding and S. Schneider (eds) *Social Science Research and Climate Change: An Interdisciplinary Appraisal*. Dordrecht: D. Reidel Publishing Company.

——(1997) *Laboratory Earth: The Planetary Gamble We Can't Afford to Lose*. New York: HarperCollins.

Shove, E. (2010) 'Social Theory and Climate Change: Questions Often, Sometimes and Not Yet Asked, Theory', *Culture and Society*, 27(2–3): 277–88.

Smith, N. (1984) *Uneven Development*. 1st edn. Oxford: Blackwell.

——(2011) 'Uneven Development Redux', *New Political Economy*, 16(2): 261–5.

Swyngedouw, E. (2010) 'Apocalypse Forever? Post-Political Populism and the Spectre of Climate Change', *Theory, Culture & Society*, 27(2–3): 213–32.

Uzzell, D. and Räthzel, N. (2013) 'Introducing a New Field: Environmental Labour Studies'. In N. Räthzel and D. Uzzell (eds) *Trade Unions in the Green Economy: Working for the Environment*. London: Routledge.

Vlachou, A. (1994) 'Reflections on the Ecological Critiques and Reconstructions of Marxism', *Rethinking Marxism*, 7(3: 112–28.

Yin, R. (2003) *Case Study Research: Design and Methods*. London: Sage Publications.

2 Climate politics and the potential for climate solidarity

Introduction

The aim of this chapter is to evaluate three of the most important ways that climate change is framed in social science literature and to integrate this understanding with employment relations theories. Each interpretation – articulated by their foremost exponents and trenchant critics – offers a distinctive answer to the question of how society can avoid the most dangerous aspects of climate change. The first section evaluates the dominant discourses – the market-oriented, neoliberal account of climate politics and the widely held ecological modernisation elucidation. This section also sketches an alternative, Marxist explanation, concentrating on the structures and processes within capitalism that drive climate change. The second section examines the neglected social agency of organised labour, exploring the latent possibilities of solidarity and social movement unionism. The third section assesses whether trade unions represent significant ecological actors. It extends this potential to climate politics, outlining the extent to which trade unions can be regarded as strategic climate actors. Overall, the chapter seeks to develop a synthesis, fusing a range of climate epistemologies with trade unions as carbon actors.[1]

Climate politics: between capitals, states and classes

Neoliberal climate political economy

The dominant approach to climate change frames the physical science evidence (distilled by the Intergovernmental Panel on Climate Change, IPCC) within already established economic and political assumptions. The political economy of carbon is increasingly conducted by, through and for markets (Newell and Paterson 2009: 80). The orientation towards markets is a neoliberal approach. Among the central elements of neoliberalism is a 'near worship of the "self-regulating market"' (Heynen *et al.* 2007), a market 'increasingly wide in its geographic scope, comprehensive as the governing mechanism for allocating all goods and services, and central as a metaphor for organising and evaluating institutional performance'. Neoliberalism involves minimally 'the subjection of more-and-more areas of social and environmental life to the logics of capital accumulation' (ibid.: 15).

William Nordhaus (1977) originated the characterisation of greenhouse gas emissions as externalities, whereby rational agents acting in their own self-interest despoil the common-pool resource of the Earth's atmosphere by using it as a global greenhouse gas sink. Climate change within the neoliberal, market framing is held to be an instance of the tragedy of the commons (Bunzl 2009). The atmosphere is regarded as a public good, owned by no one with identifiable individual property rights. Markets are considered 'neutral' entities, which 'lock out lobbying and rent-seeking' (Helm 2013: 57, 180). On this basis, Nicholas Stern (2007: 1) describes climate change as 'the greatest market failure ever seen'. Subsequently he surmised that the economics of cost 'points us to the importance of market-related mechanisms, and to a price on greenhouse gases, as the best ways to promote the search for the cheapest ways of achieving these emissions reductions targets' (Stern 2009: 99). Correcting market failure with market instruments is the *sine qua non* of neoliberal climate politics.

The idea that carbon emissions have costs and benefits naturally leads on to the idea that 'CO_2 is a commodity', which can be valued and traded like any other. This means 'it has a price, which is the outcome of supply and demand, and is amenable to application of the traditional economic tools of valuation' (Helm 2005: 15). Nordhaus summed up this approach in pithy fashion:

> Whether someone is serious about tackling the global-warming problem can be readily gauged by listening to what he or she says about the carbon price ... Economics contains one fundamental inconvenient truth about climate-change policy: For any policy to be effective in slowing global warming, it must raise the market price of carbon, which will raise the prices of fossil fuels and the products of fossil fuels ... the 'carbon footprint' is automatically calculated by the price system.
>
> (Nordhaus 2008: 20–2)

The core objective of neoliberal climate policy is 'to internalise the social cost of carbon in firms' decisions, such that firms profit when they adopt cleaner modes of production' (Hepburn 2009: 365). Neoliberal advocates argue that the market system provides a more effective, efficient and equitable solution to climate change than traditional command and control regulation (Solomon and Heiman 2010). However, there is considerable debate about which market mechanisms should be relied upon. One candidate is carbon taxes, which involve setting a price for greenhouse gases and leaving it to emitters to choose how much to emit (Parry 2005). Another instrument is emissions trading, in which an emissions ceiling or cap is set and the price is determined by the trading of permits (Grubb 1989; Victor 1991).

The most prominent example is the European Union's Emissions Trading Scheme (EU ETS), with similar schemes under discussion internationally.

The neoliberal approach recognises that an effective policy to mitigate or adapt to global warming requires international collective action. If the climate is regarded as a global public good, in the absence of a central authority to impose sanctions, actors can 'free-ride' on each other's efforts to mitigate emissions. There is significant disagreement over the Kyoto Protocol. Some scholars defend the Kyoto regime, not least because it had ensured that 'opposition to market mechanisms on ideological grounds is now confined to the fringes of the climate-change debate' (Depledge and Yamin 2009: 441–2). However, others conclude that Kyoto ultimately failed to get key states to participate, to make participants comply and to require parties to reduce emissions substantially (Barrett 2009).

Many authors emphasise the importance of business as a special interest group in climate politics (Falkner 2008; Pinkse and Kolk 2009). Stern (2007: 518, 644) praises multinational companies for taking the lead in demonstrating 'how profits can be increased while reducing emissions from industrial activities'. He concludes that with the right incentives, 'the private sector will respond and can deliver solutions'. Stern (2009: 99) predicts considerable climate action involving private firms. Climate policy is about 'enabling markets and private-sector initiatives to work well'. If markets are deemed the most desirable social structures, then privately owned firms are conceived as the central agents for mitigating and adapting to climate change.

Critique of neoliberal climate political economy

A range of scholars have subjected the neoliberal approach to significant criticism. First, reducing climate change to a matter of allocating property rights, cost-benefit analysis and pricing risks through carbon taxation or emissions trading cannot adequately quantify the magnitude of climate change. The underlying fallacy is that market forces lead by themselves to intrinsically good outcomes (Barker 2008). This central conceit is 'Adam's fallacy' (originating with Adam Smith), that through the creation of a separate economic sphere of the market, private selfishness turns into public altruism (Foley 2006; Jaeger et al. 2008). Far from the invisible hand leading to the reduction in carbon emissions, the 'invisible foot' promotes unintended harm and social misery (Spash 2002: 6). Rather than correcting market failure, climate policy requires alternatives to markets.

A second criticism is that market-based climate policy prescriptions are expected to fail in practice. The Kyoto Protocol fails because it is the wrong type of instrument relying on the wrong agents exercising the wrong sort of power to create, from the top down, a carbon market (Prins and Rayner 2007). Joseph Hansen (2009) advised the Australian government that its proposed cap-and-trade scheme was 'the temple of doom', whose 'fecklessness' was proven by Kyoto. He decried the agreement for taking a decade to implement, as countries extracted concessions that weakened even mild goals. Naomi Klein (2014: 77) argues that the UN's climate negotiations are 'subservient' to the global trading system. The United Nations Framework Convention on Climate Change's (UNFCCC) Article 3 states that 'measures taken to combat climate change, including unilateral ones, should not constitute … a disguised restriction on international trade', while similar language appeared in the Kyoto Protocol.

EU ETS is the flagship for carbon markets and a suitable test of their effectiveness. The early phases of EU ETS are credited with reducing emissions by between 2 per cent and 5 per cent (Ellerman *et al.* 2010; Laing *et al.* 2013). Although these modest reductions partly reflected the price signal created by the scheme, in reality, the economic recession rather than the cap was the main driver of emissions cuts. The collapse of the European carbon price and the absence of a paradigm-shifting transition in energy generation suggest that market mechanisms are at best insufficient and at worst a distraction from more radical measures.

A third criticism is that market mechanisms exacerbate existing inequalities. Market-based systems of distribution have an 'inherent bias' in favour of wealthy parties and they tend to remove power from those who already lack resources. If permits are allocated on the basis of historical or current emission levels, polluters will not pay. Instead firms will be rewarded for their records of pollution and will be able to maximise their rewards by 'exploiting their informational advantages and abilities to manipulate data to their advantage'. Carbon trading makes policy-makers responsive to multinational corporations, not local populations (Baldwin 2008: 201–4).

In the EU ETS, rent or 'supra-normal profits' accrue to the companies involved and because most of the companies involved are private, the gain is accrued to shareholders and not the wider public, as might be the case with a state-owned company (Convery 2009: 128–9). Grandfathering means emissions trading permits are allocated free of charge. This is highly regressive, creates windfall gains for shareholders and involves transfers of revenue to higher-income households at the expense of others (Parry 2004: 365–6). If the emissions cap is tight, a higher carbon price means the cost of heating, transport, food and other essential goods and services will rise substantially, driving more people into 'fuel poverty'. A candid verdict on the early efficacy of EU ETS was provided by a Citigroup executive: 'Prices up, emissions up, profits up … so, not really. Who wins and loses? All generation-based utilities – winners. Coal and nuclear-based generators – biggest winners. Hedge funds and energy traders – even bigger winners. Losers … ahem … consumers!' (Tickell 2008: 50).

The neoliberal framing is further criticised for leaving the structures of global and national capitalism intact, while empowering private capitals. Yet capital is too internally fractured and too interdependent on fossil fuels to have a consistent interest in tackling climate change. Fossil fuel capitals often seek weaker regulation, and some promote climate denial. Renewable energy or construction capital may favour a stronger policy to enhance their profitable opportunities. The insurance industry is ambiguous: as an institutional investor, these firms depend on returns from companies that would suffer from stringent emission targets. However, insurers also fear that extreme weather events might lead to huge pay-outs. The market is not a neutral entity; it is underpinned by contradictory and competitive relations between different fractions of capital that make business an unreliable and sometimes unwilling agent for tackling climate change. And capitalist states enforce neoliberalism, tipping the balance of class forces in favour of capital (Harvey 2005).

Advocates of carbon markets suggest that at least some business actors – such as finance – have an interest in preventing the impacts of climate change and of the instruments designed to avoid these effects. It seems obtuse to put the same actors responsible for the recent economic downturn in charge of reducing greenhouse gas emissions. A deeper problem is the interdependence of financial capital and fossil fuel corporations, from their relations of ownership and control to the flows of revenue. One hundred large companies between them have produced nearly two-thirds of the greenhouse gas emissions generated since the dawn of the industrial age. Fifty of those firms are privately owned – mostly oil companies and coal producers – while another 31 are state-owned companies operating on a capitalist basis (Heede 2014).

Fossil fuel companies have perhaps five times the reserves of coal, oil and gas on their balance sheets and are allocating billions to developing more reserves. In climate terms these assets are unburnable: they will have to be left in the ground to avoid breaching the proposed carbon budget of 2°C. If so, these corporations (whether privately owned or state-run on a capitalist basis) are fantastically overvalued at present. The New York and London stock markets are becoming more carbon-intensive, as financiers bet on further inaction on climate change (Carbon Tracker and the Grantham Research Institute 2013). This represents the predicament of the neoliberal approach: either a carbon bubble leading to financial collapse, or continued profitable fossil fuel burning with dire climate consequences.

Ecological modernisation climate political economy

Ecological modernisation represents a distinct framing within environmental sociology and politics, distinguished from neoliberal and Marxist accounts (Mol *et al.* 2009). It also underpins populist narratives by some Green politicians, journalists and NGO leaders, such as the Green New Deal (Elliott *et al.* 2008). Ecological modernisation utilises familiar metaphors such as 'win–win' co-benefits, 'low-hanging fruit' and 'technological crutches'. Three key features of ecological modernisation stand out: (1) an emphasis on state and non-state actors as significant agents for constructing climate alliances; (2) greater sensitivity to the social implications of climate policy; and (3) a wider range of instruments alongside market mechanisms.

First, ecological modernisation is more inclusive of a wide range of actors, with the state coordinating the efforts of firms and other stakeholders in a more unified effort to tackle climate change. The role of the state is pivotal to this framing of agency, the 'master discourse' that serves to legitimate other discourses (Cass and Pettenger 2007). Ecological modernisation, at least in its stronger formulations, necessarily involves the active engagement of the state, requiring strategic planning and structural change at the macroeconomic level (Murphy and Gouldson 2000).

But non-state actors also have a vital role to play in climate policy formation (Paterson 1996; Newell 2000). The progress of climate capitalism depends on 'an awkward alliance of technocratic civil servants, opportunistic environmental NGOs and profit-seeking financiers' (Newell and Paterson 2010: 165). The Low-Carbon Society project highlights key stakeholders including business, the investment community, technology vendors, local government and consumers (Strachan *et al.* 2008). It requires a 'climate change advocacy coalition' including environmental advocacy groups, scientists, journalists, agency personnel, legislators, cabinet members and renewable energy technology leaders (Pralle 2009).

Some non-state actors can be understood as social movements. Environmental social movements have four typical characteristics: (1) they are based on informal networks; (2) those involved share a set of beliefs and a collective identity; (3) they are involved in collective challenges and may threaten their opponents with sanctions; and (4) they use protest tactics (Doherty *et al.* 2000). Britain has the 'oldest, strongest, best organised and most widely supported' environmental lobby in the world. The top ten environmental NGOs exceed five million supporters, with many putting resources into climate change campaigning (Rootes 2009: 201–2). In the UK during the first decade of the new millennium, fresh climate bodies such as the Stop Climate Chaos Coalition, the Campaign against Climate Change and Climate Camp emerged as distinct organisations (Saunders 2008; 2012; Graham-Leigh 2014).

A second distinctive feature of ecological modernisation is its engagement with important aspects of climate justice.[2] Climate change impacts are likely to be unjust and may create new vulnerabilities, while actions taken to adapt to climate change can themselves have important justice implications. This applies to both *procedural justice*, meaning the degree of recognition and participation of different actors; and *distributive justice*, which refers to the distribution of the beneficial and adverse effects of climate change and adaptation (Adger *et al.* 2006: 3–4, 14). The vectors of climate justice tend to run between states in the Global North and the Global South, or between generations (Büchs *et al.* 2011). Aubrey Meyer advocates the 'contraction and convergence' approach to account for inequalities between states (Cromwell and Levene 2007). Climate justice is articulated by various activist networks intervening at climate talks (Chatterton *et al.* 2013).

The UK experience illustrates a third feature of ecological modernisation, namely the mix of instruments deployed. Although the Blair-led Labour government stressed the context of neoliberal globalisation for British political economy, its environmental policies are 'best understood as an attempt to implement something like an ecological modernisation agenda' (Barry and Paterson 2004: 767; see also Jacobs 1999). Before coming to power, Labour promised to cut national CO_2 emissions by 20 per cent by 2010, while in government it agreed at Kyoto to reduce greenhouse gases by 12.5 per cent by 2012 compared with 1990 levels. In 2001, the Labour government introduced the Climate Change Levy, a tax on fossil fuel sources, offset by a reduction in employers' National Insurance contributions and investment in renewable energy through the Carbon Trust. It also established the UK Climate Impacts Programme, introduced Climate Change Agreements, the Renewables Obligation, the Energy Efficiency Commitment (later the Carbon Emissions Reduction Target) and a UK emissions trading scheme (Carter and Ockwell 2007). The Labour government also created the Department for Energy and Climate Change (DECC) in 2008.

The Climate Change Act 2008 is an 'original and forward-looking proposal … making the UK [the] first country to make long-ranging and ambitious targets legally binding' (Lorenzoni *et al.* 2008: 106–7). The Act committed the UK to emissions reductions of 34 per cent by 2020 and 80 per cent by 2050, created a carbon budgeting system to cap emissions over five-year periods, established an expert body, the Committee on Climate Change, and mandatory emissions trading for large non-energy-intensive commercial and public organisations, the Carbon Reduction Commitment. Labour's mix of market instruments and regulation was symptomatic of the ecological modernist framing.

Critique of ecological modernisation climate political economy

Ecological modernisation has been subject to a range of criticism. Even its proponents recognise concerns with its undertheorised notions of power, limited attention to social contexts or ethical issues, neglect of emancipatory concerns and failure to link environmental reform with some aspects of social justice (Mol and Jänicke 2009). The first significant criticism concerns the role afforded to the state. Private interest theory emphasises the pressure of self-interested business groups to 'capture' regulators and legislators, which may explain why the record of climate change regulation in many countries is mixed at best (Bartle 2009). At present, the main political strategy seems to be the implementation of measures that target a broad range of emissions sources 'while not antagonising business groups or electorates' (Compston 2009: 659). State action is essential in order to tackle climate change, but capitalist states cannot permanently restrain the animal spirits of capital.

If the Labour government's climate change policy is taken to represent ecological modernisation, then the results were disappointing. Although the UK ranked as one of the more successful states in integrating climate change into national politics, its targets, strategy and specific policies have been criticised. The UK formally met its Kyoto target, though the promise of a 20 per cent cut in CO_2 emissions was not achieved, despite the economic slowdown. Consumption-based accounts (which include imported emissions from international trade) showed an average 1 per cent annual *increase* in UK emissions between 1990 and 2009 (Barrett *et al.* 2013: 454). The problem was due to

> the [Labour] government's predisposition towards ecological moder-
> nisation and market mechanisms that focus on incremental change, and
> its tendency to shy away from bolder actions that politicians may believe
> (in some cases incorrectly) will be resisted by corporate sectors or the
> electorate.
>
> (Lorenzoni *et al.* 2008: 119)

A second concern with ecological modernisation is the limited leverage that non-state actors have against capital and states. The lack of enforceable sanctions available to non-state actors constrains their ability to act as effective accountability enforcers. Civil regulation produces forms of accountability that are 'often temporary, unenforceable, subject to tokenism and publicity cycles' and are 'as likely to reflect the campaign priorities of vocal or media savvy groups' as address the largest and most serious contributors to climate change (Newell 2008: 148–9). A further limitation is a tendency to accommodate to states and to the dominant interests of business, to secure funding and gain legitimacy. None of the visible agents designated by ecological modernisation appears to have both the interest and the capacity to tackle climate change adequately. Capital has power, but is internally antagonistic and pursues other objectives. States do not rise above the fray of competing social actors. NGOs may have a more resolute ideological commitment to tackling climate change, but they lack the capacity to oppose capital all the way down.

Furthermore, ecological modernisation also fails to address differentiated liabilities between classes within states in the context of climate change (Baer 2006). The IPCC's second assessment report acknowledges that most early climate models did not provide insight into income distribution or employment issues. The poorest people are more vulnerable to climate change because 'lower-income households are more likely to live in higher-risk areas, marginal lands and floodplains; they have fewer resources to cope and have much lower rates of insurance cover; they may also suffer from poorer health and resistance' (Gough 2008: 328–9). Ecological modernisation's technocratic greening of industrial production has been 'silent on the experiences of developing countries in equity and poverty issues' (Bäckstrand and Lövbrand 2006).

Finally, ecological modernisation suffers from the same shortcomings as neoliberalism, namely, the failure to grasp the underlying causes that give rise to climate change, its reliance on market mechanisms and business actors, and the reinforcing of existing inequalities. Although ecological modernisation proposes a broad alliance of agents to tackle climate change, the direction of its policy is dictated by capital and states. Ecological modernisation has a tendency to dissolve into softer representations of neoliberalism (Bailey and Wilson 2009). In the UK context, this was epitomised by the evolution of government climate policy. The Conservative–Liberal Democrat coalition began in 2010 displaying considerable continuity with the previous Labour government, retaining the Climate Change Act and aiming to be the 'greenest government ever'. By mid-term, Conservative ministers had lurched in a neoliberal direction by championing fracking, while Prime Minister David Cameron allegedly told his closest advisors to 'get rid of the green crap' on energy taxes. Ecological modernisation's emphasis on a more climate-friendly capitalism places as off-limits the radical reorganisation of society towards ecologically sustainable collective production (Vlachou 2004: 943).

Towards a Marxist political economy of climate change

Karl Marx lived before anthropogenic climate change was established in physical science, though he did attend some of John Tyndall's lectures and may have heard him expound on the greenhouse effect (Burkett 2006: 176). Nonetheless, a contemporary Marxist framing provides vital insights into the social structures and processes that drive climate change, the uneven impacts it has on people's lives and the potential agents capable of tackling it. In Chapter 1, Smith's daring hypothesis that labour is pivotal to ecological politics was proposed as the starting point for a more adequate framing of relations between climate and society. If this is accepted, then core Marxist concepts can be used to understand important aspects of climate change.

First, the key Marxist concept for understanding different forms of society is the mode of production, consisting of a specific combination of productive forces and production relations (Callinicos 1987a). The productive forces include the labour process, the technical combination of labour power (the capacity to work) and the means of production employed in order to transform nature and to produce use-values, thereby determining a particular level of productivity. Production relations are the relationship of the direct producers to the means of production and their labour power, the nature of any non-producing owners and the mode of appropriation of surplus labour from the direct producers by any such owners. Modes of production rest on a particular relationship with nature. The market does not exist in nature; rather, under capitalism it is labour that turns nature into commodities (Altvater 2006). Changing society also changes relations with nature. Natural conditions of production are integral to the productive forces/production relations, not set apart from them. There is therefore no 'second contradiction' outside of the productive forces/production relations distinction (Spence 2000).

Second, 'the specific economic form in which unpaid surplus-labour is pumped out of direct producers determines the relationship between rulers and ruled' (Marx 1981: 927). It is the basis of exploitation and arises from society's particular relations of production. The mode of surplus extraction determines the class structure, so that classes are defined by their objective relationship to the means of production and labour power and to other classes. This exploitation gives rise to class struggle, or at least the potential for it in all class societies. Third, exploitation informs the particular form of political domination and is therefore the basis for Marxist theories of states, international relations and ideology. The Marxist conception of 'uneven and combined development' incorporates the significance of international relations into a theory of capitalist world development and creates an opening for a social theory of 'the international' (Callinicos and Rosenberg 2008). Marxists generally regard the state as a form of social relations and view capitalism as a political moment within global capitalist social relations. States and state managers seek to act in the interests of capital in general rather than for particular factions of capital to resolve crises within the circuit of capital (Burnham 2001). States are nevertheless vital sites of political strategy in international geopolitics and in domestic affairs. They play an integral role in extending capitalist social relations of production, shaping capital accumulation and mediating class struggles (Jessop 2007). Since 1945, global capitalism has emerged under the superintendence of the US imperial state, involving the further internationalisation and interpenetration of capitals and most other states (Panitch and Gindin 2012).

In the capitalist economy, employment relations between people necessarily acquire the form of the value of things, and can appear only in this material form; social labour can only be expressed in value. The point of departure for research 'is not value but labour, not the transactions of market exchange as such, but the production structure of the commodity society, the totality of production relations among people' (Rubin 1972: 62). Capital is a social relation (not simply material things), value-in-motion, which extracts surplus labour (in the form of surplus value) from workers who produce commodities under the veil of wages. Exploitation is opaque. Social relations of production under capitalism are fetishised or reified, and Marxist political economy attempts to uncover the relationships between people that are mystified by the relations between things such as commodities, money and capital. Under capitalism, there is a systematic tendency for workers' capacity to work (labour power) as well as the 'free gifts of nature' to take the form of commodities and this explains capitalism's expansive vitality. A society organised on capitalist lines cannot deny this drive for capital accumulation. This is the source of capitalism's dynamism, but also its folly. If capitalism is principally about the production, appropriation and distribution of surplus value, and the competitive drive for capital accumulation, then the capitalists' insatiable thirst for profit knows no bounds – and certainly no ecological limits.

Capital extracts surplus labour from workers and this valorisation process shapes and refashions the labour process. One means of extracting more surplus value is simply for the capitalists to force workers to work longer. Marx called this the creation of absolute surplus value, or *the formal subsumption of labour to capital*. Assuming that the costs of reproducing the worker (the proportion of time spent producing for their means of subsistence) remains the same, the extra hours of work will create extra surplus value for the capitalist. However, what distinguishes capitalism is the development of more dynamic ways of extracting surplus labour, making the labour process more productive, more intensive or more efficiently organised (Saad Filho 2003). This process Marx called the creation of relative surplus value, or *the real subsumption of labour to capital*. The three forms discussed in *Capital* are cooperation, the division of labour and the introduction of machinery. The strategy of relative surplus value is to increase productivity in order to drive down the value of labour power. Increased productivity allows capital to extract more surplus value from the same sum of new value added. With real subsumption, capital really takes control of the labour process and forces workers to cooperate with each other, often in a common workplace but certainly as part of an interdependent production process. The tasks workers are expected to carry out are specialised, so that more can be done in a given working day. The application of machinery is imposed to speed up and simplify the production process. Individual capitalists recognise that by transforming the labour process they can appropriate higher-than-average returns, extracting additional surplus value and through its reinvestment, accumulate greater and greater capital. The process of the concentration and centralisation of capital extends the capitalist mode of production spatially, incorporating new means of production and turning other direct producers into workers. Ever more areas of social life are enclosed and commodified.

Boyd, Prudham and Schurman (2001: 557) extend these insights about the exploitation of labour to ecological degradation and posit the concepts of *the formal and real subsumption of nature to capital*. Under the formal subsumption of nature, firms confront nature as 'an exogenous set of material properties and bio-/geophysical processes', but are unable to directly augment natural processes and use them as strategies for increasing productivity. In contrast, with the real subsumption of nature, 'firms are able to take hold of and transform natural production and use this as a source of productivity increase' (ibid.: 565). In adapting these concepts from notions of the formal and real subsumption of labour, these scholars highlight some of the different ways in which biophysical systems are industrialised and can be made to operate as productive forces themselves. The real subsumption of nature involves altering biophysical properties so that it offers enhanced possibilities for capital accumulation. For example, in agriculture and forestry, 'hybridisation and now genetic modification are two key technologies in subsuming nature to the demands of capitalist firms'.

With real subsumption, capital circulates through nature as opposed to around it. Biological systems are made to act as actual forces of production (Castree 2008: 146).

It is possible to extend these conceptions further to explain the drives that generate climate change, to what might be called *the subsumption of climate to capital*. The formal subsumption of climate means the release of polluting gases into the air, into rivers and the sea, the scourging of the earth for raw materials, the mining of coal and metals. It means the by-products of capital accumulation are dumped into ecological sinks. For energy, it means the utilisation of available fossil fuel sources of power to drive the production process in factories. The advent of factory night shifts, forcing waged labour to work extended hours, was simultaneously a draw on energy resources for power and lighting. Therefore, the formal subsumption of labour to capital coincided with the initial, formal subsumption of nature and the climate to capital.

However, it was the real subsumption of labour to capital that really spurred the transformation of the climate and broke the energy budget. The process of replacing living labour with machinery – the product of other, past labour – required an enormous expansion of energy to power such labour processes. Christie (1980: 16) has argued that capital increasingly needs energy 'as it uses machinery to protect its ownership of property … to control workers; to control production; to deskill production processes; to speed up production; to speed up transport'. Capital needs more energy as it uses more machinery 'to increase relative surplus value while decreasing working class power in the process of class struggle'. Because capital needs machinery to expand the accumulation of surplus value, and because it needs machinery to 'substitute' or control workers in struggle, capital therefore needs energy. Overall, energy powers the ongoing technological revolution, often giving capital the upper hand in the class struggle (Keefer 2010).

Increased throughput and substitution of energy for machines in place of labour mean 'a more rapid depletion of high-quality energy sources and other natural resources, and a large amount of wastes dumped into the environment'. Expanding scales of production, which are a corollary of the valorisation logic of capitalist production, 'normally coincide with greater throughput of raw materials and auxiliary substances', especially fossil fuels (Foster 2002: 45). The metabolic rift approach to climate change connects the rise of capitalism and especially the development of industrial capital to the expansion of anthropogenic CO_2 emissions, 'exploiting the historic stock of energy that was stored deep in the earth and releasing it back into the atmosphere' (Clark and York 2005: 403).

This process might be called *the real subsumption of climate to capital*. Fossil energies are particularly congruent with capitalist production because of their flexibility, fitting capitalist society's particular relationship to nature (Altvater 1993). Technical change may lead to energy-saving machines and less carbon-intensive energy generation, but, under capitalism, only if it is profitable to do so. Accumulation requires capital to reduce the circulation time of commodities produced, to get them sold faster in order to realise the surplus value needed for further accumulation. In the *Grundrisse*, Marx (1986) highlighted the 'annihilation of space by time' – the development of more streamlined and just-in-time labour processes, faster forms of transport to take commodities and workers (and capitalists) to their workplaces – hence the development of fast trains, faster ships, cars and later aeroplanes. This process helps to explain the growth in emissions from transport and communications (York *et al.* 2003). One virtue of the Marxist approach is its ability to burrow down to deep social processes that drive the generation of greenhouse gas emissions. Commodification, accumulation and exploitation – essential to the capitalist mode of production – drive huge, unplanned technical changes, which require enormous inputs of energy, land and materials. Efforts to reduce accelerating quantities of greenhouse gas emissions run up against this logic of capital, from which there is only limited room to escape. It is the structures prevalent within capitalism that simultaneously drive emissions and prevent its ruling agents (both capital and states) from adequately tackling climate change.

When orthodox economists designate anthropogenic climate change as market failure, an unfortunate side-effect of economic growth, they miss 'the systemic mechanisms by which market relations produce social and ecological harm' (Mason 2010). Instead, there is a major explanatory gain from applying critical political economy approaches to the understanding of climate change. In particular, Marxism provides a 'plausible account of the role of power relations in driving carbon-intensive (and socially dislocative) economic development paths'. The worldwide structural lock-in to the fossil fuel-intensive mode of production is not the outcome of a natural play of market forces or pluralistic decision-making, but 'the result of the political dominance of capitalist interests in determining the social allocation of resources' (ibid.: 151–2). If scholars pride themselves on pondering the great questions of our time, they must be 'willing to ask whether the very form of social and economic life – capitalism – is not an underlying cause of climate change' (Wainwright 2010: 987–8). If society is to successfully avoid the most dangerous aspects of climate change, then the critique of capitalism (rather than accommodating to it) is the logical starting point.

Critique of Marxist climate political economy

Many scholars acknowledge the insights of Marxist perspectives, which explain rising greenhouse gas emissions by capitalism's long-term tendency to expand the scale of production and by the associated increase in material and energy throughput. However, they argue that this approach suffers from some similar limitations to pro-capitalist accounts. Marxism is apparently too abstract to explain differences in the emissions of particular states or capitals, nor is sufficient to explain 'capitalism's capability to adapt and adjust to changing external conditions, including the foreseeable end of fossil fuels' (Koch 2012: 37–8). Capitalism also provides the near-term context for any immediate response to climate change; in short, the urgent need to mitigate emissions cannot wait for systemic, structural transformation (Boyd *et al.* 2011).

Some prominent environmental scholars (Daly 2007; Victor 2008; Jackson 2009) argue that ecological limits, including climate change, require a steady-state economy or 'degrowth', the planned reduction of economic output. They believe that 'combating climate change equitably will include an unprecedented degrowth, with a dramatic restructuring of the state and a reconfiguration of work' (Kallis *et al.* 2012: 174). However, degrowth exponents operate within the boundaries of capitalism, leaving markets and private ownership of the means of production largely intact. Degrowth advocates define capital as a static stock of physical wealth, whereas for Marxists, 'capital is a process' (Blauwhof 2012: 255–6). Steady state proposals under capitalism feed 'an abstract notion of growth divorced from the specific form that this takes' and focused 'almost exclusively on scale and relatively little on system' (Foster *et al.* 2010: 203). The accumulation of capital is a systemic necessity. Capitalism can either grow or collapse: it cannot degrow voluntarily. Growth, in the sense of the production of more and more use values, is not the goal of capitalist production. The objective of capital is profit. A socially just, steady state economy is possible, but not feasible within the social relations of capitalism.

Nor is a Marxist approach simply maximalist, demanding socialism or nothing. It does not deny that capitalists have some interest in climate conditions. The intensification of global warming is expected to have adverse effects on capitalist firms and economies, which will register as increases in costs, values and prices, leading to changes in profits, rents and wages. If the climate is a condition of existence for capitalist production, then natural resources constitute elements of constant and variable capital in this production. Even when natural conditions and resources are not commodified, they still affect the value of commodities through their impact on labour productivity (Vlachou and Konstantinidis 2010). Marxist accounts leave room for reforms, albeit as palliatives compared to the scale of transformation necessary.

Capitalist states can use market instruments to partially account for climate change. Burkett (1999: 19, 94, 98) argues that the tendency to undervalue natural conditions remains, because of the distinction between use value and exchange value, and the divergence between value and prices under capitalism. He argues that Marx's rent theory recognises that 'exchange values may be assigned to valueless but scarce and monopolisable natural conditions' (ibid.), but the value–nature contradiction 'cannot be resolved by private rents or by grafting green tax and subsidy schemes onto an economic system shaped and driven by money and capital' (ibid.). The market view presupposes that the price form can adequately represent nature's use value, but capitalism's goal of profitable accumulation and its inherent competitiveness make it 'impossible to adequately regulate greenhouse gas emissions through market channels and their political superstructures' (ibid.). Neoliberal climate policy involves the increased commodification of nature and spatio-temporal fixes linked to financial markets, which largely displaces emissions rather than manage their reduction (Bond 2012).

A Marxist analysis also allows room for regimes of capitalism other than neoliberalism (such as ecological modernisation), which may tackle climate change more adequately. Meaningful reforms to reduce emissions can be fought for and won in the short term, without overturning the entire structure of global capitalism. A transitional politics bridges the gap between reform and revolution. But without large-scale structural transformation and collectivist, democratic, social relations of production, mitigating climate change in the long term is highly unlikely. Having a more transformatory goal helps shape the kind of demands to make, the reforms fought for, the alliances formed and dictates the partners in the alliances. The immediate political significance of the critique of neoliberal capitalism is to reject claims that capital and its representatives are the necessary social actors to which climate policy must defer. Instead, in the short term, capital will have to be driven through regulation, pressure and mobilisation to undertake the necessary climate mitigation and adaptation measures. And the driver of these reforms is simultaneously the agent driving the transformation of social production relations – the organised working-class movement.

Workers and climate change: between market, society and class

This section extends Smith's (2011: 262) 'outrageous proposal' to put labour at the centre of climate politics. Such a move requires a deeper engagement with the concept of class.[3] Class means, first, a general description of structures of material inequality and, second, actual or potential social forces, or social actors, which have the capacity to transform society. Marx distinguished between class-in-itself and class-for-itself (Crompton 1998: 11).

Workers and social agency

The Marxist conception of class starts from exploitative production relations, so that classes begin with the common positions within the social relations of production. Ste Croix (1981: 43–4) defined class as essentially a relationship of 'the collective social expression of the fact of exploitation, the way in which exploitation is embodied in a social structure'. By exploitation, he meant 'the appropriation of part of the product of the labour of others' (ibid.). Under capitalism this involves the appropriation of surplus value. Class is defined as an objective, antagonistic relationship based on exploitation and formed in production, rather than primarily by occupation, income or status (Callinicos 1987b). Under capitalism, exploitation is a particularly explosive form of social relations, first, because it constitutes

> a social relation which simultaneously pits the interests of one group against another and which requires their ongoing interaction, and second it confers on upon the disadvantaged group a real form of power with which to challenge the interests of exploiters.
>
> (Wright 2005: 25)

Exploitation is not simply a matter of theft or exceptionally low wages, but of social production relations masked by the wage form, as well as an explanation for the origin of profits.

Guglielmo Carchedi (1987) argues that classes in capitalist society are derived from the social relations of production, consistent with Marx's labour theory of value. The capitalist class or bourgeoisie is formed by all those who exploit, have real economic ownership of the means of production, perform the global function of capital and derive their income from surplus value. The working class or proletariat are all those who do not own the means of production, perform the function of the collective worker, are exploited and who consequently are paid a wage. The extent of this wage is determined by the value of their labour power. Workers are either paid back part of the value they themselves produced or are paid out of the surplus value produced in the productive spheres. Intermediate classes perform some of the global functions of capital (such as the control and surveillance or workers) without owning the means of production. High-level managers and supervisors occupy 'contradictory class locations' (Wright 1978: 63). These core class relations define both the structures that predominate in capitalist society as well as the most significant agents within it.

Erik Olin Wright (2005: 20–2) introduces a number of useful distinctions that clarify the nature of class. Class interests are 'the material interests of people derived from their location-within-class-relations'. An account of these interests provides a crucial theoretical bridge between the description of class relations and the actions of individuals within those relations. Class consciousness is the subjective awareness people have of their class interests and the conditions for advancing them. Class formations are collectivities formed in order to facilitate the pursuit of class interests, ranging from highly self-conscious organisations such as political parties and trade unions to much looser forms of collectivity such as social networks and communities. As long as exploitation exists and inequalities derived from it persist, there remains the potential for workers to coalesce and organise around those interests for collective action.

The working class is the privileged social agent because of its historically constituted nature as the exploited collective producer within the capitalist mode of production. As the exploited class, it is caught in a systematic clash with capital, which cannot generally and permanently satisfy its needs. As the main producing class, it has 'the power to halt – and within limits redirect – the economic apparatus of capitalism, in pursuit of its goals' (Mulhern 1984). And as the collective producer, it has 'the objective capacity to found a new, non-exploitative mode of production' (ibid.: 22–3). This combination of interest, power and creative capacity distinguishes the working class from every other social and political force in capitalist society. Working-class movements have more consistently than any other social collectivity set themselves on the side of various progressive causes. No other identifiable social force can match the labour movement's record of emancipatory struggles, either in 'the breadth of their visions, the comprehensiveness of the liberation they have sought, or in their degree of success' (Wood 1986: 185–6). This account elevates the working class to a unique position as the essential progressive agent of social change under capitalism, with the best prospects of winning struggles for reforms within it, as well as developing new social relations to replace it.

However, for several decades there has been a feverish retreat from this kind of working-class politics, which for some has scholars turned into a rout. Class is regarded as dead or at least dying, no longer coherent, empirically verifiable or relevant (Pakulski and Waters 1996). Some Green thinkers also share these objections, embracing ecology while bidding farewell to the working class (Gorz 1983). The working class in this interpretation is 'no longer the central agent of progressive social, cultural, and political change' (Eckersley 1992: 123–4). Indeed, for some theorists, there is 'no privileged agent of ecosocialist transformation' (Kovel 2007: 241).

Yet as Beverley Skeggs (1997: 6–7) argues cogently, to abandon class as a theoretical tool does not mean it has ceased to exist; only that some scholars do not value it. When class is abandoned, workers' experiences are silenced and their lives ignored. To think that 'class does not matter is only a prerogative of those unaffected by the deprivations and exclusions it produces' (ibid.). To make class invisible is to abdicate responsibility for the effects it produces – and to abandon vital political actors. In terms of its global social weight, the waged working class has grown both absolutely and relative to other classes. The global waged working class appears to have at least doubled in size in the past three decades. Far from disappearing, the majority of the world's direct producers now probably do waged work rather than (or alongside) work for themselves in peasant agriculture (McNally 2010: 51–3, 134). Recent decades have witnessed one of the greatest migrations in history, with the majority of humanity now living in urban environments where waged labour predominates. Far from disappearing, waged labour remains essential to global capitalism.

Class struggles take place on three fronts: the economic, the political and the ideological.[4] Class originates in the economic sphere with exploitation, but whether it leads to workers' collective action depends on a wider range of political and ideological pressures, both from the context and from within the workers' organisations. The attainment of class consciousness leading to collective action is therefore never automatic or inevitable, nor does it assume workers have a privileged position of perception with regard to social relations. Once class consciousness is treated as 'an unstable, shifting, and indeterminate faculty', it is possible to show how 'sociologically speci-fied class capacities could be made to materialise in action and effects' (Eley and Nield 2007: 173). Gramsci (1971: 641) conceived of 'contradictory con-sciousness', where elements of class consciousness coexist alongside ideas uncritically absorbed from capitalist society.

Working-class politics is not restricted to scarcely attainable levels of revolutionary class consciousness. A more modest standard of class agency is proposed, whereby organised labour as a potential social force and climate agent starts from contemporary conditions. In particular, this dimension of class focuses on elements of independent organisation, participation and representation that are separate from and sometimes antagonistic to employers and the state. A further element of class agency in this respect is the mobilisation of trade unionists and other workers to take action, both at work and outside the workplace, on matters of climate interest. These activities, which take a multiplicity of forms from official industrial action to demonstrations and direct action, are a vital part of what it means to regard workers as climate actors. In terms of ideology and the articulation of demands, the focus is on workers and their organisations confronting the private ownership and control of means of production, particularly in energy and transport, where the bulk of greenhouse gas emissions are gen-erated. Challenges to existing social relations include clashes over property relations, struggles over the frontiers of control at work and, at a lower level, over the distribution of gains and losses. Although class should not be reduced to occupation, demands for socially (and ecologically) useful types of employment, improved conditions at work and other occupational issues are an important part of the class analysis of climate change.

Trade unions in employment relations

There is a wide range of theories in employment relations, suggesting an essential plasticity to trade unionism. Allan Flanders (1970: 15) perceived the tension between unions functioning as a 'vested interest' and their role as 'swords of justice'. Trade unionism generates a series of contradictions, for example, between conflictual oppositionists and cooperative partners. The foundations of the economic appreciation of trade unions as bargaining agents within the labour market were laid by Beatrice and Sidney Webb (Webb and Webb 1920: 1), who defined unions as 'a continuous association of wage earners for the purpose of maintaining or improving the conditions of their employment'. Their contemporary, the American trade union leader Samuel Gompers, summed up this approach economistically as 'pure-and-simple' trade unionism. An alternative, political characterisation of trade unionism considers these organisations as essentially political agents operating in an economic environment. Trade unions act in two areas: the state and the labour market (Streeck and Hassel 2003: 335–7). Such a stance feeds the notion of unions as social partners, who promote more co-operative relations with employers as well as government regulation of the labour market (Heery 2002).

Marx provided another perspective, considering trade unions as a means of organising the working class as a class-for-itself. In *The Communist Manifesto*, he lauded the combination of workers into trade unions. He regarded unions as 'ramparts of resistance' against capital and as 'organising centres of the working class in the broad interest of its complete emancipation'. The task of trade unions was to prove that 'the working classes are bestriding the scene of history no longer as servile retainers, but as independent actors, conscious of their own responsibility' (Marx [1847] 1976a: 210; [1848] 1976b; 1985a: 192; 1985b: 54).

Richard Hyman (2001: 3–4) attempts to capture the variable geometry of trade unionism: whether unions are a bargaining agent, a social partner, a mobiliser of discontent, or all of these at one and the same time. He argued that trade unions face in three directions. As associations of employees, they are concerned to regulate the wage labour relationship, the work performed and payments received. Unions cannot ignore the market. But as organisations of workers, they embody a conception of collective identity that distinguishes them from employers. Whether or not they endorse an ideology of class division and class opposition, 'unions cannot escape a role as agencies of class'. Yet unions also exist and function within a social framework, which they may aspire to change but which constrains their current choices. Survival necessitates 'coexistence with other institutions and other constellations of interest'. Unions are part of society.

Hyman points to three major ideal types of European trade unions in their dealings with: (1) the market; (2) society; and (3) class. In the first, unions are perceived as labour market institutions engaged in collective bargaining; in the second, unions focus on improving workers' conditions and status in society, advancing social justice and equality; and, in the third, they are schools of class conflict in the struggle between capital and labour. He illustrated these with reference to employment relations in Britain, Germany and Italy. Hyman (2012) accepts that his conception was a stylised model, which necessarily oversimplified and underplayed differences between trade unions within any national context. However, the framing provides a useful heuristic for evaluating trade union engagement with climate change.

Hyman (1997: 515) further suggests that to become strategic agents, unions have to answer three fundamental questions: 'whose interests they represent, which issues they embrace as relevant for the task of representation, and what methods and procedures they adopt in undertaking this task'. Whether unions act strategically depends partly on their organisational capacity: the ability to assess opportunities for intervention, to anticipate changing circumstances, to frame coherent policies and to implement these effectively. Strategy requires a long-term perspective and is closely related to leadership. Strategic thinking is 'reflexive and imaginative, based on how leaders have learned to reflect on the past, pay attention to the present, and anticipate the future' (Hyman 2007: 198–9). Trade unions are structurally constrained, but nevertheless collectively make strategic choices.

Trade unions face a range of structural and contextual constraints because they operate within capitalist society and face not only individual employers but states, the media and a range of institutions often hostile to even their minimal goals. They also face internal, agential constraints as a result of their organisational forms. The 'iron law of oligarchy', whereby union officials become managers of discontent or 'labour lieutenants of capital', is not automatically subdued by the 'iron law of democracy'. Unions may take the line of least resistance and seek to consolidate organisation around traditional core constituencies, or seek to 'compensate for the decline in former strongholds by appealing to distinctive interests of the new elite sections of the changing workforce'. This will inevitably confirm unions' status as 'a vested interest defending the position of the relatively advantaged'. The alternative is to assert trade unions' role as a popular movement, developing the capacity 'to represent the losers as well as the beneficiaries from economic restructuring' (Hyman 2004: 25, 28). Trade unions embody the latent force of organised labour, but whether they utilise this power greatly depends on how their members and leaders frame their goals and the methods they employ to reach them.

Reimagining solidarities and social movements

Whether trade unions can act for workers' interests in general and for more universal human interests depends to high degree on how their members and leaders perceive the idea of solidarity. Working-class interests are socially constructed and trade unions play an important role in constituting these interests. Hyman (1999: 94) argues that some notions of workers' interests rest on 'imagined' or 'mechanical solidarities', so that expressions of the general interests of the class have sometimes been representations of the particular interests of relatively protected sections. Instead he proposed a trade unionism based on more 'organic solidarities', particularly on the reassertion of the rights of labour against the imperatives of capital, to integrate and promote a far broader set of interests than previous movements (Simms 2012).

Rebecca Johns (1998: 256) argues that some solidarity campaigns are designed to confront the class relations between workers and employers 'regardless of the consequences for any particular locale within the space-economy', what she called 'transformatory solidarity'. However, other actions, dubbed 'accommodationist solidarity', while giving the outward appearance of seeking to defend common class interests, 'are actually protesting about particular workers' privileged positions within the spatial division of labour and may have nothing to do with challenging the extant class relations of capitalism' (ibid.). Andrew Herod (2002: 98–9) argues that some international trade union campaigns are politically regressive and designed 'to preserve the vaunted position of some workers in the global economy'. Sometimes sections of capital and labour might construct vested interests in spatial fixes that are complementary to one another. On these occasions, 'workers may participate in cross-class coalitions not as dupes of capital but as fully aware social actors who perceive their own futures as being dependent upon the success or failure of local boosterism and who act accordingly' (ibid.). Solidarity in the progressive sense of the term cannot be assumed: it is a path consciously chosen and has to be constituted through struggle.

Social movement theory provides insights into forms of solidarity and the role of trade unionism as a form of social movement (Tarrow 1998; Kelly 2005). The concept of 'social movement unionism' originated as a description of militant unions, notably in South Africa. As a theoretical development seeking to overcome existing models of economic or political unionism, it is generally credited to Peter Waterman, though he would reject the conception set out here.[5] Kim Moody (1997: 4–5, 276) extends the original interpretation of social movement unionism to the international arena in the context of neoliberal globalisation. He argued that social movement unionism aspires to be 'deeply democratic', because that is the best way to mobilise the strength of numbers and to apply maximum economic leverage. Such unions are militant in collective bargaining, in the belief that retreat only leads to further defeats. Social movement unions emphasise solidarity – 'an injury to one is an injury to all' (ibid.). They are grounded at the workplace level, where organisation is powerful. They are political, acting 'independently of the retreating parties of liberalism and social democracy', fighting for all the oppressed and enhancing their own power in the process by taking a universal, global outlook. Social movement unions 'ally with other social movements, but provide a class vision and content that make for a stronger glue than that which usually holds electoral or temporary coalitions together' (ibid.). Democracy, solidarity, militancy, internationalism, independence, workplace organisation and activism: these are the crucial values that constitute social movement unionism.

Integral to social movement unionism is the belief that unions should act in concert with other progressive social forces and particularly new social movements. Coalitions involve 'discrete, intermittent, or continuous joint activity in pursuit of shared or common goals between trade unions and other non-labour institutions in civil society, including community, faith, identity, advocacy, welfare, and campaigning organisations' (Frege *et al.* 2004: 137–8). Implicitly, this conception opposes joint union action with state agencies, mainstream political parties and between unions and employers – though it allows for a wide range of united actions, alliances and campaigns.

Lowell Turner (2006: 87, 93) suggests that trade unions should look in the direction of ecology, because it is 'difficult to imagine preservation of the earth and a broadening of human rights unless unions join such coalitions as enthusiastic proponents and partners'. Social movement unionism in the context of climate change would therefore involve transformative, collective solidarity action in pursuit of emancipatory goals together with other progressive allies.

Workers and ecology: a natural synergy?

The social and economic role of trade unions may be tacitly acknowledged, but there are few advocates of the notion that workers can be climate agents. On matters of ecology, organised labour has largely been consigned to the recycling bin of history. Neoliberal scholars believe that trade unions support environmental regulation only in so far as it benefits their members' health or jobs, and that rents from environmental regulation may be shared through the bargaining process (Yandle 1985: 430). Unions calling for carbon taxes are regarded as 'foul-weather allies' or 'Cheshire Cats', retaining their own job security while foisting unemployment on other (often non-unionised) workers (Fredriksson and Gaston 1999: 666).

Trade unions' climate policy has been considered fleetingly within the framework of neoliberal political economy. Boom (2002a: 241–2) argues that 'environmental policy is not the core interest of unions, and hence, they often have no policy on this issue'. However, where they do, 'workers prefer direct regulation because this gives the highest level of employment'. Boom (2002b: 273) discusses union policy with respect to carbon emissions trading. Trade unions may prefer no emissions trading, because 'if the industry has low abatement costs, international emissions trading may mean a loss of jobs'. However, if emissions trading leads to higher profits for industry, this will give unions 'a greater opportunity to press for higher wages for their members'. Hence trade unions could support emissions trading. But Boom also expected they would reject a cap on trading, because 'such a cap will increase the cost of compliance for industry'. These claims appear incongruent: unions may either oppose or support carbon trading while opposing caps on emissions, even though some sort of cap is essential to these trading schemes. Orthodox economic theory seemed largely unable to conceptualise a coherent climate interest for workers.

Similarly, some proponents of ecological modernisation have rejected a worker-based approach to ecological questions. Mol and Spaargaren (2000: 41) believe that global environmental risks are 'democratic', in the sense that they make no distinction between social classes, so 'traditional class differences are no longer adequate to understand the distribution of these risks among the population'. For these scholars, nobody can escape the greenhouse effect or other environmental hazards. Rather, now is found 'the tendency that socio-economic categories (classes) and environmental risks no longer run parallel by definition' – all members of society have to deal with modern environmental risks one way or the other. John Barry (2013: 227–8) argues that the labour movement has uncritically embraced orthodox economic growth and capital accumulation, and consequently had 'an overly narrow focus on issues around formal employment, pay and conditions', supporting coal production, nuclear power and airport expansion. Unions have often 'explicitly mis-portrayed environmental conservation issues in terms of "jobs versus the environment" and sided with political forces for unsustainability – such as the nation-state and corporations – against environmentalists'. The trade union movement has become 'effectively depoliticised and divorced from a vision of its purpose as the fundamental transformation of social, economic and political structures within society'.

These objections all boil down to one crucial area: whether workers and their organisations have a coherent interest in ecological matters. In the case of neoliberal market thinkers, workers' interests are reduced to narrow, particular and sectional economic motives, in keeping with their instrumental view of rational actors. In the case of ecological modernisation, workers' interests have no particularity at all; they are simply dissolved into a wider general interest. Most green political thought echoes these positions while rejecting politics based on class, whether rooted in the limited goals of trade unionism or wider transformatory socialist ambitions.

The exploitation-based conception of waged labour is the best means to reconstruct the interests of workers with respect to ecology. Approaching ecological politics through the lens of class, defined in terms of exploitation, does not preclude other lenses such as race and gender (Newell 2005). Anthropogenic climate change can be conceived as the world's affluent benefiting at the expense of the world's poor, a relationship that 'can be plausibly described as exploitation' (Vanderheiden 2009: 45–6). Paul Burkett posits the working class as the social agent with the special interest and strategic power to tackle ecological questions:

> The working class is the agency whose everyday life-activities and (individual and collective) struggles are rooted in, but not limited to, capitalism's dominant form of productive activity: wage-labour and capital accumulation. It is the only systemically essential group that directly experiences the limitations of purely economic struggles over wages and working conditions as ways of achieving human development, given the increasingly communal and global character of the environmental problems produced by capitalist production. It is therefore the only agency capable not just of envisioning but of practically undertaking a planned and life-guided recombination of economic and environmental reproduction. But to lead this project it must struggle not just for the demarketisation of production and its necessary conditions, but for its own collective taking, holding and utilisation of these conditions and their conversion into means of sustaining human development. This includes

a practical grasp of scientific knowledge. Without such a thoroughgoing disalienation, which necessarily involves a long historical epoch of struggle, the demarketisation of production will only lead to new forms of alienation and capitalisation, and new forms of the metabolic rift as occurred for instance in the Soviet Union.

(Burkett 2006: 300)

More concretely, the working class bears a disproportionate share of the harm due to environmental destruction, giving workers 'a clear interest in environmental protection'. This includes the effects of environmental degradation on health and other quality of life issues, as well as the siting of hazardous, environmentally undesirable facilities close to working-class communities. Further, policies designed to protect the natural environment 'tend to impose a greater economic burden on the working class'. Some research has demonstrated that 'environmental concerns are widespread among the working class and that lower-income people are actually more willing than others to sacrifice economic expansion in favour of environmental protection' (Obach 2004: 29–31).

Workers, as the principal victims of ecological degradation, have a special interest in tackling the source of this damage. It is precisely the same mechanisms that give rise to exploitation (a longer working day, the reorganisation and mechanisation of the labour process) that also give rise to ecological damage. These analogous, simultaneous processes have a common root in the drives of capital. Victor Silverman (2004: 133) put it succinctly: 'By understanding the domination and exploitation of workers and of nature is inextricable, labour environmentalists situate humans within the natural. Exploitation is the unifying term, which makes the common enemy common.' This implies that workers, who have the incentive to mitigate and ultimately abolish their own exploitation, also have a significant and privileged stake in abolishing the processes that give rise to the degradation of the natural environment. Herein lies the real value of 'class-as-exploitation' – it posits working-class agency as potentially capable of embracing the general, universal interest of ecology as its own special interest.

Workers are likely to be among those most vulnerable to the physical impacts of climate change and to have fewer resources to adapt to climate change, given their levels of wages and limited access to means of production. However, workers are also likely to be the victims of government policies designed to tackle climate change, especially those that shift the costs of mitigation and adaptation from capital onto labour. Workers are expected to struggle against the impacts of climate change and climate policy, generating class struggles between antagonistic social actors. Climate politics will become another terrain on which class struggles are played out (Vlachou 2000; 2005; Brunnengräber 2006). These struggles may take the form of workplace-based strikes and other forms of industrial action, or they may involve working-class communities battling particular climate policies in their locality. They may take a political form in clashes over taxation and fiscal policy, particularly when this impacts on employment.

Trade unions as climate actors

Trade unions as ecological actors

If workers suffer disproportionately from ecological problems and from market- and state-led efforts to internalise the damage, then one might expect to encounter workers organising collectively to resist these impacts. In some circumstances, workers' and trade unions' contributions to environmental protection have been narrow and limited. European research in the 1990s found that trade unions played a rather reactive role with regard to environmental issues. Trade union strategies were 'concentrated on the core issues of interest representation: growing or steady income and ensuring optimal employment and working conditions, in the main guaranteed by economic growth and post-war prosperity' (Gregory *et al.* 1996: 442). Yet worker engagement with ecological issues can be traced back at least as far as the nineteenth century, notably to William Morris.[6] Environmental labour historians highlight some outstanding examples of trade union action on ecological issues across the globe, where workers allied with environmentalists to form significant and effective coalitions. For example, in the 1980s, UK trade unions took action against the use of pesticides and on dumping of nuclear waste at sea (Mason and Morter 1998).

Probably the most impressive working-class-based ecological movement to date was led by Australian construction workers (Mallory 2005). In the first half of the 1970s, the New South Wales Builders' Labourers Federation (BLF) imposed around 50 'green bans' in the Sydney area in support of environmental campaigns, in an archetypal form of social movement unionism (Burgmann and Burgmann 1998). BLF secretary Jack Mundey dismissed the myth that 'the environment movement is the preserve of the do-gooding middle class'. He argued that: 'It is the workers who are most affected by the deterioration of the environment and it is therefore up to the trade union movement to give it a higher priority to fighting to improve it' (Burgmann 2000: 98). In its scope and effectiveness, the green bans movement has yet to be surpassed as an exemplar of trade union ecological mobilisation.

However, the BLF were not alone in radically reconfiguring trade union ecological politics.[7] During the 1970s, a significant number of workplace rank-and-file union organisations in Britain produced workers' plans, in response to employers' restructuring and unemployment. These plans invariably questioned the logic of capitalist production for profit and asserted the need for 'socially useful production' – often making explicitly pro-ecology proposals. Probably the most famous was the Lucas Aerospace Corporate Plan, published by the cross-union combine committee in 1976 (Wainwright and Elliott 1982; see Chapter 3 for further discussion). While it would be mistaken to equate these peaks with an inevitable trajectory, the examples nevertheless demonstrate the potential of organised labour in eco-logical matters and that ecological interests are a recognisable emergent property of trade unions in certain conditions.

Räthzel, Uzzell and Elliott (2010) recognise the relevance of these Lucas-inspired workers' plans for trade unions confronting climate change in today's conditions. At the turn of the new century, some trade union representatives grasped both the epochal importance of climate change, for the sake of their own members, their class and for wider society. Some seized the moment to reorientate themselves for organisational renewal and turned outwards towards new alliances. For others, more immediate and sectional matters continued to dominate. Snell and Fairbrother (2010: 413, 421) argue that the social, economic and industrial implications of climate change 'provide possibilities for unions to renew themselves with a new sense of purpose'. Some unions are in the process of constructing a 'politico-ecological' role for themselves that 'expresses a "green" vision for the future of work' (ibid.). However, they still need to protect the interests of the workers and members they represent, whose lives depend upon the con-tinuation and expansion of economic activity. Similarly, Uzzell and Räthzel (2013b: 255) highlight the conjunctural importance of climate change for trade unions, a moment when they recognise that 'it could be decisive for their future, not only in terms of the effects it will have on jobs, but also for the impact it could have on international solidarity'. Union representatives may be discovering and even embracing a new sense of purpose, but they have to do so within the context of existing global production relations.

With ambition, organised labour has the potential to play a hegemonic role in climate politics. Only a large, sustained coalition of labour and environmental movements can 'reveal the interconnectedness of climate change with the class aspects of modern capitalist societies at a global level' (Vlachou and Konstantinidis 2010: 47). It is not possible to stop climate change without trade unionists because 'environmentalists cannot do it on their own'. A mass climate movement 'has to include and mobilise large numbers of working-class people'. Not all workers are union members, but 'the easiest way to mobilise workers is still through the unions' (Neale 2008: 251–2). Trade unions could become powerful motivators for climate action by working with 'third sector' organisations such as local community groups (Hale 2010: 263–4). The potential of union solidarity on climate matters, as well as some of the possible contradictions in union climate action, is evident from the discourses employed by some unions internationally.

Trade unions and climate discourses

Trade unions are now beginning to receive some scholarly attention as cli-mate actors, after a long period of neglect. Although a principal social actor in the labour process, trade unions have largely been ignored in climate

debates (Patenaude 2011). Trade union leaders and their members conceptualise climate change using a variety of tropes to produce a mélange of
responses. Räthzel and Uzzell (2011: 1221) offer a synthesis of the frames
used by unions to articulate their climate politics, based on interviews with
key officials. First, the *technological fix* discourse looks to improved technology to safeguard jobs and protect the environment. However, this approach
does not address the social context in which technological innovations are
embedded. The 'social effects of technological development, like reduced
employment, are naturalised' (ibid.). Second, the *social transformation* discourse proposes a comprehensive policy in which environmental protection
and societal change are interconnected. Workers' fears of losing their jobs
are understood in broader terms, acknowledging that 'transforming production
must take into account socially constructed images of work and professions,
including social power relations' (ibid.).

Third, Räthzel and Uzzell (ibid.: 1221–2) register the *mutual interests* discourse, which focuses on the legitimacy of workers' immediate interests. It
aims to resolve the contradiction between jobs and the environment by
entering into a horizontal dialogue with workers about 'how their immediate
interests can be redefined and reconciled rather than abandoned'. It replaces
an abstract morality with a focus on interests, cooperation and solidarity.
The fourth framing is dubbed the *social movement* discourse. It includes
workers' immediate interests, but places them within a broader notion of
general interests. It conceptualises unions as representing not only the interests of workers at work, but society as a whole. Further, Räthzel and Uzzell
also discerned an embryonic new perspective of nature in trade union discourses, bridged by a South Africa trade unionist who talked about 'the
metabolic rift between nature and humans'.

Romain Felli (2014: 381–4) examines international trade union discourses
on climate change and identifies three essential strategies: (1) the deliberative;
(2) collaborative growth; and (3) the socialist. The *deliberative* strategy is
associated with 'a non-conflictual understanding of social relations' and
despite claims to reject neoliberalism, the acceptance of market solutions 'is
central to this strategy'. The core rationale is the emphasis on 'adaptation' to
change. This strategy has led to 'accommodating the worse consequences
of climate change for workers in a situation in which fundamental property
relations are left unchallenged'. The *collaborative growth* strategy assesses the
constraints of climate change essentially in terms of the costs and benefits
associated with climate policies, notably the employment effects of the losses
and gains of national competitiveness due to climate regulations. It uses the
rhetoric of cost-cutting through energy efficiency and other environment-
friendly measures, and also offers hope for the growth of 'green' companies
and sectors. As Felli (ibid.: 387) points out, competitiveness 'presupposes
competitiveness against others (including other workers)'. By contrast, the
socialist strategy solves the climate crisis through the transformation of the
social relations of production and not just the implementation of new or

stronger regulations. The possibility of organising democratic control over the economy is 'the essential element distinguishing the socialist from other strategies' (ibid.: 389, 391).

Snell and Fairbrother (2011: 87–90) examine the activities of four Australian unions, each representing different formulations of climate politics. The Australian Workers' Union, which represents workers in primary and traditional manufacturing industries, promotes a partnership approach. It has been a vocal opponent of emissions trading, arguing that the Australian government should only introduce it if a global scheme is implemented, because of the threat of carbon leakage. The Construction, Forestry, Mining and Energy Union adopts a jobs-defence position, while lobbying strongly for federal government funding for carbon capture and storage projects. The Electrical Trades Union, representing workers in power generation, prefers to encourage the development of renewable energy. Finally, the Australian Manufacturing Workers Union argues for a comprehensive industrial policy, laying the foundations for a just transition to a low-carbon economy. Even though it is likely to lose members if carbon-intensive industries reduce or close their operations, this union is considered to have the most progressive union environmental policy.

Similar discourses have been found in other case studies of unions elsewhere. The Canadian Auto Workers (CAW), for many years regarded as a model social movement union and now part of the Unifor union, appears before the merger to have accommodated to the same kind of market pressure as some Australian unions. The CAW found itself at the intersection of several important political tensions, a clear conflict between 'the vested interests of the auto-industry membership in defending their existing (and increasingly scarce) jobs' and the 'global ecological interest in averting catastrophic climate change by transforming the industry in which they work, the transportation system, and the urban infrastructure built around it'. This was evidenced by CAW leaders' support for automakers' decisions to produce sports utility vehicles in Canadian plants, hostility towards Japanese hybrid vehicles and distancing themselves from the Canadian environment movement (Hrynyshyn and Ross 2011: 17, 22).

The United Steelworkers of America (USW) demonstrates competing tensions between its own conception of steelworkers' interests with regard to climate change, and those found within ecological modernisation and neoliberal discourses. As early as 1980, a resolution at a USW convention presaged the threat of global warming. In 1990, it adopted a report forewarning that climate change 'may be the single greatest problem we face'. The USW has articulated 'a particular version of ecological modernisation that seeks to renew post-war Fordist relations between labour, the state, and domestic capital – especially so-called green industries'. This 'green new dealism' does not fundamentally challenge capitalism, but it does 'oppose the free-market logic of neoliberalism' and the downward pressures on pay and conditions (Nugent 2011: 60–1).

Further evidence of a range of climate discourses at work has emerged from research into 'climate champions', which in the UK context are employees who are given a voluntary, unpaid, but semi-official climate watchdog role by their employer. Swaffield and Bell (2012: 249–50, 258) found that these champions 'consistently constructed the process of social change in neoliberal terms' and 'do not challenge the limits that neoliberalism imposes on how we can tackle the problem of climate change'. However, participants also used a different set of discourses when asked about their own reasons for involvement in the scheme, appealing to ideas of justice, responsibility to future generations and 'doing the right thing'. Lewis and Juravle (2010: 490–1) found three distinct discourses articulated by climate champions: (1) the neoliberal view that free markets can solve environmental problems; (2) advocacy of some kind of government intervention; and (3) a 'dissenter' view. A dissenter argues that 'the interests of capital, land (environment) and labour are not the same – they are constantly in conflict'. The idea that everyone to sit down and thrash it out among friends is 'flawed … typically labour and more recently the environment, will always tend to be on the losing side' (ibid.).

This threefold division between market, state and dissenter discourses is similar to the one utilised in this book. Of course, any such synthesis risks conflating important and contradictory ways in which the climate is framed. However, as Hulme (2009) points out, there do appear to be some strong and distinct meta-narratives for the social construction of climate change, with significant differences of assessment and political conclusions arising from them.

Trade unions as strategic climate actors

Neoliberal and ecological modernisation discourses are hegemonic in the current social constructions of climate change. The neoliberal framework conceptualises climate political economy in terms of market failure and concludes that market-based instruments are the principal tools to solve the problem. The role of the state in the neoliberal interpretation is confined largely to making the conditions for markets to function, for example, by establishing property rights for emissions trading or by imposing carbon taxes. This framing looks mainly to private business actors to respond to price signals and change the behaviour of firms. The ecological modernisation discourse accepts the predominant role for markets, but also provides scope for command and control measures, regulation and other non-market instruments in climate policy by the state. This framing extends beyond business and government actors to include non-state actors, such as environmental NGOs and even occasionally trade unions. The Labour government's climate policy between 1997 and 2010 was located between neoliberalism and ecological modernisation, while global climate policy emanating from the UNFCCC also appears on the same terrain.

A Marxist critique of the dominant climate political economy reveals the absence of class dimensions within these discourses. This is reflected in a largely uncritical acceptance of existing structures and institutions as adequate to tackle climate change. In particular, the dominant framings elide the connections between capitalism as the world's dominant political and economic system and the causes of climate change. With an inadequate grasp of the real generative mechanisms driving the burning of fossil fuels, there is no systematic discussion of how to transform and reconfigure social relations to create a low-carbon economy. Class is also largely missing from assessments of the impacts of climate change, from evaluations of the effects of climate policy, and from analyses of social agents capable of tackling the issues. Workers are largely ignored, both as interested parties affected by climate change and policy, but also as active agents in remaking social climate relations.

If workers are understood as exploited waged labourers, then it is possible to establish their real interests and powers in nature–society relations, including climate change. However, working-class interests are not mechanically transposed into working-class organisations, nor must ecological matters inevitably translate into working-class action. This chapter suggests the potential for trade unions, as workers' organisations within existing political and economic structures, to come to terms with ecological questions. Hyman's (2001) trichotomy of trade union identities and discourses between market, society and class is the primary conception used in this study. It is not an abstract normative model, but one that coalesces real structures, social agencies and ideological discourses. The relevance of this model for ecological questions has been noted (Räthzel and Uzzell 2011). In employment relations terms, business unionism prioritises labour market issues such as collective bargaining and the representation and protection of occupational interests. By contrast, integrative unionism emphasises wider social justice, political reform and social integration. The class moment is distinguished by a more anti-capitalist orientation, with workers' class interests advanced through militant socio-political mobilisation.

This model can be extended by mapping the ecological and climate discourses onto trade unions. This mapping associates neoliberal climate discourse with the market pole; ecological modernisation with the social integration pole; and the Marxist perspective with the class pole (see Figure 2.1). Using this model, it is possible to deepen our understanding of the policies, behaviours and practices of trade unions with respect to climate change. Trade unionists approaching climate change primarily as a market issue tend to emphasise similar concerns to their employers, including the impact on competitiveness, profitability and employment. These union representatives are generally supportive of market-based instruments such as emissions trading, though they are mindful of the effects on the viability of the businesses in which they organise. Their climate solidarity will tend to be 'accommodationist' towards employers, in the sense defined by labour geographers. Taking neoliberal globalisation as given and in the absence of a

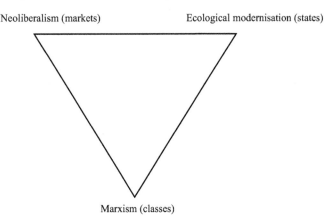

Neoliberalism (markets)   Ecological modernisation (states)

Marxism (classes)

Figure 2.1 The variable geometry of climate political economy

global compact, they are likely to fear the effects of 'carbon leakage' for employment.

By contrast, trade unionists orientated towards social integration often embrace the discourse of ecological modernisation, with its pursuit of co-benefits and win–wins for social partners. They tend to look to the state for an active industrial policy, one that promotes low-carbon technologies and new green jobs, especially in renewable energy. They are concerned with the wider social justice impacts of climate policy, including the effects of higher prices on fuel poverty and with adaptation to climate changes already underway. These union representatives are likely to 'accommodate' more closely with their local states. Finally, other trade unionists take a more explicitly class-orientated approach. They are more critical of existing efforts to tackle climate change and are unwilling to entrust action solely to states and markets. In particular, they underline the question of who pays and conceive of existing climate policy as taking measures at the expense of workers. These trade unionists emphasise radical alternative structures and social relations, both domestically and internationally, even when staying within the boundaries of states and capital (such as the workers' plans). They avoid collaboration with employers and the state, but seek an independent stance based on identifiable class interests. They will probably ally with community and other organisations in coalitions and engage in more militant tactics on matters of 'transformative' solidarity.

The attitude to climate change represents a strategic choice for trade unionists: the framing of interests, the modes of representation and the methods used to engage with it are likely to depend on individual unions' organisational capacity, leadership reflexivity and their chosen orientation within the market–class–society triangle. The approach does not ignore differentiation between and within trade unions. Union leaderships may pursue strategies incongruent with the general interests of workers, in particular, by juxtaposing their members' perceived interests to those of other workers. Similarly, different unions may conceive of climate solidarity in various ways and make diverse alliances or coalitions in framing their own stance on climate change. These strands can be tested empirically by assessing UK trade unions' climate practice over the past three decades.

Conclusion

The dominant framings of climate change across the globe are largely between neoliberalism and ecological modernisation, with Marxism as very much a minority interpretation. Such a three-way division is inevitably somewhat stylised. Nevertheless, neoliberalism, ecological modernisation and Marxism capture vital elements of market, state and class that are unavoidable elements in any social science attempt to comprehend contemporary climate change.

The current impasse of climate politics can be traced to the misframing of vital matters by the dominant discourses of neoliberalism and ecological modernisation. If market failure really is the cause of emissions' proliferation, then it seems obtuse to rely on the same capitalist societal structures and the same social agents (largely business actors, and ironically facilitating states) to resolve the problem. Similarly, while ecological modernisation appears to offer the possibility of a reformed, state-led and technologically rearmed capitalism, this framing does not challenge the dominance of market imperatives or the processes that give rise to climate change. A Marxist approach offers a distinct framing of climate social relations and structures, centred on labour. The valence of this approach resides in its ability to identify and explain the social processes that have accelerated greenhouse gas emissions over the last two and a half centuries. The real subsumption of climate to capital parallels the transformation of the labour process by the production of relative surplus value, unconstrained by climate imperatives.

Politically, this approach has the advantage of naming the 'enemy' of climate change as the structures of capitalist production and thereby rejects efforts designed to tackle climate change through the profit-seeking firms. Understanding capitalism as an exploitative, class society is an important ingredient for climate politics, because class is vital for understanding the differential impacts of climate change on societies and communities. Workers are among the most vulnerable groups susceptible to the effects of climate change. Workers are also likely to bear the brunt of governments' and employers' policies designed to tackle climate change in their own way. These tendencies are likely to give rise to class struggle over climate matters. A further advantage of the Marxist approach is a sharper focus on political subjects and forces, which points towards a more adequate account of the social agency required for climate politics.

Trade unions are often regarded as quintessential working-class organisations, given their social composition: their members are workers who live by selling their labour power for wages. Trade unions may be class formations, but whether they adequately represent class interests depends upon their members, their leadership, their internal democracy and political orientation. Some trade unions, their leaders, activists and members have been able to articulate a distinctive class-based ecology in certain conditions. The high points historically of these efforts are probably the 'green bans' movement in Australia and the workers' plans in the UK during the 1970s. There are some signs that trade unions across the globe are beginning to grapple with the implications of climate change. As expected, unions exhibit a wide range of responses to climate change, which depend heavily on the industries they organise in, their leadership and the ability of rank-and-file members to debate the issues. Trade union climate politics can be usefully understood as lying between the market, social (or state) and class structures in which they operate. Whether unions can become outward-facing social movements that incorporate climate change into their core mission is possible, but contingent on the circumstances they work in and the strategies they pursue. This potential can be tested empirically and is examined in the following four chapters.

Notes

1 Rayner, Malone and Thompson (1999) suggest a market-institutional-egalitarian triangulation, which resembles the employment relations trichotomy of markets, society and class developed by Hyman (2001).
2 The environmental justice movement has deep roots in African-American, indigenous and other working-class community struggles (see Bullard 1990).
3 Ekers and Loftus (2013: 239) warn that there is no universal subject that labours; rather, there are particular classed, gendered and racialised groups that are involved in the production of nature across time and space.
4 This conception, attributed to Engels, was developed by Lenin in *What Is to Be Done?* (Lih 2008: 697ff.) and adopted by Gramsci (1978: 287–8).
5 Waterman (2001: 26 n.8) would now reject the interpretation given here as 'workerist', arguing that 'the assertion of the working class's vanguard role in the struggle against neoliberalism would seem to be empirically in error and prescriptively counterproductive'. However, Waterman (2008: 307) conceded that 'whilst labour is not the privileged bearer of the new global solidarity, it is essential to it'.
6 William Morris identified working-class action as essential to protect the environment. Shortly after his conversion to socialism, he looked forward to a time 'when the workmen of some manufacturing district will strike to compel their masters to consume their own smoke' (Meier 1978: 425). Morris made the point more explicitly in a public lecture on 12 December 1882:

> I have taken note of many strikes, and I must needs say without circumlocution that with many of these I have heartily sympathised: but when the day comes that there is a serious strike of workmen against the poisoning of the air with smoke or the waters with filth, I shall think that art is getting on indeed.
>
> (Lemire 1969: 51)

7 Mundey visited the UK in 1975 and helped spark a struggle to defend the central post office in Birmingham, which involved an unusual alliance between the UCATT building workers union and the local Victorian Society (Burgmann and

Burgmann 1998: 284). The late Peter Carter, a key union organiser in Birmingham at the time, kindly provided press (Carter, pers. comm., 24 April 2008).

References

Adger, N., Paavola, J. and Huq, S. (2006) 'Towards Justice in Adaptation to Climate Change'. In N. Adger, J. Paavola, S. Huq and M. Mace (eds) *Fairness in Adaptation to Climate Change*. Cambridge, MA: MIT Press.

Altvater, E. (1993) *The Future of the Market*. London: Verso.

——(2006) 'The Social and Natural Environment of Fossil Capitalism', *Socialist Register*, 43: 37–59.

Bäckstrand, K. and Lövbrand, E. (2006) 'Planting Trees to Mitigate Climate Change: Contested Discourses of Ecological Modernization, Green Governmentality and Civic Environmentalism', *Global Environmental Politics*, 6(1): 50–75.

Baer, P. (2006) 'Adaptation: Who Pays Whom?' In N. Adger, J. Paavola, S. Huq and M. Mace (eds) *Fairness in Adaptation to Climate Change*. Cambridge, MA: MIT Press.

Bailey, I. and Wilson, G. (2009) 'Theorising Transitional Pathways in Response to Climate Change: Technocentrism, Ecocentrism, and the Carbon Economy', *Environment and Planning A*, 41(10): 2324–41.

Baldwin, R. (2008) 'Regulation Lite: The Rise of Emissions Trading', *Regulation and Governance*, 2: 193–215.

Barker, T. (2008) 'The Economics of Avoiding Dangerous Climate Change. An Editorial Essay on The Stern Review', *Climatic Change*, 89: 173–94.

Barrett, J., Peters, G., Wiedmann, T., Scott, K., Lenzen, M., Roelich, K. and Le Qur, C. (2013) 'Consumption-Based GHG Emission Accounting: A UK Case Study', *Climate Policy*, 13(4): 451–70.

Barrett, S. (2009) 'Climate Treaties and the Imperative of Enforcement'. In D. Helm and C. Hepburn (eds) *The Economics and Politics of Climate Change*. Oxford: Oxford University Press.

Barry, J. (2013) 'Trade Unions and the Transition from "Actually Existing Unsustainability": From Economic Crisis to a New Political Economy Beyond Growth'. In N. Räthzel and D. Uzzell (eds) *Trade Unions in the Green Economy: Working for the Environment*. London: Routledge.

Barry, J. and Paterson, M. (2004) 'Globalisation, Ecological Modernisation and New Labour', *Political Studies*, 52(4): 767–84.

Bartle, I. (2009) 'A Strategy for Better Climate Regulation: Towards a Public Interest Orientated Regulatory Regime', *Environmental Politics*, 18(5): 689–706.

Blauwhof, F. (2012) 'Overcoming Accumulation: Is a Capitalist Steady-state Economy Possible?' *Ecological Economics*, 84: 254–61.

Bond, P. (2012) 'Emissions Trading, New Enclosures and Eco-Social Contestation', *Antipode*, 44(3): 684–701.

Boom, J-T. (2002a) 'Interest Group Preference for Instruments of Environmental Policy: An Overview'. In C. Böhringer, M. Finus and C. Vogt (eds) *Controlling Global Warming: Perspectives from Economics, Game Theory and Public Choice*. Cheltenham: Edward Elgar.

——(2002b) 'Interest Group Preference for Emissions Trading Scheme'. In C. Böhringer, M. Finus and C. Vogt (eds) *Controlling Global Warming: Perspectives from Economics, Game Theory and Public Choice*. Cheltenham: Edward Elgar.

Boyd, E., Boykoff, M. and Newell, P. (2011) 'The "New" Carbon Economy: What's New?' *Antipode*, 43(3): 601–11.

Boyd, W., Prudham, S. and Schurman, R. (2001) 'Industrial Dynamics and the Problem of Nature', *Society and Natural Resources*, 14(7): 555–70.

Brunnengräber, A. (2006) 'The Political Economy of the Kyoto Protocol', *Socialist Register*, 43: 213–30.

Büchs, M., Bardsley, N. and Duwe, S. (2011) 'Who Bears the Brunt? Distributional Effects of Climate Change Mitigation Policies', *Critical Social Policy*, 31(2): 285–307.

Bullard, R. (1990) *Dumping in Dixie: Race, Class and Environmental Quality*. 1st edn. Boulder, CO: Westview Press.

Bunzl, M. (2009) 'Climate and the Commons: A Reappraisal', *Climatic Change*, 97: 59–65.

Burgmann, M. and Burgmann, V. (1998) *Green Bans: Red Union: Environmentalism and the New South Wales Builders Labourers' Federation*. Sydney: New South Wales Press.

Burgmann, V. (2000) 'The Social Responsibility of Labour Versus the Environmental Impact of Property Capital: The Australian Green Bans Movement', *Environmental Politics*, 9(2): 78–101.

Burkett, P. (1999) *Marx and Nature: A Red and Green Perspective*. Basingstoke: Macmillan.

——(2006) *Marxism and Ecological Economics: Toward a Red and Green Political Economy*. Leiden: Brill Academic Publishers.

Burnham, P. (2001) 'Marx, International Political Economy and Globalization', *Capital & Class*, 75: 103–12.

Callinicos, A. (1987a) *Making History*. London: Polity.

——(1987b) 'Introduction'. In A. Callinicos and C. Harman, *The Changing Working Class*. London: Bookmarks.

Callinicos, A. and Rosenberg, J. (2008) 'Uneven and Combined Development: The Social-Relational Substratum of "the international"? An Exchange of Letters', *Cambridge Review of International Affairs*, 21(1): 77–112.

Carbon Tracker and the Grantham Research Institute (2013) *Unburnable Carbon 2013: Wasted Capital and Stranded Assets*. London: Carbon Tracker and the Grantham Research Institute.

Carchedi, G. (1987) *Class Analysis and Social Research*. Oxford: Basil Blackwell.

Carter, N. and Ockwell, D. (2007) *New Labour, New Environment? An Analysis of the Labour Government's Policy on Climate Change and Biodiversity Loss*, Report for Friends of the Earth, Centre for Ecology, Law and Policy. York: University of York.

Cass, L. and Pettenger, M. (2007) 'Conclusion: The Constructions of Climate Change'. In M. Pettenger (ed.) *The Social Construction of Climate Change*. Aldershot: Ashgate.

Castree, N. (2008) 'Neoliberalising Nature: The Logics of Deregulation and Reregulation', *Environment and Planning A*, 40(1): 131–52.

Chatterton, P., Featherstone, D. and Routledge, P. (2013) 'Articulating Climate Justice in Copenhagen: Antagonism, the Commons, and Solidarity', *Antipode*, 45(3): 602–20.

Christie, R. (1980) 'Why Does Capital Need Energy?' In P. Nore and T. Turner (eds) *Oil and Class Struggle*. London: Zed Books.

Clark, B. and York, R. (2005) 'Carbon Metabolism: Global Capitalism, Climate Change and the Biospheric Rift', *Theory and Society*, 34: 391–428.

Compston, H. (2009) 'Introduction: Political Strategies for Climate Policy', *Environmental Politics*, 18(5): 659–69.

Convery, F. (2009) 'Reflections: The Emerging Literature on Emissions Trading in Europe', *Review of Environmental Economics and Policy*, 3(1); 121–37.

Crompton, R. (1998) *Class and Stratification*. London: Polity.

Cromwell, D. and Levene, M. (eds) (2007) *Surviving Climate Change: The Struggle to Avert Global Catastrophe*. London: Pluto.

Daly, H. (2007) *Ecological Economics and Sustainable Development*. Cheltenham: Edward Elgar.

Depledge, J. and Yamin, F. (2009) 'The Global Climate-Change Regime: A Defence'. In D. Helm and C. Hepburn (eds) *The Economics and Politics of Climate Change*. Oxford: Oxford University Press.

Doherty, B., Paterson, M. and Seel, B. (2000) 'Direct Action in British Environmentalism'. In B. Seel, M. Paterson and B. Doherty, *Direct Action in British Environmentalism*. London: Routledge.

Eckersley, R. (1992) *Environmentalism and Political Theory: Toward an Ecocentric Approach*. London: UCL Press.

Ekers, M. and Loftus, A. (2013) 'Revitalizing the Production of Nature Thesis: A Gramscian Turn?' *Progress in Human Geography*, 37(2): 234–52.

Eley, G. and Nield, K. (2007) *The Future of Class in History: What's Left of the Social?* Ann Arbor, MI: University of Michigan Press.

Ellerman, D., Convery, F. and de Perthuis, C. (2010) *Pricing Carbon: The European Union Emissions Trading Scheme*. Cambridge: Cambridge University Press.

Elliott, L. *et al.* (2008) *A Green New Deal*. London: New Economics Foundation.

Falkner, R. (2008) *Business Power and Conflict in International Environmental Politics*. Basingstoke: Palgrave Macmillan.

Felli, R. (2014) 'An Alternative Socio-Ecological Strategy? International Trade Unions' Engagement with Climate Change', *Review of International Political Economy*, 21(2): 372–98.

Flanders, A. (1970) *Management and Unions: The Theory and Reform of Industrial Relations*. London: Faber.

Foley, D. (2006) *Adam's Fallacy: A Guide to Economic Theology*. Cambridge, MA: Harvard University Press.

Foster, J. (2002) *Ecology Against Capitalism*. New York: Monthly Review Press.

Foster, J., Clark, B. and York, R. (2010) *The Ecological Rift: Capitalism's War on the Earth*. New York: Monthly Review Press.

Fredriksson, P. and Gaston, N. (1999) 'The "Greening" of Trade Unions and the Demand for Eco-taxes', *European Journal of Political Economy*, 15: 663–86.

Frege, C., Heery, E. and Turner, L. (2004) 'The New Solidarity? Coalition Building in Five Countries'. In C. Frege and J. Kelly (eds) *Varieties of Unionism: Strategies for Labor Movement Renewal in the Global North*. Oxford: Oxford University Press.

Gorz, A. (1983) *Ecology as Politics*. London: Pluto.

Gough, I. (2008) 'Introduction: JESP Symposium: Climate Change and Social Policy', *Journal of European Social Policy*, 18(4): 325–31.

Graham-Leigh, E. (2014) 'The Green Movement in Britain'. In M. Dietz and H. Garrelts (eds) *Routledge Handbook of the Climate Change Movement*. London: Routledge.

Gramsci, A. (1971) *Selections from the Prison Notebooks*. London: Lawrence and Wishart.

——(1978) *Selected Political Writings, 1921–26*. London: Lawrence and Wishart.

Gregory, D., Hildebrandt, E., Le Blansch, K. and Lorentzen, B. (1996) 'Industrial Relations and the Environment: Some Theses', *Transfer*, 2(3): 440–8.

Grubb, M. (1989) *The Greenhouse Effect: Negotiating Targets*. London: Royal Institute for International Affairs.

Hale, S. (2010) 'The New Politics of Climate Change: Why We Are Failing and How We Will Succeed', *Environmental Politics*, 19(2): 255–75.

Hansen, J. (2009) 'Worshipping the Temple of Doom. Letter to Martin Parkinson, Secretary of the Australian Department of Climate Change', 4 May.

Harvey, D. (2005) *A Brief History of Neoliberalism*. Oxford: Oxford University Press.

Heede, R. (2014) 'Tracing Anthropogenic Carbon Dioxide and Methane Emissions to Fossil Fuel and Cement Producers, 1854–2010', *Climatic Change*, 122(1–2): 229–41.

Heery, E. (2002) 'Partnership Versus Organising: Alternative Futures for British Trade Unionism', *Industrial Relations Journal*, 33(1): 20–35.

Helm, D. (2005) 'Climate-Change Policy: A Survey'. In D. Helm (ed.) *Climate-Change Policy*. Oxford: Oxford University Press.

——(2013) *The Carbon Crunch. How We're Getting Climate Change Wrong – and How to Fix It*. New Haven, CT: Yale University Press.

Hepburn, C. (2009) 'Carbon Taxes, Emissions Trading and Hybrid Schemes'. In D. Helm and C. Hepburn (eds) *The Economics and Politics of Climate Change*. Oxford: Oxford University Press.

Herod, A. (2002) 'Organizing Globally, Organizing Locally: Union Spatial Strategy in a Global Economy'. In J. Harrod and R. O'Brien (eds) *Global Unions? Theory and Strategies of Organized Labour in the Global Political Economy*. London: Routledge.

Heynen, N., McCarthy, J., Prudham, S. and Robbins, P. (2007) 'Introduction: False Promises'. In N. Heynen, J. McCarthy, S. Prudham and P. Robbins (eds) *Neoliberal Environments: False Promises and Unnatural Consequences*. London: Routledge.

Hrynyshyn, D. and Ross, S. (2011) 'Canadian Autoworkers, the Climate Crisis, and the Contradictions of Social Unionism', *Labor Studies Journal*, 36(1): 5–36.

Hulme, M. (2009) *Why We Disagree About Climate Change: Understanding Controversy, Inaction and Opportunity*. Cambridge: Cambridge University Press.

Hyman, R. (1997) 'Trade Unions and Interest Representation in the Context of Globalisation', *Transfer*, 3(3): 515–33.

——(1999) 'Imagined Solidarities: Can Trade Unions Resist Globalisation?' In P. Leisink (ed.) *Globalization and Labour Relations*. Cheltenham: Edward Elgar.

——(2001) *Understanding European Trade Unionism: Between Market, Class and Society*. London: Sage.

——(2004) 'The Future of Trade Unions'. In A. Verma and T. Kochan (eds) *Unions in the 21st Century: An International Perspective*. Basingstoke: Palgrave Macmillan.

——(2007) 'How Can Trade Unions Act Strategically?' *Transfer*, 13(2): 193–210.

——(2012) 'Will the Real Richard Hyman Please Stand Up?' *Capital & Class*, 36(1): 151–64.

IPCC (1995) *Climate Change 1995: Impacts, Adaptations and Mitigation of Climate Change*. Cambridge: Cambridge University Press.

Jackson, T. (2009) *Prosperity Without Growth: Economics for a Finite Planet*. London: Earthscan.

Jacobs, M. (1999) *Environmental Modernisation: The New Labour Agenda*. London: The Fabian Society/College Hill Press.

Jaeger, C., Schellnhuber, H. and Brovkin, V. (2008) 'Stern's Review and Adam's Fallacy', *Climatic Change*, 89: 207–18.

Jessop, B. (2007) *State Power: A Strategic-Relational Approach*. Cambridge: Polity.

Johns, R. (1998) 'Bridging the Gap between Class and Space: U.S. Worker Solidarity with Guatemala', *Economic Geography*, 74(3): 252–71.

Kallis, G., Kerschner, C. and Martinez-Alier, J. (2012) 'The Economics of Degrowth', *Ecological Economics*, 84: 172–80.

Keefer, T. (2010) 'Machinery and Motive Power: Energy as a Substitute for and Enhancer of Human Labour'. In K. Abramsky (ed.) *Sparking a Worldwide Energy Revolution: Social Struggles in the Transition to a Post-Petrol World*. Edinburgh: AK Press.

Kelly, J. (2005) 'Social Movement Theory and Union Revitalisation in Britain'. In S. Fernie and D. Metcalf (eds) *Trade Unions: Resurgence or Demise?* London: Routledge.

Klein, N. (2014) *This Changes Everything: Capitalism vs the Climate*. London: Allen Lane.

Koch, M. (2012) *Capitalism and Climate Change: Theoretical Discussion, Historical Development and Policy Responses*. Basingstoke: Palgrave Macmillan.

Kovel, J. (2007) *The Enemy of Nature: The End of Capitalism or the End of the World?* London: Zed Books.

Laing, T., Sato, M., Grubb, M. and Comberti, C. (2013) *Assessing the Effectiveness of the EU Emissions Trading System*, Centre for Climate Change Economics and Policy Working Paper 126. Leeds: CCCEP.

Lemire, E. (ed.) (1969) *The Unpublished Lectures of William Morris*. Detroit: Wayne State University Press.

Lewis, A. and Juravle, C. (2010) 'Morals, Markets and Sustainable Investments: a Qualitative Study of "Champions"', *Journal of Business Ethics*, 93(3): 483–94.

Lih, L. (2008) *Lenin Rediscovered: What Is to Be Done? in Context*. Chicago: Haymarket.

Lorenzoni, I., O'Riordan, T. and Pidgeon, N. (2008) 'Hot Air and Cold Feet: The UK Response to Climate Change'. In H. Compston and I. Bailey (eds) *Turning Down the Heat: The Politics of Climate Policy in Affluent Democracies*. Basingstoke: Palgrave Macmillan.

Mallory, G. (2005) *Uncharted Waters: Social Responsibility in Australian Trade Unions*. Annerley: Greg Mallory.

Marx, K. ([1847] 1976a) 'The Poverty of Philosophy', *MECW*, vol. 6. London: Lawrence and Wishart.

——([1848] 1976b) 'The Communist Manifesto', *MECW* 6. London: Lawrence and Wishart.

——(1981) *Capital*, vol. III. Harmondsworth: Penguin.

——(1985a) 'Instructions for the Delegates of the Provisional General Council: The Different Questions, August 1866', *MECW*, vol. 20. London: Lawrence and Wishart.

——(1985b) 'Address to the National Labor Union of the United States, 12 May 1869', *MECW*, vol. 21. London: Lawrence and Wishart.

——(1986) 'Outline of the Critique of Political Economy (Rough Draft of 1857–58)', *MECW*, vol. 28. London: Lawrence and Wishart.

Mason, M. (2010) 'Critical Salvoes in the Corporate Greenhouse', *Environmental Politics*, 19(1): 149–54.

Mason, M. and Morter, N. (1998) 'Trade Unions as Environmental Actors: A Case Study of the UK Transport & General Workers' Union', *Capitalism, Nature, Socialism*, 9(2): 3–34.

McNally, D. (2010) *Global Slump: The Economics and Politics of Crisis and Resistance*. Oakland, CA: PM Press/Spectre.

Meier, P. (1978) *William Morris: The Marxist Dreamer*. Atlantic Highlands, NJ: Harvester Press.

Mol, A. and Jänicke, M. (2009) 'The Origins and Theoretical Foundations of Ecological Modernisation Theory'. In A. Mol, D. Sonnenfeld and G. Spaargaren (eds) *The Ecological Modernisation Reader: Environmental Reform in Theory and Practice.* London: Routledge.

Mol, A. and Spaargaren, G. (2000) 'Ecological Modernisation Theory in Debate: A Review', *Environmental Politics,* 9(1): 17–49.

Mol, A., Spaargaren, G. and Sonnenfeld, D. (2009) 'Ecological Modernisation: Three Decades of Policy, Practice, and Theoretical Reflection'. In A. Mol, D. Sonnenfeld and G. Spaargaren (eds) *The Ecological Modernisation Reader: Environmental Reform in Theory and Practice.* London: Routledge.

Moody, K. (1997) *Workers in a Lean World.* London: Verso.

Mulhern, F. (1984) 'Towards 2000, or News from You-know-where', *New Left Review,* I(148): 5–30.

Murphy, J. and Gouldson, A. (2000) 'Environmental Policy and Industrial Innovation: Integrating Environment and Economy through Ecological Modernisation', *Geoforum,* 31(1): 33–44.

Neale, J. (2008) *Stop Global Warming: Change the World.* London: Bookmarks.

Newell, P. (2000) *Climate for Change: Non-State Actors and the Global Politics of the Greenhouse,* Cambridge: Cambridge University Press.

——(2005) 'Race, Class and the Global Politics of Environmental Inequality', *Global Environmental Politics,* 5(3): 70–94.

——(2008) 'Civil Society, Corporate Accountability and the Politics of Climate Change', *Global Environmental Politics,* 8(3): 122–53.

Newell, P. and Paterson, M. (2009) 'The Politics of the Carbon Economy'. In M. Boykoff (ed.) *The Politics of Climate Change: A Survey.* London: Routledge.

——(2010) *Climate Capitalism: Global Warming and the Transformation of the Global Economy.* Cambridge: Cambridge University Press.

New Labour (1997) *Because Britain Deserves Better: The Election Manifesto.* London: The Labour Party.

Nordhaus, W. (1977) 'Economic Growth and Climate: The Carbon Dioxide Problem', *The American Economic Review,* 67(1): 341–6.

——(2008) *A Question of Balance: Weighing the Options on Global Warming Policies.* New Haven, CT: Yale University Press.

Nugent, J. (2011) 'Changing the Climate: Ecoliberalism, Green New Dealism, and the Struggle over Green Jobs in Canada', *Labor Studies Journal,* 36(1): 58–82.

Obach, B. (2004) *Labor and the Environmental Movement: The Quest for Common Ground.* Cambridge, MA: MIT Press.

Pakulski, J. and Waters, M. (1996) *The Death of Class.* London: Sage.

Panitch, L. and Gindin, S. (2012) *The Making of Global Capitalism.* London: Verso.

Parry, I. (2004) 'Are Emissions Permits Regressive?' *Journal of Environmental Economics and Management,* 47: 364–87.

——(2005) 'Fiscal Interactions and the Case for Carbon Taxes over Grandfathered Carbon Permits'. In D. Helm (ed.) *Climate-Change Policy.* Oxford: Oxford University Press.

Patenaude, G. (2011) 'Climate Change Diffusion: While the World Tips, Business Schools Lag', *Global Environmental Change,* 21(1): 259–71.

Paterson, M. (1996) *Global Warming and Global Politics.* London: Routledge.

Pinkse, J. and Kolk, A. (2009) *International Business and Global Climate Change.* London: Routledge.

Pralle, S. (2009) 'Agenda-Setting and Climate Change', *Environmental Politics*, 18(5): 781–99.

Prins, G. and Rayner, S. (2007) *The Wrong Trousers: Radically Rethinking Climate Policy*. London: MacKinder Programme for the Study of Long Wave Events, LSE and Institute for Science, Innovation and Society, University of Oxford.

Räthzel, N. and Uzzell, D. (2011) 'Trade Unions and Climate Change: The Jobs Versus Environment Dilemma', *Global Environmental Change*, 21(4): 1215–23.

Räthzel, N., Uzzell, D. and Elliott, D. (2010). 'Can Trade Unions Become Environmental Innovators?' *Soundings*, 46: 76–87.

Rayner, S., Malone, E. and Thompson, M. (1999) 'Equity Issues and Integrated Assessment'. In F. Tóth (ed.) *Fair Weather? Equity Concerns in Climate Change*. London: Earthscan.

Rootes, C. (2009) 'Environmental NGOs and the Environmental Movement in England'. In N. Crowson, M. Hilton and J. McKay (eds) *NGOs in Contemporary Britain*. Basingstoke: Palgrave Macmillan.

Rubin, I. (1972) *Essays on Marx's Theory of Value*. Montréal: Black Rose Books.

Saad Filho, A. (ed.) (2003) *Anti-Capitalism: A Marxist Introduction*. London: Pluto.

Saunders, C. (2008) 'The Stop Climate Chaos Coalition: Climate Change as a Development Issue', *Third World Quarterly*, 29(8): 1509–26.

——(2012) 'Reformism and Radicalism in the Climate Camp in Britain', *Environmental Politics*, 21(5): 829–46.

Silverman, V. (2004) 'Sustainable Alliances: The Origins of International Labor Environmentalism', *International Labor and Working-Class History*, 6: 118–35.

Simms, M. (2012) 'Imagined Solidarities: Where Is Class in Union Organising'? *Capital & Class*, 36, 1, 97–115.

Skeggs, B. (1997) *Formations of Class and Gender: Becoming Respectable*. London: Sage.

Smith, N. (2011) 'Uneven Development Redux', *New Political Economy*, 16(2): 261–5.

Snell, D. and Fairbrother, P. (2010) 'Unions as Environmental Actors', *Transfer*, 16 (3): 411–24.

——(2011) 'Toward a Theory of Union Environmental Politics: Unions and Climate Action in Australia', *Labor Studies Journal*, 36(): 83–103.

Solomon, B. and Heiman, M. (2010) 'Integrity of the Emerging Global Markets in Greenhouse Gases', *Annals of the Association of American Geographers*, 100(4): 973–82.

Spash, C. (2002) *Greenhouse Economics: Value and Ethics*. London: Routledge.

Spence, M. (2000) 'Capital against Nature: James O'Connor's Theory of the Second Contradiction of Capitalism', *Capital & Class*, 72: 81–109.

Ste Croix, G. (1981) *The Class Struggle in the Ancient Greek World*. London: Duckworth.

Stern, N. (2007) *The Economics of Climate Change*. Cambridge: Cambridge University Press.

——(2009) *Blueprint for a Safer Planet: How to Manage Climate Change and Create a New Era of Progress and Prosperity*. London: The Bodley Head.

Strachan, N., Foxon, T. and Fujino, J. (2008) 'Policy Implications from the Low-Carbon Society (LCS) Modelling Project', *Climate Policy*, 8: S17–S29.

Streeck, W. and Hassel, A. (2003) 'Trade Unions as Political Actors'. In J. Addison and C. Schnabel (eds) *International Handbook of Trade Unions*. Cheltenham: Edward Elgar.

Swaffield, J. and Bell, D. (2012) 'Can "Climate Champions" Save the Planet? A Critical Reflection on Neoliberal Social Change', *Environmental Politics*, 21(2): 248–67.

Tarrow, S. (1998) *Power in Movement: Social Movements and Contentious Politics*. Cambridge: Cambridge University Press.

Tickell, O. (2008) *Kyoto 2*. London: Zed Books.

Turner, L. (2006) 'Globalization and the Logic of Participation: Unions and the Politics of Coalition Building', *Journal of Industrial Relations*, 48(1): 83–97.

Uzzell, D. and Räthzel, N. (2013a) 'Introducing a New Field: Environmental Labour Studies'. In N. Räthzel and D. Uzzell (eds) *Trade Unions in the Green Economy: Working for the Environment*. London: Routledge.

——(2013b) 'Local Place and Global Space: Solidarity across Borders and the Question of the Environment'. In N. Räthzel and D. Uzzell (eds) *Trade Unions in the Green Economy: Working for the Environment*. London: Routledge.

Vanderheiden, S. (2009) *Atmospheric Justice: A Political Theory of Climate Change*. Oxford: Oxford University Press.

Victor, D. (1991) 'Limits of Market-Based Strategies for Slowing Global Warming: The Case of Tradeable Permits', *Policy Sciences*, 24: 199–222.

Victor, P. (2008) *Managing Without Growth: Slower by Design, Not Disaster*. Cheltenham: Edward Elgar.

Vlachou, A. (2000) 'The Economics of Global Warming: A Critical Assessment'. *Rethinking Marxism*, 12(4): 90–116.

——(2004) 'Capitalism and Ecological Sustainability: The Shaping of Environmental Policies', *Review of International Political Economy*, 11(5): 926–52.

——(2005) 'Environmental Regulation: A Value-Theoretic and Class-Based Approach', *Cambridge Journal of Economics*, 29(4): 577–99.

Vlachou, A. and Konstantinidis, C. (2010) 'Climate Change: The Political Economy of Kyoto Flexible Mechanisms', *Review of Radical Political Economics*, 42: 32–49.

Wainwright, H. and Elliott, D. (1982) *The Lucas Plan: A New Trade Unionism in the Making?* London: Allison & Busby.

Wainwright, J. (2010) 'Climate Change, Capitalism, and the Challenge of Transdisciplinarity', *Annals of the Association of American Geographers*, 100(4): 983–91.

Waterman, P. (2001) 'Trade Union Internationalism in the Age of Seattle'. In J. Wills and P. Waterman (eds) *Place, Space and the New Labour Internationalisms*. Oxford: Basil Blackwell.

——(2008) '"Social Movement Unionism" in Question: Contribution to a Symposium', *Employee Responsibilities and Rights Journal*, 20(4): 303–8.

Webb, S. and Webb, B. (1920) *The History of Trade Unionism*. London: Longman.

Wood, E. (1986) *The Retreat from Class*. London: Verso.

Wright, E. O. (1978) *Class, Crisis and the State*. London: Verso.

——(2005) 'Foundations of a Neo-Marxist Class Analysis'. In E. Wright (ed.) *Approaches to Class Analysis*. Cambridge: Cambridge University Press.

Yandle, B. (1985) 'Unions and Environmental Regulation', *Journal of Labor Research*, 6: 429–43.

York, R., Rosa, E. and Dietz, T. (2003) 'A Rift in Modernity? Assessing the Anthropogenic Sources of Global Climate Change with the STIRPAT Model', *International Journal of Sociology and Social Policy*, 23(10): 31–51.

3 Trade unions, climate and employment in a neoliberal world

Introduction

The 'jobs versus the environment' dichotomy appears to be the most intractable problem facing trade union engagement with climate change at the international, national, regional and local scales. Neoliberal political economy has tended to follow the OECD's (1997: 33) widely quoted assessment that the net effect of environmental policies on employment is 'on the whole ... slightly positive'. Climate change and climate policy are expected to trigger 'widespread structural adjustment' and episodes of 'creative destruction', with significant implications for employment in the near and medium term. But mainstream economists believe that in the long run, climate change has 'the potential to create many more jobs than it destroys' (Fankhauser et al. 2008: 421–2, 427). These economists expect the amount of 'churn' – job destruction and job creation linked to climate mitigation – to be about 0.5 per cent of total employment, which they regard as 'quite small compared with the overall "churn" that normally occurs in a market economy'. Some studies suggest that recycling carbon tax revenues to reduce labour market taxes 'could offset or more than offset all adverse impacts of climate action on employment' (GCEC 2014: 38). This view of employment expresses a certain technocratic optimism that markets can be made to work and that no problem is too great for the private sector.

However, there are contradictions within the neoliberal treatment of the occupational impacts of climate policy. In orthodox economic theory, 'if climate policy consists solely of a carbon charge with no simultaneous market reforms or compensating tax cuts, overall impacts on GDP, disposable income and jobs are negative' (Krause et al. 2003: 91). Complex general equilibrium models used in climate policy studies 'assume a perfect labour market and ignore unemployment issues'. This representation 'contrasts with the imperfections of real-world labour markets' (Guivarch et al. 2011: 769–70). An OECD assessment of climate mitigation policy estimated that fossil fuel and coal mining sectors in Europe could lose more than 30 per cent of their jobs. Overall it suggests that 'job destructions and creations' would only be 'equalised' at the aggregate level labour markets where 'full flexible', meaning that workers would pay in the form of lower wages. With 'strong wage rigidities', employment declines – and models 'do not account for the potential economic damages from climate change'. The OECD suggested recycling emissions trading revenues to help create jobs without workers losing purchasing power (Chateau *et al.* 2011: 20–1, 25–7).

For the most part, these analyses simply ignore the presence and role of trade unions, treating workers as passive victims of market forces. Where trade unions are discussed in the context of environmental policy, they are conceived as campaigning to protect existing jobs, rather than supporting reforms that might lead to higher levels of employment overall, but would involve job losses in some sectors (Jacobs 1997). 'Wage rigidities' occur when workers in declining economic sectors 'are unable or unwilling to move into more rapidly growing sectors', yet are still able to maintain their nominal wages. Similarly, another type of wage rigidity 'keeps the wage of sector specific labour at the economy wide wage of mobile labour, even though the sectoral demand for that labour has dropped' (Babiker and Eckaus 2007: 602). In both cases, unions are blamed.

Other economists argue that stronger environmental regulation has a limited effect on competitiveness because it encourages efficiency and innovation. Such regulation may lead to some employment gains at certain scales, in individual firms, sectors, states and globally (Porter and van der Linde 1995). Some scholars (Carter 1997: 196) argue that 'trade union fears about the employment implications of green policies are addressed by means of an environmental "New Deal" that would create thousands of new jobs in industries such as recycling, energy efficiency and environmental protection'. This treats workers as recipients of paternalistic benevolence on the part of states that are correcting market failures.

This chapter analyses international trade union discussion of climate change and employment. International trade union bodies such as the International Trade Union Confederation (ITUC, formerly ICFTU), the Global Unions (such as the International Transport Workers' Federation, ITF), regional bodies such as the European Trade Union Confederation (ETUC) and national centres such as the Trades Union Congress (TUC) in the UK do not directly organise workers. But to some extent they indirectly represent workers as workers and have a democratic representative structure (Felli 2014). The chapter examines the employment implications of climate change for workers and asks whether the demand for green jobs can be rendered coherent by trade unions. It analyses the meaning and significance of the demand for a 'just transition' to a low carbon economy and suggests that the dominant union articulation is framed in ecological modernisation terms. It investigates the kind of low-carbon transition that trade unionists have envisaged and whether the outcomes differ from those found in the dominant framings. The first section sets out union discussion of the apparent climate and employment trade-off. The second section evaluates the distinctive union framing of the climate and employment relationship in terms of just transition. The third section sets out a more class-focused approach, through assessing union demands for energy democracy, climate jobs and socially useful work.

Unions, climate and green jobs

Unions, climate and employment: a natural synergy?

Trade unions have long had to grapple with the implications of climate change for employment, as well as the employment prospects for workers in the context of climate policy. The immediate answer to the jobs versus climate dilemma was well expressed in a pioneering global warming statement by the United Steelworkers of America union in 1990: 'In the long run, the real choice is not jobs or environment. It's both or neither' (Foster 2010: 234). However, the dichotomy cannot be written off quite so easily and for unions it is potentially fraught with contradictions. This is well illustrated by the ITUC's campaign Unions4Climate. The statement includes neoliberal demands for 'supporting a carbon price to make renewable energy, green buildings and retrofits competitive', ecological modernisation calls for partnership and climate justice, as well as more class-focused demands for solidarity and workplace climate action (ITUC 2014b: 3). The statement indicates that the 'contradictory consciousness' identified by Gramsci is operative in union climate politics.

Trade unions have foregrounded the employment implications of climate change. Philip Pearson, the TUC policy officer responsible for climate change over the last decade, articulated one of the principal complaints from trade unionists, namely that the IPCC and the UNFCCC COP process 'has never taken a close look at the world of work, nor systematically explored climate impacts on human settlements and human rights' (Pearson 2010b).[1] In the absence of authoritative investigation by these bodies, international trade unions have undertaken much of the work themselves. An ETUC analysis of the IPCC's fifth assessment report concludes that the impacts from climate change on employment are 'many and varied, direct and indirect'. It identifies that threats to ecosystems such as forests and oceans will affect economic sectors like agriculture, fisheries, mining, energy production, pulp and paper and tourism. Such threats originate from climate change itself and from water, land and energy management strategies as the climate changes. Extreme weather events, rising temperatures and disease will impact on international trade and reduce labour productivity in many areas. In the twenty-first century, 'climate change impacts will slow economic growth and poverty reduction, further erode food security and trigger new poverty traps' (Scott 2014: 6). It concludes that workers need to be integrated into mitigation and adaptation strategies.

In 2007, the ETUC produced the most significant study to date of the occupational impacts of climate change (Dupressoir 2007). It was framed in ecological modernist terms. The report estimated the expected changes resulting from climate change would be an overall net gain in employment of 1.5 per cent by 2030 for the sectors considered, though it was critical of the OECD and other studies, which, it said, took an 'incomplete account of the effects on employment'. The potential cost of the transition for workers in the 'losing' sectors 'is not appreciated, nor is the vulnerability of some categories of workers in relation to the opportunities for re-skilling' (ibid.). The study identified a general risk that 'the jobs that arise in new businesses in new services and products will be less well-paid, with less secure employment conditions, than in established branches'. Trade unionists believed that it was necessary, 'not only to promote the development of renewable energy sources and energy efficiency to secure or create jobs, but also to monitor the quality of those jobs' (ibid.: 37, 73). The report warned that if not anticipated and dealt with appropriately, the largely underestimated questions of occupational transitions and training would 'represent a significant roadblock to sectoral transformation required by European emissions reduction targets' (ibid.). It recommended the development of 'social accompaniment measures' to reassure workers and enable them to adapt to the structural changes in skills associated with the process of reducing greenhouse gas emissions (ibid.: 179–80, 187).

The ETUC report was undertaken after a decade of requests for an authoritative analysis of the occupational implications of climate change and climate policy. The ICFTU (forerunner of the ITUC) intervened in the Kyoto negotiations, arguing that trade unions were concerned about 'the job losses and other costs that will be caused to workplaces and communities by measures designed to meet current and more ambitious post-2000 targets and deadlines'. The ICFTU advised that 'failure to plan for deep cuts in greenhouse gas emissions will also have grave consequences for working people and their families' (ICFTU 1997: 1). At COP6 at The Hague in 2000, an agreement was reached committing 'representatives of trade unions and business to work together for more research into the employment and social implications of climate change' (Gereluk and Royer 2001: 15). However, it would take nearly a decade before major international institutions devoted serious attention to the issue, while it continued to be marginal to the UNFCCC process.

Trade union discussion in Britain in the late 1980s and early 1990s in the TUC in the UK also began to articulate the distinctive occupational dimension of the environment and climate change. An early report stated that 'trade unions have a special role and responsibility because most external environmental concerns originate in the workplace – giving unions a front-line environmental responsibility' (TUC 1990a: 50). A TUC submission to government declared that it was not clear 'what the potential is for environment-linked jobs'. Union leaders said it was not known whether higher environmental standards would push up costs and lead to plant closures. However, the document suggested that even if 'actual loss or gain of jobs due to environment policies may be small nationally, they could be significant at the sectoral level and within local communities' (TUC 1990c: 16). Another early TUC submission emphasised 'the absence of any real discussion or assessment of the employment and income effects of measures to combat global warming' (TUC 1991a: 22). The more positive framing of environmental-related employment matters was expressed in the language of sustainable development. At the 1990 Congress, Diana Warwick (AUT) argued that: 'We need a new concept ... that includes sustainable employment and sustainable living standards' (TUC 1990b: 354). However, these fertile lines of enquiry petered out as the economy went into recession and other concerns took hold.

In the UK, there was another flurry of activity around the employment implications of climate change in the mid-1990s. Union officials discussed jobs and the environment at a conference on 22 November 1996. A Labour Research Department (LRD) report commissioned for the conference stated that 'there is scarcely any data to suggest that plant closures have been primarily, let alone exclusively, caused by environmental considerations'. A UK study of plant closures at the time suggested that in only one case out of 193 were environmental costs listed as an important factor. The report referred to an earlier gathering of trade union officials, which had discussed pollution arising from burning alternative fuels in the cement industry. Len McCluskey, then a TGWU national officer for the cement industry, reported:

> We listened to all sides of the argument and the discussions got pretty explosive at times ... This conference provides one model of how a union may go about facing up to its environmental responsibilities and developing sustainable jobs. We are key 'stakeholders' in the environment now.
>
> (TUC 1996: 4, 8)

This was the context in which trade unions grappled with the implications of the Kyoto Protocol.

European trade unions supported the Kyoto Protocol, although the AFL-CIO in the United States opposed it. All unions warned of the likely employment impacts of tackling climate change (Stanley 2008). TUC leaders felt that the trade union presence at Kyoto 'pushed the question of employment up the agenda' and focused on 'how to avoid the dilemma of jobs versus the environment'. They recognised that to deal with climate change, transitional measures would have to be discussed beyond company level, including at EU and international levels. Union delegates 'stressed the dangers to jobs of not acting on climate change and also the need to ensure a just transition in economic sectors where climate change policies will have an employment impact' (TUC 1998a). The TUC's strategy included a multi-stakeholder approach, 'wherein companies develop dialogue with "interested parties", including their own workforce and through a structured system of representation'; an employment impact assessment that includes 'the possible costs to jobs of making environmental improvements' and the need to ensure a just transition with 'an equitable distribution of costs' (ibid.: 154, 156). The adoption of the 'just transition' formulation was important and followed other similar international union statements (see next section). However, at the time, 'just transition' was underdeveloped.

A UK union seminar in October 1998 discussed the expected employment repercussions of Kyoto and indicated some difficulties unions faced. Delegates from the energy workshop reported that 'job security was likely to be the key issue for trade unions'. If reaching targets set by the Kyoto agreement meant job losses, 'this would be difficult for the unions'. Delegates pointed out that 'job losses would almost certainly be in different places and involve different people to job gains and that this could impose substantial strains on local economies and on the trade unions' (TUC 1998b). However, the issue was not resolved satisfactorily. The Trade Union Sustainable Development Advisory Committee (TUSDAC), formed as a liaison body between unions and government after Kyoto, solicited a study from the government on the employment implications of environmental policy, though again the results were not conclusive (Coates 2000). There was frustration that neither international institutions nor national governments were addressing these concerns.

At the turn of the century, the IPPR think tank produced a further study for TUSDAC on the 'jobs and environment' debate (Hewett and Foley 2001). The study found 'no evidence to support the argument that environmental policy has damaged the competitiveness of any country', though in specific economic sectors 'there will be job losses as well as gains' (ibid.). Researchers argued that 'numerous studies have shown positive employment effects for moving the UK energy market towards greater use of renewables and improved energy efficiency', because most of the low carbon technologies are more labour-intensive than conventional fossil fuels. However, the majority of these studies have been 'commissioned by trade associations or environmental groups', which meant there could be 'a perception of bias in their findings'. Instead, they proposed that TUSDAC 'commission an independent assessment of the employment potential of a low carbon economy' (ibid.: 2–3, 26). It took a further five years before pan-European trade unions would begin to fill the gap.

At the beginning of the twenty-first century, high-level union discussion began to evolve away from older framings in terms of sustainable employment towards the more fertile conception of just transition. Union officials suggested that 'the terminology of sustainable development – even the phrase itself – cloaks rather than lays bare its message' (TUSDAC 2003: 2). They claimed that there was a general feeling in workplaces that sustainable development was like rocket science, 'theoretically complex, difficult to understand, time-consuming and expensive, necessitating the introduction of convoluted systems and massive upheaval' (ibid.: 4). Union leaders recognised that a different framing needed to be found. The presence of more trade union representatives at the UNFCCC's conferences of the parties meant the employment implications of climate change globally became a matter of more widespread discussion and was framed in universal, internationalist terms.

Climate change, carbon leakage and employment in a neoliberal world

One long-standing concern identified by trade unions was the potential for job losses due to climate measures in energy-intensive industries such as steel, ceramics, cement and lime manufacture, aluminium, basic inorganic chemicals and other industries, which employed 800,000 people in the UK. The fears of 'job-kill' came particularly from workers in more developed states that had experienced a decline in manufacturing industry and manufacturing jobs since the 1970s. At the turn of the century, British union officials stated that 'the industries most exposed to adverse effects are energy intensive industries … ' The paper industry is 'both energy and labour intensive and could be affected more seriously', while 'energy producing industries will also be affected' (TUC 1999: 1). These discussions suggest a genuine fear among unions that many workers would lose their jobs as a by-product of climate policy.

In the UK, the TUC and the Community, GMB, Unite and Unity unions allied with employers' lobbyists, the Energy Intensive Users Group (EIUG) to outline these uncertainties, which became more acute after the economic downturn across much of the world economy. They published a report, *The Cumulative Impact of Climate Change Policies on UK Energy Intensive Industries* (Waters Wye Associates 2010) to inform government policy on issues such as employment, taxation and the carbon floor price. TUC officials argue that the combined impact of the government's climate change policies imposed significant costs on the UK's energy-intensive industries. Jobs essential to a low-carbon future were at risk and 'without urgent review, current policies could see some prime UK companies leave the UK for good' (ibid.). A key threat was carbon leakage, which 'could be the net result – the loss of jobs, investment and our ability to regulate carbon emissions – as competitors with fewer controls on emissions benefit' (Pearson 2010b).

A second study, *Technology Innovation for Energy Intensive Industry in the UK* (Vallack *et al.* 2011), argued that 'there is a compelling rationale for government to develop an industrial low carbon manufacturing policy, in particular for the energy intensive sector' (TUC 2011a: 74). A third study, *Building Our Low-Carbon Industries*, warned that 'jobs and investment could be lost to overseas competitors' because of higher energy costs for firms and a 'less business-friendly government policy' in the UK (TUC 2012). The report recommended that the government should 'share the burden of environmental taxes across the economy, creating a more favourable climate for high energy companies with more tax relief on energy costs' (Pearson 2012b). A further report, *Walking the Carbon Tightrope* (Orion Innovations

2014), called for 'immediate further action on the carbon tax, and for a new tripartite Energy Intensive Industries Council to develop a long-term strategy for the energy-intensive industries' (TUC 2014a: 13).

These anxieties, articulated in sectional terms within the UK trade union movement, cannot be dismissed lightly, not least because they are made in the context where the market dominates and where government safety nets for displaced workers are extremely limited or non-existent. The loss of the UK's last remaining aluminium smelter in the north-east of England and the closure of a steel plant in north Kent underlined the ongoing retrenchment of these industries (TUC 2014b: 2). Although research found mixed evidence of carbon leakage (Sato *et al.* 2013), the fears were sufficient to drive the TUC and some unions into an explicit alliance with business. The TUC added its name to an employers' letter to *The Times* in February 2014 highlighting the impacts of the Renewables Obligation (RO) and feed-in-tariffs on firms' energy costs, calling for more compensation for the energy-intensive industries (Pearson 2014a). The TUC went as far as to claim the carbon price floor had become 'a strategic mistake, disadvantaging UK industry' for its impact on 'the competitiveness and sustainability of UK industry relative to the EU and rest of the world'. These unions argued that a way should be found 'to phase out the difference between the UK and EU carbon price' (TUC 2014b: 2). Although this stance appeared to baulk at aspects of neoliberal climate policy, it was not opposition to market mechanisms as such. Rather it compromised the principle of 'polluter pays' – in this case the greenhouse gas emissions that are a by-product of productive processes.

Unions, green jobs and ecological modernisation

As global unions began to engage more seriously with climate change, they went significantly further than the binaries of job protection versus 'sustainable employment', in order to make a distinctive and coherent contribution to policy. Unions found the language of ecological modernisation – emphasising the green economy, green growth, 'green-collar' and green jobs – provided a better means to come to terms with the employment implications of climate change (Jones 2008). In the context of economic slowdown, the slogan 'cut carbon, not jobs' encapsulated the linkage between climate policy and employment.

The ITUC explicitly promotes an ecological modernisation discourse based on the green economy and green jobs (ITUC 2012). It defines the green economy as one where 'investment in sustainable production and in cleaner technologies is shaped by key principles of social justice, social protection, and decent work' (ibid.). A green job 'reduces the environmental impacts of enterprises and economic sectors to sustainable levels, while providing decent work and living conditions to all those involved in production, and ensures workers' rights are respected' (ibid.). Green jobs include traditional environmental jobs such as making solar panels, manufacturing wind turbines, water conversation and sustainable forestry. They also include 'retrofitting related jobs in the construction and public transport sectors, and making energy efficiency improvements in manufacturing plants, along with services supporting all industries' (ibid.). A decent job 'ensures safe work, fair wages, respect for workers' rights and social protection'. The report analysed seven industries in 12 countries across Asia-Pacific, Africa, the Americas and Europe and claimed that investing 2 per cent of GDP in the green economy could create up to 48 million new green jobs over five years (ibid.: 3).

International trade union officials grappled with the potential of green jobs, particularly as this tied in with government pledges to create hundreds of thousands of such jobs as part of economic recovery. The AFL-CIO trade union federation launched a national Centre for Green Jobs at the 'largest-ever' labour-green movement conference organised with the Blue-Green Alliance (Pearson 2009a). In Copenhagen in 2009, the ITUC argued that the priority was 'to create green and decent jobs, transform and improve traditional ones and include democracy and social justice in environmental decision-making processes'. Trade unions pledged to work 'towards the transformation of all jobs into environmentally-friendly and socially-decent jobs'. Green jobs were 'a first step towards the transformation' (ITUC 2009a: 10, 12). The emerging union narrative dovetailed with wider ecological modernisation discourses of the green economy and green growth.

The ITUC contributed to an earlier United Nations Environment Programme (UNEP) green jobs publication. The report defined green jobs as 'work in agricultural, manufacturing, research and development (R&D), administrative, and service activities that contribute substantially to preserving or restoring environmental quality'. It anticipated that employment would be affected in at least four ways as the economy oriented towards greater sustainability. First, additional jobs would be created, such as in the manufacturing of pollution-control devices. Second, some employment would be replacements, such as shifting from fossil fuels to renewables. Third, certain jobs may be eliminated without direct replacement. Fourth, many existing jobs, such as plumbers, electricians, metal workers, and construction workers, 'will simply be transformed and redefined as day-to-day skill sets, work methods, and profiles are greened'. The report estimated that at least 2.3 million workers were employed internationally in green jobs, with over 20 million such jobs globally by 2030 (UNEP 2008: 3–4).

International trade union discussion over green jobs began in the 1990s, often in dialogue with environmental NGOs. At the ICFTU conference in 1992, environmentalists appealed to trade unions to fight 'jobs *versus* the environment' with 'jobs *for* the environment' and to build global support for 'green jobs, not pink [unemployment] slips' (Greenpeace International 1992; Jenkins and McLaren 1995; Jacobs 1995). Unions in Denmark promoted green jobs to counter the 'jobs versus environment' illusion. Trade union officials argued that green jobs 'must form part of a two-pronged response to

job dislocation that will occur in a transition to a sustainable economy'
(Gereluk and Royer 2001: 9–10). Investment in sustainable jobs 'can provide
alternative employment, but usually in the long-term; hence the need for a
short-term strategy to ensure a "just transition"'(ibid.). UK unions also took part
in discussions about green jobs during this period. A report by Friends of the
Earth, working with the GMB and Unison trade unions, promoted an integrated
approach, with job gains not confined to new specialist 'green' jobs, but a
'mix of skilled, semi-skilled and unskilled occupations'. In classic ecological
modernist terms, the focus was on 'identifying the combination of policies that
can realise this "win–win" potential most effectively' (Barry *et al.* 1998: 2–3).

This positive approach to green jobs continued as climate change moved
to the centre of environmental discussions. The 2010 TUC Congress
pledged its support for 'a campaign for one million green jobs' (TUC 2010b:
20), while the TUC's climate change conference in 2011 was entitled *Green
Jobs: No Turning Back* (Pearson 2013b). The British–German Trade Union
Forum held a gathering of trade union delegates on green jobs on 2–3 July
2009. At the event, Martin Jänicke argued for a programme of ecological
modernisation to create millions of new jobs. He said:

> The rapid growth of renewable energy sources in Germany shows that
> this changeover does not only make sense in ecological terms; with the
> right political management, the economy and the labour market can also
> benefit hugely from this 'Green New Deal'.
>
> (Doelfs 2009: 6)

However, the conference found it difficult to come up with an unambiguous
definition of green jobs. One of the UK delegates, Jane McCann from the
GMB, warned against 'making an ideological issue of the term green job in
the debate about an ecological renewal of manufacturing industry'. The trade
unions should not get into a debate that 'set bad old jobs against good new
ones. A job is a job'. (ibid.: 6)

These discussions indicate that there is no consensus on what constitutes
a 'green' job. Loosely, green jobs may be regarded as those 'associated with
environmental objectives and policies'. Some definitions of green jobs focus
on 'occupations and skills with an identifiable environmental focus', but
most centre on 'employment in industries (or specific projects) the products
of which are deemed to be of environmental benefit' (Bowen 2012: 3). Other
scholars divide them into 'light green' jobs that remedy ecological decline;
'ecologically modernist' jobs that involve technological innovation; and
'deep green' jobs that preserve ecological integrity (Crowley 1999: 1021).
However, the narrative of green jobs remains peculiarly imprecise. While
green jobs are widely discussed in the media, they are neither well defined
nor perhaps precisely definable (Kouri and Clarke 2012). The ambiguities
were well summed up by the Labour government's announcement of its low-
carbon industrial strategy. Business Minister Peter Mandelson claimed that

the British economy already supported 880,000 'low-carbon jobs' and was poised to create a further 400,000 green jobs by 2015 (DECC 2009). However, an assessment published by *The Times* revealed the 'extraordinarily loose' definition of the term, with jobs in the supply and manufacture of animal bedding, providing equestrian surfaces and in the recycling of footwear, slippers and carpet wear counted as green jobs (Pagnamenta 2009).

Räthzel, Uzzell and Elliott (2010: 78) found some distrust of green jobs within international union ranks. Green jobs are not necessarily well paid, safe, and secure and 'decent' jobs. A Canadian delegate told them that green jobs was a term from the environmental movement, not the labour movement. This suspicion was expressed even more strongly by another interviewee, who explained that steel jobs were not 'brown jobs' because renewable energy sources like wind turbines still required steel. A green boss 'is still a boss. A green capitalist is still a capitalist.' This suggests a more profound critique, namely that green jobs are one component of a new green capitalism that is trying to avoid fundamental change through an emphasis on expanding markets and new technologies (Cock and Lambert 2013). Barry (2013) argues that green jobs take for granted the assumption that economic growth is the right approach and it does not particularly challenge the system of production that has led to climate change, though this was contested by union officials (Stanley 2010). Snell and Fairbrother (2010) examine the Illawarra Green Jobs Project in Australia, a collaboration between regional government, local business and union leaders to develop sustainable green jobs. Although presented as a progressive initiative, it looked like the kind of local boosterism labour geographers had warned of. Uzzell and Räthzel (2013a: 8; 2013b: 242) argue that the demand for green jobs appears to lead to 'shallow reforms' rather than transcending present forms of production. They also recognise that it is difficult for progressive trade unionists to put climate change on their unions' agenda when workers say, 'I will die quicker from not having a job than from climate change.' Redefining disparate occupations as 'green jobs' provides no security for workers fearful of unemployment.

Ecological modernisation discourse appears cognisant, at least rhetorically, of the employment implications of the proposed climate transition. Conceptions of 'green jobs' appear more congruent with trade union concerns about the employment impacts of climate change and climate policy. They also seem consistent with ecological modernisation framings of the role of the state, of non-state actors and climate justice. Union discussions of green jobs at least have the semblance of a global perspective. Union debates provide 'a broad working class perspective, emphasising areas of employment growth that are skilled, well paid and sustainable'. Three principles of green jobs have emerged from unions: (1) whether the job is environmentally sustainable; (2) whether it is a quality job in the sense of being well-paid and secure; and (3) when it replaces another, non-green job, whether it is located in the same community and targeted to the same worker (Pearce and Stilwell 2008: 131–2).

As attractive as the slogan 'green jobs' may appear, the conception has thus far lacked clarity of definition and at times seemed ambiguous. Efforts to demarcate the boundary between green jobs and non-green jobs have yielded few theoretical gains. Steel production may not seem particularly green and it is certainly energy-intensive, with a significant carbon footprint.

But as Jacque Hatfield (Community) told TUC Congress delegates, 'The crazy thing is that our manufacturing base should be the key to a low carbon economy. After all, you can't make the wind turbine without making steel' (TUC 2011b: 37). In many respects, the greening of all work and of the economy as a whole, making every job subject to the metric of its environmental impact, is a more coherent option. A more holistic approach is one that trade unionists have taken in discussions of the concept of just transition.

Just transition

The origins of just transition

The concept of just transition is the most distinctive trade union framing of climate change politics to date. Although usually expressed in ecological modernisation terms, it also has significant class undertones and draws together a range of themes found in the climate literature from a trade union perspective. The idea is usually attributed to Tony Mazzocchi, an official from the Oil, Chemical and Atomic Workers Union (OCAW) in the United States.[2] According to his biographer, Mazzocchi developed the idea from the late 1960s, after he realised that 'there was no way to protect workers and society from toxic substances without banning them'. But banning these products would cause workers to lose their jobs. Mazzocchi's jarring solution was 'for society to pay workers not to make poisons', because 'conversion had its limits' (Leopold 2007: 413).

Mazzocchi took inspiration from his own experience to find a solution for workers displaced from their jobs in the name of the environment. The Serviceman's Readjustment Act of 1944 (known as the GI Bill) was designed for demobilised soldiers and provided an income, health benefits and college tuition fees for four years. Mazzocchi was one of its beneficiaries. He first adapted this idea after discussions with environmentalists about the fate of nuclear weapons workers. In the 1980s, Mazzocchi called the proposal for a four-year income and benefit guarantee for chemical and atomic workers 'the Superfund for Workers'. After environmentalists complained that the term superfund had too many negative connotations, the name of the plan was changed to just transition (ibid.: 309, 417). Mazzocchi also organised an early US union conference on global warming and helped publish *Global Warming Watch* in 1988, regarded as 'the first publication on the implications of climate change for American workers'. The OCAW faced the closure of whole industries deemed too environmentally unsustainable to continue. While federal money provided millions of dollars to clean up contaminated land, there was no compensation set aside for workers displaced by the closures. Mazzocchi commented that they 'treat dirt better than workers'. He also pointed out that 'working people aren't going to commit economic suicide in order to advance the enhancement of the environment' (ibid.: 433).

The term 'just transition' emerged in union discourse in 1995, when two Mazzocchi protégés, Les Leopold and Brian Kohler, spoke at the International Joint Commission on Great Lakes Water Quality. The immediate hook was the phase-out of toxic organochlorines, which involved 'sunsetting' jobs in the chemical manufacturing sector (Young 2003). In 1996, the Communications, Energy and Paperworkers Union of Canada passed a resolution at its conference, calling for the creation of a just transition programme. The union argued that a structured programme was necessary, otherwise 'workers in the affected industries and the communities that rely on the income of those workers would pay the price of change. Workers do not have the options of writing off losses, collecting insurance or re-investing elsewhere' (Kohler 1996).[3] The OCAW's 1997 conference committed itself to 'fair and just transition to sustainable production that protects both health and safety and the environment, as well as workers' livelihoods'. It would make corporations more accountable and make 'the just transition fund a reality, including agreement on working with allies in other unions and in the environmental and environmental justice communities' (TUC 2008c: 19).

Mazzocchi's thinking was explicitly taken up in wider international union discussions on climate change. In 1991, TUC environment advisor Paul Hackett argued for 'special assistance provided to aid any redeployment and enhance job creation' (TUC 1991b: 1). He warned that 'in vulnerable industries such as mining and chemicals special assistance should be provided where appropriate through a national adjustment fund' (ibid.). He said that additional funding could be made available through 'a work environment superfund, supported by government and employers' (ibid.: 6–7). Hackett (1991: 25, 22) pointed explicitly to trade unions and environmental groups in the US that had been lobbying 'for just such a fund to provide for improved health and safety, education, training, retraining and retraining and research'. It would also offer 'income support and assistance for workers who suffered as a result of environmental adjustments' (ibid.). A superfund was 'the only viable way to resolve the conflict between the public interest in a clean environment and the workers'interest in employment protection' (ibid.). He said the TUC was exploring the idea of a working environment fund based on the Swedish system, where a payroll levy of 0.15 per cent is placed on employers to underpin workplace research and training.

The concept of just transition reached international climate circles at the Kyoto conference in 1997. The ICFTU told the gathering that in response to measures to tackle greenhouse gas emissions, 'workers will demand an equitable distribution of costs through "just transition" policies that include measures for equitable recovery of the economic and social costs of climate change programmes' (ICFTU 1997: 1). Companies, which had profited from unsustainable practices, 'must assume their share of responsibility, but any mechanism to insure this must be carefully structured to avoid further adverse employment effects' (ibid.). The ICFTU warned that union support for targets that affect the workplace and community 'will be contingent on the existence of "just transition" measures that provide, as a minimum: income protection, redundancy procedures, re-employment, and education and retraining' (ibid.: 5–6).

Although this articulation of just transition was largely defensive, it would set the tone for future union interventions into international climate talks. At COP4 in Buenos Aires in 1998, the ICFTU called for a programme of 'transition measures' to provide for 'income protection, redundancy procedures, redeployment, education and re-training, coupled with job creation in energy conservation, as well as in green job creation', to overcome the 'diabolical dilemma of jobs versus the environment' (ICFTU 1998). Global union federations also adopted the formula. In November 1999, the International Federation of Chemical, Energy, Mine and General Workers' Unions, which includes workers from energy-intensive industries, adopted the just transition formula at its world congress (ICEM 2001). By the turn of the new century, just transition had become the sheath for trade union articulations of climate politics.

The development of just transition

The ITUC defines just transition as an approach 'aimed at smoothing the shift towards a more sustainable society and providing hope for the capacity of a green economy to sustain decent jobs and livelihoods for all'. The ITUC Congress in 2010 declared just transition to be 'the' approach to tackling climate change. The gathering committed unions to 'promoting an integrated approach to sustainable development through a just transition', including social progress, environmental protection and economic needs, democratic governance, respect for labour and other human rights and gender equality (Rosemberg 2010: 141–2).

The promotion of just transition coincided with the increasing size of trade union delegations at COPs. The ITUC had participated from its inception in the annual COP process, though with a relatively small presence in the early years. According to participants, nine union delegates attended COP7 in 2001, four went to COP8, 21 to COP9, 31 to COP10, 57 at COP11, 32 attended COP12 and 91 delegates lobbied the Bali COP13 in 2007 (UNEP/Sustainlabour 2008: 102). At the turn of the century, the ETUC called for an 'equitable social transition', taking account of the social impacts of climate change and prevention policies and their effects on employment, and a transition programme consisting of training, income support, and relocation funds for workers at risk of losing their job (ETUC 2004: 19, 41).

Just transition was promoted at the first Trade Union Assembly on Labour and the Environment held on 15–17 January 2006 in Nairobi (UNEP 2007). At the Bonn climate talks in May 2007, for the first time, unions secured explicit reference to the importance of employment creation in the conclusions of the Ad Hoc Working Group on future Kyoto commitments (TUSDAC 2007). In December 2007, the union delegation statement to the Bali climate talks called for just transition 'to ensure that the urgent measures which must be taken are done in a way which are fair and just' (TUC 2008d: 6–7).

The process of elaborating the concept of just transition in some detail was enhanced by a TUC pamphlet, *A Green and Fair Future: For a Just Transition to a Low Carbon Economy* (TUC 2008c). It defined just transition as 'a way that workers can support the environmental clean-up without the worry of job loss ... Just transition forces employers to take responsibility for workers and keep communities intact.' The pamphlet sought to 'assess the impact that moving towards a less carbon-intensive economy will have on jobs, skills and employment opportunities, and will explore how the transition itself can be rendered socially just' (ibid.: 14). Just transition should 'embody principles of equality, social justice and workforce participation'. It was intended to be a 'truly visionary' intervention, designed to ensure that 'all the conditions exist for a genuinely just transition to a low carbon economy' (ibid.: 1).[4]

The pamphlet stated that a shift to a low-carbon economy was 'not just necessary but increasingly inevitable'. Previous industrial transformations had often had retrograde consequences for workers. It highlighted the likely 'job churn' from the transition to a low-carbon economy. First, newly created jobs may not go to those whose jobs were threatened as the result of environmental measures. Second, there were concerns about the effectiveness of some re-skilling/retraining programmes. Third, newly created jobs may be of a poorer quality – in terms of pay, conditions and/or seniority – than the jobs they replace. Finally, many energy-intensive industries are concentrated in relatively small geographical areas, therefore there was a real danger that 'environmental transition will have a disproportionate effect on particular communities' (ibid.). Just transition assumed that 'ensuring social justice in the transition to a low-carbon economy cannot be based on the vain hope that the market alone will provide' (ibid.). By demanding just transition, unions recognised that support for environmental policies was 'conditional on a fair distribution of the costs and benefits of those policies across the economy' and because support for environmental change was required from all sections of society, 'so the costs of that change must fall proportionately on all sections' (ibid.). Government intervention was needed to provide flexible support packages, including 'consultation requirements; education/training/re-skilling; compensation to cover relocation costs or living costs for those finding new work or who are facing significant change in the nature of their work' (ibid.: 1–3). The pamphlet argued that just transition would pay for itself in the long term, though some measures would require initial or ongoing investment to make them possible. A possible source of funding was the massive revenue stream from the auctioning of allowances under the EU ETS (ibid.: 11).

TUC officials endeavoured to render just transition operational for international and domestic policy. They argued that just transition embodied

> a set of guiding principles to ensure the development of a green economy brings the maximum benefit to working people: the right consultation mechanisms from the workplace to the highest levels of government; the right skills and training strategy; innovation policies; and the right financial support for new low-carbon technologies.
>
> (TUC 2008a: 74–5)

Pearson argued that just transition meant 'consultation between stakeholders – governments, unions, industry, communities – at global and national level', plus 'massive investment in green jobs and skills. Change through consent. Environmental rights at work. Social protection for the most vulnerable. And a massive transfer of funds to the South for climate impacts we can't avoid' (Pearson 2009b). The TUC launched the pamphlet at its climate change conference on 16 June 2008, in front of two hundred delegates and Defra Environment Minister Hilary Benn (TUC 2008c: 5, 6). It would also contribute to international discussions in the run-up to COP14 in Poznań.

A significant breakthrough on just transition was made at COP14 in Poznań, in Poland in 2008. The trade union delegation, chaired by Philip Pearson and composed of more than 100 delegates from 40 countries, supported action to tackle climate change as a priority for a new trade union internationalism. The UNFCCC granted the ITUC the formal status of an 'official constituency' in the COP process. The ITUC said this was an important step forward, providing better access to the UN officials and placing it on an equal footing with other observer groups representing business, research institutes and NGOs (ITUC 2008). A draft text acknowledged many of the core trade unions' demands, with references to 'assessing labour market impacts and adopting transition measures, promoting labour-management initiatives for greener workplaces; and using labour policies to identify opportunities for green jobs, greening existing jobs, and phasing out unsustainable jobs' (UNFCCC 2009: 59).

At the Bonn climate talks in June 2009, Pearson reported that just transition resonated because it was about 'recognising and planning fairly and sustainably for the huge changes that adaptation to climate change will have for our economies' (Pearson 2009c). In a further post, he argued that the shift to a low-carbon economy could go either way. It could 'displace many, bring change without benefits to many'. Or through 'concerted efforts by trade unions, working people and communities, working with their governments and employers, create the conditions for a just transformation, bringing quality employment and hopefully benefits to the wider informal sectors' (Pearson 2009d). The draft text ahead of the crucial Copenhagen conference included the trade union call for a just transition to a low-carbon future in its *Shared Vision* document. The text stated:

> An economic transition is needed that shifts global economic growth patterns towards a low emission economy based on more sustainable production and consumption, promoting sustainable lifestyles and climate-resilient development while ensuring a just transition of the workforce. The active participation of all stakeholders in this transition should be sought, be they governmental, private business or civil society, including the youth and addressing the need for gender equity.
>
> (TUC 2009c: 1)

Just transition was also acknowledged at the national level. Climate Minister Ed Miliband told the TUC Congress that 'it will not just be the TUC position that we need a just transition, but it will be this Labour government's position that we argue for at the Copenhagen Summit this December' (TUC 2009b: 124). However, as events unfolded in Copenhagen, it became clear that unions, along with other NGOs, civil society and even state actors, were in fact outside the real negotiations. Pearson blogged that hopes were briefly aroused, when 'perhaps for the first time' ever at the UN, governments discussed the relevance of workers' issues in an international agreement. He added that union delegates had urged governments 'to put the issues of just transition and decent work on the table. And last night, albeit in closed session, we hear from various reports that governments gave explicit support for a just transition to a low-carbon future' (Pearson 2009f)! Therefore, trade union representatives expressed understandable frustration, as they and other climate activists were shut out of the talks, and the UN's original text was eclipsed by the Accord.

The ITUC expressed 'dismay' at the outcome of the Copenhagen Climate Summit, though its officials tried to remain upbeat. ITUC President Sharan Burrow expressed its 'satisfaction' that the process 'recognised the importance of a just transition as a driver for decent work and good quality job creation'. The fact that the UNFCCC had endorsed the *Shared Vision* text, including the strategically important just transition clause, was something unions could carry into further negotiations and potential agreement (ITUC 2009b). Internationally, the EU acceded to the ETUC's demand for a high-level forum for dialogue between the European social partners on climate change and the transition to a low-carbon economy. The forum, composed of ten members on the employers' side, ten on the trade unions' side and ten members representing the European Commission, held its first meeting on 13 May 2011.

In the UK context, the formation of the Forum for a Just Transition and, to an extent, the Conservative–Liberal Democrat Coalition government's

Green Economy Council (which included union representatives), meant that just transition appeared to be on the verge of institutionalisation. TUC officials argued that the Forum for a Just Transition, the joint unions–business–government body announced in 2009, brought together the key elements of just transition (TUC 2010a). It was 'both a table, and a place at the table itself' (Pearson 2009e). Just transition was defined in terms of formal consultation with unions, green and decent jobs, education and training, diversification, social protection measures and respect for human rights (TUC 2009a). Just transition was reduced to five key principles: (1) union voice ('consultation between representatives from trade unions, business, government and voluntary organisations on the shift to a green, low-carbon economy'); (2) green and decent jobs; (3) green skills; (4) respect for labour and human rights; and (5) 'strong and efficient social protection systems' (TUC 2010a: 64; TUC 2014c: 3). This formulation, boiled down for government consumption, was some way from Mazzocchi's original, more radical conception of just transition.

As union officials advanced just transition on the international and domestic stages, they also began to use it as a euphemism for reconfiguring the whole economy after the 2008 economic downturn. TUC officials promoted the demand for the Robin Hood tax on financial transactions as a suitable instrument for funding just transition measures internationally (Pearson 2010a; Tudor 2010). Just transition is about 'recognising and planning fairly and sustainably for the huge changes that climate change policies will have for our whole economy' (TUC 2010c: 2). At the Cancún talks, Pearson argued that the climate crisis, 'like the financial turmoil, stems from an unsustainable economic model'. The union vision of a just transition sought to counterbalance the market 'with progressive principles of decent work and union voice' (Pearson 2010e). Just transition had become the defining notion within high-level union narratives.

Just transition went through further vicissitudes at global climate gatherings. The UN text that went forward to COP16 in December 2010 recognised that addressing climate change required a 'paradigm shift towards building a low emission society', which would need to ensure 'a just transition of the workforce that creates decent work and quality jobs' (Pearson 2010d). However, delegates found on arrival in Cancún that in an apparent bid to simplify its negotiating text, the UN had 'deleted almost all the references to labour and human rights issues' (Pearson 2010f). Although the *Shared Vision* document did eventually commit to 'promoting a just transition of the workforce, the creation of decent work and quality jobs in accordance with nationally defined development priorities', uncertainty was evident (Pearson 2010g). More than 250 trade union representatives from around the world attended the Durban COP17, where the formulation remained in favour of 'a just transition of the workforce, and the creation of decent work and quality jobs' (Pearson 2011a, 2011b). Just transition was mentioned once in the Rio+20 statement, but unions were outraged by the deletion of women's reproductive rights from the final draft (Pearson 2012a).

The Global Commission on the Economy and Climate also used the language of just transition, though it did not envisage an active role for workers and trade unions (Pearson 2014b).

Philip Pearson reflected on the progress made on just transition at the COPs. From Cancún onwards, the UN had included just transition and decent work in its conference decisions. Gradually, the idea had taken hold, to the point where in Bonn in June 2013, 'a key UN committee has devoted a whole session to discussing the key principles involved – social partnership with a place at the table for trade unions, the vital role of green jobs and skills to support green growth and tackle global poverty' (Pearson 2013a). The process also yielded some important acts of solidarity. The TUC, Unison and Prospect backed climate projects in Ghana, Sierra Leone and Bangladesh and helped their union delegates to attend the global climate gatherings (Pearson 2010d).

Perhaps the most symbolic gesture took place literally on top of the world. Dorje Khatri from the Unitrav Nepalese union of trekking, travels, rafting and airline workers ascended Mount Everest on 26 May 2011 to plant the ITUC flag almost 9 kilometres above sea level. The act was a dramatic fusion of climate concern with workers' rights, drawing attention to the ongoing effect of climate change on the mountain, the threat of floods and landslides for communities below and the continued exploitation of the sherpas. The gesture was all the more tragic because only three years later Dorje Khatri was killed by an Everest avalanche (ITUC 2011, 2014a).

The personal tragedy was preceded by political calamity at the Warsaw climate talks in 2013. The so-called 'corporate COP', preceded by an official coal summit, also saw the publication of the UN's outline climate change treaty. International union officials denounced the draft as neither 'politically smart, nor responsible'. The common threads linking the main objectives of the treaty to cut emissions, provide finance and support adaptation provided 'no space for bringing Decent Work, Just Transition, social justice, or the need to transform economies into the next agreement', the ITUC said (Pearson 2013c). The union delegates joined a walk-out with NGOs and other campaigners disgusted at their exclusion from the process (Pearson 2013d). The 'emerging policy architecture' for agreement in Paris 2015 suggests states' emissions reduction contributions is likely to be 'nationally-determined' and not legally binding under international law. If this move may encourage the largest emitters (particularly China and the United States) to participate, it will also confine just transition to policy within but not between states (Green 2014: 5). The limits of the just transition strategy seem to have been reached.

The limits of just transition

The chastening experience of Copenhagen, as well as changes of government in states such as the UK, have meant that just transition has not been institutionalised. Crucial just transition support, training and funding mechanisms have not been embedded in government policy or international law during this period. Key actors in government and in individual unions are cognisant of these limitations. A Labour government advisor told the TUC's just transition project, 'whilst there are jobs to be had in all that, that can't be the crux of the argument'. As they candidly put it, 'The government actually sees its role as not directly intervening and creating a diversification agency and saying this factory is closing, we'll help them get to new carbon, low-carbon production' (Interviewee Omega 2007). Similarly, the failure to agree a successor treaty to Kyoto (including the just transition clause) suggests that just transition is a long way from becoming government policy, never mind reality.

Even the weaker version of just transition advocated by TUC leaders did not entice the Labour government or most employers to consummate the kind of partnership they had hoped for. The relationship between the partnership approach and just transition is problematic: given the scale of transformation required, it is questionable whether such a just transition is ever likely. If someone has to pay, then it is simply impossible to ally with every other actor. Senior TUC officials were committed to the partnership approach. One interviewee in the TUC just transition project argued for partnership on pragmatic grounds: 'I don't see a problem with it [partnership], but you always have to remember that even the best of partners fall out from time to time.' They added: 'And then if you take the opposite view that you wouldn't have a partnership, you're always in confrontation, aren't you? So I think there's a lot of merit in partnership, but it has to have clear rules and guidelines' (Interviewee Delta 2007). Another interviewee went further, argued that 'partnership has a place within a framework that recognises common objectives. And clearly it's been the case that the common objective thus far has been achieving growth, achieving consumer power, and that's obviously been driving emissions.' They added that the big issue was 'how much our current levels of consumption can be maintained in a low-carbon economy'. They stated:

> I don't think they can, but that just underlines more and more the need for a shared understanding on the part of government and on the part of corporations, on the part of workers, on the part of trade unions, for a new goal.
>
> (Interviewee Gamma 2007)

However, whether it is possible for business, government and unions to have common goals in a just transition is precisely the point – particularly when the former did not appear to want 'partnership' beyond window-dressing.

Just transition was visible at the highest levels of the trade union movement, even if it was largely ignored by employers. It did not resonate deeply with governments of all political stripes either: the rhetoric was not embraced by the Conservative–Liberal Democrat Coalition government at

Westminster from 2010, which had a rather different transition in mind for austere times. Perhaps more damningly, just transition did not permeate very far lower down the trade union movement, beyond the officials and the activists to be embraced by ordinary members. Given that just transition was in its infancy during this period, it is perhaps unfair to expect it to have gained a wider resonance. At Copenhagen, the 100,000-strong demonstration became a mobilising slogan, with banners and stickers stating 'Unions have solutions: just transition' and 'Union solidarity: just transition' (Pearson 2009g). But this was a relatively small part of a much larger mobilisation.

The just transition concept was developed by trade unionists in an attempt to grapple with both threats to existing jobs and the opportunities for new employment. Snell and Fairbrother (2013: 149) ask two pertinent questions about the potential and limitations of just transition: first, what are the conditions for such a transition to be just; and second, 'what capacities do unions have to influence economic and political conditions in such a way that "just transition" can be actualised?' Peter Rossman (2013: 58) argues that just transition has two shortcomings. First, it can 'underestimate the extent to which current technologies are embedded in power relations that require more than rational arguments to transform'; and second, just transition 'tends to overlook that rights are never granted, but always fought for'. The experience of just transition in the British labour movement in the first decade of the century provides some support for these claims.

Comments from senior union officials for the just transition project illustrate the limits. Just transition is presented as a matter of long-term sagacity, rather than challenging existing relations of production. One interviewee said:

> I'm not quite sure I like the concept of just transition, but I think it's useful to a certain extent. But I think that what you have to do then is as the government has done for energy, is to think ahead 40 or 50 years actually.
> (Interviewee Beta 2007)

They added: 'So I think we haven't had that, have we, that sort of very long-term, part of the government do it, they call it foresight' (ibid.). Another interviewee put it in terms of unions coping with changes beyond their control. They said:

> Theoretically, I don't think the 'no change' model is an option. I don't think you can say we're not going to accept any job losses, period. I don't think trade unions are able to stick any kind of flag in any kind of sand in this economy or any other kind of economy.

They added:

> That's not how things have ever worked before and it's not going to be the case in the future. You can't help thinking that the changes that

do emerge will emerge in the way that they've always done, in an incremental way.

(Interviewee Gamma 2007)

Other tensions with the formulation of just transition also became evident during this period. The 2008 TUC Congress recognised:

> Trade unions can play a major role in educating everyone about the causes of climate change, the likely impact and the need for a planned and just transition to a low-carbon economy that will see substantial changes from the nature and type of employment that currently exists.

(TUC 2008b: 20)

Michael Leahy (Community) stated: 'A just transition must not abandon trade union members. A just transition must not repeat the mistakes of Thatcher's damaging de-industrialisation. A just transition must provide a sustainable future for all: blue-collar, white-collar and green-collar.' He said: 'We all know what we want – a green and fair economy – but we cannot achieve it by a giant leap. We must take small steps and think carefully about the path that we want to choose.' Leahy warned that 'we must not give the multinationals the opportunity to become carbon tourists, seeking out countries where carbon emissions are poorly regulated. That would not provide us with a just transition' (ibid. 2008b: 128).

At the other end of the political spectrum, some senior union officials recognised the lack of radical policy proposals for thoroughgoing change at work in the sanitised version of just transition. The *Green and Fair Future* pamphlet quoted a study of environmental transition in Canada, which concluded that just transition had remained 'largely a slogan' rather than 'a well-articulated theoretical programme'. It had not taken off because 'there has been no green job creation worth the name' (TUC 2008c: 11). Even during negotiations to secure a just transition clause in the global climate agreement, this was registered. ITUC policy officer Anabella Rosemberg pointed out in the run-up to Copenhagen that 'even now, few governments really know what "just transition" means. When the phrase appears on their screens here, probably 90 per cent of them won't fully understand it. Of course, they probably won't be alone in this' (Pearson 2009c). Rosemberg (2010: 145) also acknowledged that the conception of just transition had to be widened. She argued that the just transition concept had to take into account at least three different starting points and consequent policy options: 'carbon-intensive developed countries'; 'increasingly carbon-intensive emerging economies'; and 'low-carbon, highly climate-vulnerable developing countries'. For just transition to cohere, it had to integrate the unevenness of the global economy.

In the light of these considerations and in the context of Mazzocchi's original vision, the ITUC's version of just transition appeared breezy but somewhat underdeveloped. This was well captured by Nigel Stanley, TUC head of communications, who blogged:

> I'm not sure I'm too keen on the phrase [just transition], but the idea that adaptation and the move to a low-carbon economy must be done in a way that doesn't make the world even more unfair and unequal is absolutely right. It really is jobs, justice and climate.
>
> (Stanley 2009)

However, three elements are left unstated. First, the lack of clarity on the destination of a low-carbon economy – or rather the goal of climate politics; second, whether the strategy and transitional measures are sufficient to affect such a significant transformation; and, third, what just transition implies for the alliances forged by unions with other actors. The next section explores efforts to supersede just transition by infusing it with more class-related content.

Class, climate and work

Trade unionists have highlighted the employment impacts of climate change within the context of global capitalism. There was a tangible class element to union discourse in demands for decent work and for compensation for workers who would lose out as a result of climate policy. Even weaker conceptions of just transition have class referents, pushing the boundaries of ecological modernisation discourse in the direction of workers. However, within unions internationally (including in the UK), some articulations emerged around energy democracy, specifically 'climate jobs' and socially useful work that pushed the class-based framing beyond just transition.

A more class-focused approach starts with a critique of the neoliberal and ecological modernisation framings of climate politics. Such a critique would not dismiss the efforts of high-level trade unionists to engage in international climate talks nor require their withdrawal from the process. Trade union delegates have played an important role in campaigning for emissions reductions, for funding and for solidarity between workers in the Global North and the Global South already experiencing the impacts of global warming. However, it would begin with a realistic assessment of the current impasse.

Sean Sweeney (2014: 1–2, 5) has produced a nuanced but devastating critique of the dominant union approach until now. He argues that the green economy framework has reached a 'political dead end'. Jobs and just transition have been the heart of the trade union message on climate change during the first phase. Unions have talked and acted 'as if the transition to a low carbon economy was green transition itself, was inevitable' – yet it now appears to be impossible. The high-level lobbying strategy of pursuing a 'workers clause' in a new climate agreement 'is only of value if there is an actual agreement – and therein lies the problem'. Sweeney argues that unions now need a new course – a 'pressure from below' strategy – 'anchored in both mobilising their members and building alliances with social movements who share the basic values and broad objectives of the trade union movement'. Fortunately, the resources of the international labour movement are replete with pointers towards this alternative strategy.

Beyond just transition

There is some appreciation that ends are important and union campaigning for reforms in response to climate change would have to challenge the destination of the ubiquitous 'low-carbon economy'. For the TUC's just transition project, one interviewee said:

> I strongly suspect that it will be capital that shapes the future and shapes the low-carbon economy. And I strongly suspect that we'll be fulfilling our historic role which as you know has been about getting a good deal for the workers in the context of that model. I don't think the low-carbon economy ultimately will be anything other than a capitalist economy, but it clearly has to look very different, just through necessity.
> (Interviewee Gamma 2007)

However, they also made the point that unions would 'do well to dust off our William Morris and earlier ideas about communism', because the climate debate has a silver lining: 'you can start to think about different ways of organising society. You can think about more wholesome worlds where we're not saddled with debt trying to afford the latest gadget' (ibid.). Trade unionists have to take part in the realpolitik of bargaining within the system. Yet they cannot ignore the way society is organised and avoid articulating a vision of how it might be done on different lines and following different imperatives. The classic debate between immediate reforms and a more radical transformation is also played out in climate politics.

It is important to avoid exaggerating the extent to which just transition represents a 'counter-hegemonic position' compared with the dominant framings (Nugent 2011: 62–3). But some articulations of just transition constitute a distinct, union-initiated and worker-based contribution to climate politics. The conception of a just transition is trade unions' distinctive intervention into the complex world of climate politics. It represents an effort to articulate a specific worker interest in the process, taking a long-term strategic view of the trajectory of the world economy and some of the likely restructuring ahead, in which unions will need to represent members' interests. It also suggests the kind of measures needed to ensure that the transition is not at the expense of workers' living standards. The plasticity of the concept allowed for a more radical interpretation. For example, the demand for a 'worker-led just transition' was discussed by trade unionists and climate activists, including at the Climate Camp, where it became the main slogan of the Workers' Climate Action campaign.

However, the social structures of (neoliberal) capitalism are the systemic constraint on making a transition to a low-carbon economy. Radical versions of just transition require the wholesale transformation of social relations of production, not simply technological shifts. Technology is never socially neutral. The ownership and democratic control of natural resources (particularly those which produce huge quantities of greenhouse gas emissions) are vital conditions for ensuring that any low-carbon transition is socially just, but also swift and effective. A renewed socialist vision would have to incorporate these concerns, but even low-carbon capitalism would have to overcome resistance from significant sectors of capital. Hence, the importance of social agency for just transition. At present, the trade union movement in Britain and internationally alone may not have the political and organisational leverage to enforce such a large-scale transformation. However, with clarity of vision, leadership and organisational regeneration, it is a movement with substantial strength and one potentially capable of coalescing climate activists and other campaigns to begin that process.

Workers' control and energy democracy

There is an emerging critique of eco-modernist discourses, including green jobs and just transition that stretches these conceptions in a radical direction. Sweeney (2012: 29) articulated the case for 'energy democracy', which included demands for social ownership and democratic control over energy corporations. He argued that the trade union movement can work with other social movements to develop a vision for energy to move people into action and show that 'another energy system is possible'. In 2013, some 29 unions, including national trade union centres and Global Union Federations, launched Trade Unions for Energy Democracy. The initiative advocates public direction and social ownership of energy at the local to the global scales as the basis for durable and effective alliances between unions and other social movements:

> The key to mobilising union members, workers, and individuals is for unions and their social movement allies to identify a series of bold interventions that can begin to address not just climate change but also the full spectrum of unsustainable and unjust features of political economy. A trade union approach to system change is therefore both transitional and transformative in nature … It also needs to be grounded in the historical traditions of economic democracy, worker cooperatives, credit unions and mutualism, and it is these traditions that can now be deployed in the effort to reclaim the economy and protect the planet from certain destruction. A medium-term goal, therefore, is to secure a qualitative shift towards public and social ownership of key economic

sectors, particularly energy and electrical power generation, major transportation services, energy conservation through 'climate jobs' and public works, and food production, distribution and retail. The need for action now, within the existing system, in no way negates the push for system change.

(Sweeney 2014: 14–15)

There was some recognition of these issues at ITUC level. Its statement to COP20 in Lima argued that 'democratic ownership of energy is needed' and that energy 'along with other common goods that belong to humanity (air, water) must be brought, administered and kept under public control'. Energy companies 'need to be restructured in order to allow for broad democratic control and oversight, including a strong scheme of workers' participation'. The ITUC called for a decisive move away from 'ecologically and socially destructive methods of fossil fuel extraction' (such as fracking for shale gas, tar oil exploitation) 'towards renewable energy under public and democratic control' (ITUC 2014c: 3).

Implicit in these trade union discussions of energy democracy is a challenge to the nature of work under modern capitalism. Some union climate activists questioned what production is for: for profit or for social need? Incorporating climate change within this latter, broadly defined conception of social needs meant some trade unionists acquainting themselves with earlier discussions of socially useful production. Labour movements around the world have long-standing traditions challenging the nature of work, which have raised questions about exploitation, workers' control over the labour process and the types of commodities (whether goods or services) produced at work. These debates variously perceived workers' control as the essence of industrial democracy, workers' self-activity and socialism, but for others it signified a diversion, class collaboration and ultimately the 'castration of the trade union movement' (Horner 1974; Scargill *et al.* 1978: 4). The Environmentalists for Full Employment campaign in the United States sought to tackle the 'jobs blackmail' argument juxtaposing employment to environmental protection (Kazis and Grossman 1982). Similarly, a conference of British trade unionists held on these issues in 1975, organised by the Socialist Environment and Resources Association and the Institute for Workers' Control, proposed 'socially useful production' to simultaneously tackle unemployment and environmental concerns (Kinnersly and Cooley 1976).

During the 1970s, a significant number of workplace rank-and-file union organisations in Britain produced workers' plans, in response to employers' restructuring and unemployment. These plans invariably questioned the logic of capitalist production for profit and asserted the need for socially useful production – often making explicitly pro-ecology proposals. Probably the most famous was the Lucas Aerospace Corporate Plan, published by the cross-union Combine Committee in 1976. The plan stated:

New, renewable, sources and more efficient methods of conversion must be developed. Solutions to the problem based on nuclear power give rise to new problems of health, safety and even survival. Instead R&D should focus on new sources of energy and new types of energy conversion transmission and storage.

(Wainwright and Elliott 1982: 101–2)

The stewards detailed designs for ecological heat pumps, solar and fuel cells, windmills and flexible power packs, as well as road–rail public transportation vehicles, hybrid power packs for motor vehicles and airships.

The example of the Lucas Aerospace plan was undoubtedly the most widely cited precedent, particularly because the plan raised the question of socially useful production. Wainwright and Elliott (ibid.: 107–9) explained that at first, the meaning of socially useful production tended to be 'intuitive and implicit'. However, the Lucas Combine Committee delegates spelt out an approximate definition of a socially useful product: It must not 'waste energy and raw materials, neither in its manufacture nor in its use'; it must be 'capable of being produced in a labour-intensive manner'; it must 'lend itself to organisational forms within production which are non-alienating'; and be organised 'to allow for human creativity and enthusiasm'. The Lucas stewards were not the first to have challenged the social values behind product decisions. The novelty of their initiative was that they challenged these values 'as producers as well as, as citizens, users and consumers'.

Beynon and Wainwright (1979) found that organised workers in major military contracting firms such as Vickers and Rolls Royce produced similar initiatives.[5] Other similar workers' plans emphasised renewable and environmentally friendly technologies. Workers at GEC Trafford advocated wave, wind and nuclear power, for example, in the Severn Estuary (CSE 1977). Chrysler car workers also developed this approach, demanding diversification into public transport and agricultural vehicles. A statement from Chrysler stewards stated:

The widespread ecological and environmental criticism of the private petrol-driven car as a socially irresponsible form of transport suggests to us that we must explore the feasibility of new kinds of products of a socially useful kind to harness the skills of the existing plant and machinery, and direct it away from a commodity whose profitability and usefulness is rapidly declining.

(Wainwright and Elliott 1982: 142)

These precedents were drawn upon by some sections of UK trade unions when confronted with climate change. Trade unionists attending the first Campaign against Climate Change trade union conference in 2008 discussed the Lucas plan as a model for climate campaigning, while it was explicitly discussed by the Workers' Climate Action network at its gatherings in 2008 and 2009. The Lucas example was also cited by Frances O'Grady during a TUC seminar for green workplaces day in June 2009. During the Congress debate on one million climate jobs, PCS delegate Adam Khalif (TUC 2010b: 117) hailed the *One Million Climate Jobs* pamphlet as 'a new Lucas Plan'.

Räthzel, Uzzell and Elliott (2010: 81–2, 85–6) made the connection between the Lucas experience and climate change. In interviews Räthzel and Uzzell conducted with a wide range of different trade unionists, many interviewees referred to Lucas Aerospace as a model. Like climate change prevention, the defence spending cuts during the 1970s were acknowledged as a necessary and progressive step, though with foreseeable employment consequences for workers. Lucas trade union stewards 'decided to try another way. Instead of fighting for the maintenance of the defence-related jobs, they started the struggle for the transformation of production at Lucas from military hardware to socially useful products.' Climate change has brought such contradictions even more sharply into focus, and made projects like the Lucas Plan a necessity. Common themes such as collective action, the progressive potential of technology and the importance of decent employment are particularly pertinent.

In recent years, some union reps and officials have also discussed shorter working hours, homeworking and other forms of potentially climate-friendly working patterns (LRD 2007; Flaxton 2010). Earlier proposals on reduced working hours as a means of gaining more leisure time, improved quality of life and to reduce unemployment have been extended to climate change.[6] Radical proposals were discussed to reduce hours with no loss of pay, so that capital bore the costs through reduced profits. These fertile lines of reasoning were not curtailed by the economic recession.[7] These radical union conceptions went further than ecological formulations of the job guarantee and basic income guarantee (Lawn 2009), which also challenged conventional conceptions of employment. Indeed, the defence of jobs along the lines of a Lucas climate plan arguably begin to challenge the relations of production (the largely private appropriation of nature) and implicitly the relationship between society and climate mediated by labour. The inspiration of Lucas gives trade unionists a radical edge within the emerging climate movement.

One million climate jobs

Another innovative approach to fusing climate change with occupational matters is the one million climate jobs campaign. The justification for this demand in the UK was provided by a widely circulated pamphlet, *One Million Climate Jobs*, which has appeared in three editions, published by the Campaign against Climate Change and edited by Jonathan Neale (2009, 2010; 2014). Neale (2010: 6–7) argues that the framing of 'climate jobs' differs from what politicians usually meant by green jobs. First, he narrows the focus on the type of work done: 'We mean climate jobs, not green jobs. Climate jobs are jobs that cut down the amount of greenhouse gases we put in the air and thus slow down climate change.' Green jobs could mean work in the water industry, national parks, landscaping, bird sanctuaries, pollution control and many more things. He argues: 'All these jobs are necessary. But they do not affect global warming. We mean jobs that tackle the main sources of emissions.' Second, these climate jobs would be directly employed public sector occupations. Neale criticises government policy, which simply uses subsidies and tax breaks to encourage private industry to invest in renewable energy. Climate jobs would be direct government jobs:

> The traditional approach is to encourage the market. That's much too slow and inefficient. We want something more like the way the government used to run the National Health Service. In effect, the government sets up a National Climate Service (NCS) and employs staff to do the work that needs to be done.
>
> (Neale 2010: 7)

The proposed National Climate Service would 'employ people directly in making the components for wind turbines, putting the components together, installing and maintaining the turbines, and building and working the ships we need for offshore wind'. Other indirect jobs would be created for 'workers who make the supplies and service the NCS's needs – steel for the turbines and ships, the hammers and saws for the building workers, the paint for the buses'. He suggests that further induced jobs would be created by workers' spending on 'shoes, clothes, cinema tickets, meals, cameras, fishing rods, tickets to gigs, and so on'. While the framing appears to be compatible with ecological modernisation, the sharper emphasis on workers gaining during the process of transition and on public ownership was more distinctive and class-focused. Neale argues that 'anyone who loses their job because of the new economy will be offered work in the NCS, with retraining and their old wages guaranteed'. He advocates exploring 'alternative, democratic forms of public ownership if the planet's productive resources are to meet social need and halt a slide towards ecological disaster' (Neale 2010: 8, 41). This was closer to the original, stronger conception of just transition envisaged by Mazzocchi.

Some contributors to the pamphlet are critical and others are less optimistic of some jobs considered as valuable for low-carbon energy production. This was the case for carbon capture and storage, though contributors agreed that 'some of the one million jobs be used for building the first working coal plant in the world to capture and store all its carbon'. Similarly, most contributors thought that nuclear power was too expensive and dangerous, and so they did not include new nuclear power stations in their plans. However, acknowledging that many in the trade union movement supported nuclear power on climate grounds, the authors agreed to continue discussions. However, the pamphlet is adamant that jobs in the hydraulic fracking industry were not climate jobs, estimating that their proposals would create 80 times as many climate jobs as those from fracking (Neale 2014: 25, 63).

TUC Congress in 2010 passed a resolution that included support for a campaign for one million green jobs, with key speakers adopting the 'climate jobs' approach set out in the pamphlet. Tony Kearns, CWU Deputy General Secretary, told Congress (TUC 2010b: 20, 116) that representatives from the PCS, TSSA, NUT, UCU and CWU unions, academics from Brunel and Oxford Universities and workers from Vestas had come together through the Campaign against Climate Change, 'to put down, if you like, on paper what it is that we want'. He differentiated the campaign from wider discussions of green jobs. Kearns said: 'Let us be quite clear that we are talking here about government jobs. They can be paid for ... by subsidies and tax.' He was adamant that the dominant framings had 'failed previously to deal with climate change, because they left it to the markets to decide'. Climate jobs was a narrower conception than green jobs, but potentially more fertile.

The demand for one million climate jobs is also perceived as a key mobilising tool, shaping an alliance between trade unionists, environmentalists and other activists to tackle climate concerns alongside other wider issues arising from the economic crisis. Implicitly, it is not aimed at partnership with employers or indeed with existing governments. Neale (2010: 42, 46) argues that climate jobs allowed campaigners to offer a positive way forward. Instead of simply defending this or that service, or opposing certain cuts, climate jobs 'won't just create work and save the planet – the investment has the potential to pull the economy out of crisis'. However, he warns that winning a million climate jobs would have to be fought for. Campaigning for climate jobs 'will help unite trade unionists, environmentalists, students, pensioners and the unemployed. Such a coalition will be a powerful force.' The campaign has had some success, reaching out beyond the higher levels of the unions, circulating thousands of copies of the pamphlet through trade union branches and organising events, such as the Climate Caravan to raise the profile of climate jobs during the economic downturn.

Conclusion

The employment impacts of climate change cannot be avoided if the future low-carbon economy is to be socially just. With the concept of just transition, some trade unionists began to articulate their own distinctive climate policy, based on a separate class interest that workers have on climate matters. The framing of just transition by the ITUC, ETUC, TUC and other unions during this period articulated some class concerns within the sheath of ecological modernisation. Although there is some tension between the embrace of low-carbon transformation and the defence of jobs and living standards, and over the precise means to attain a low-carbon economy, just transition does capture principles of distributive and procedural justice that underpin the trade union endeavour. The concept of just transition could be extended to every level of climate change policy, from the production process to government fiscal policy and to wider democratic governance.

Demands for energy democracy, socially useful work and public sector climate jobs can be understood as articulating a more radical desire by trade unionists to shape the form of the emerging low-carbon economy and discourses around it. Given the essential mediating role of labour in defining relations between human society and the Earth's climate (as discussed in Chapters 1 and 2), employment questions are unavoidable for climate politics. Some union discussions during this period indicated the continued relevance of class interests to any progressive and socially just vision of a low-carbon economy. A more radical interpretation of just transition will be necessary to fully capture the extent of the transformation necessary and to galvanise wider social actors around the labour movement axis.

Notes

1 The Touchstone Blog is an informal blog by TUC staff about policy issues that are in the news, or ought to be. Contributions should not be taken as formal statements of TUC policy. While written from a TUC perspective, contributions often cover areas where there is no settled TUC policy and go into areas in more detail than its formal decisions.

2 Snell and Fairbrother (2013: 147) also attribute the provenance of just transition to Leonard Woodcock's work within the UAW autoworkers union in the early 1970s.

3 I am grateful to Brian Kohler for clarifying the origins of just transition (Kohler, pers. comm., 28 October 2014).

4 The pamphlet was not without controversy. Union officials interviewed for the publication expressed a variety of opinions. Some understood that just transition was seeking to align employment and environmental concerns, while others interpreted the concept as trading jobs for the environment. One said: 'We need to be careful. This research could end up justifying the transition as "just".' They argued that the just transition concept was 'out of date for developed countries, if it ever was in date. It's not attached. It's a contradiction in terms' (Interviewee Alpha 2007).

5 Dave Elliott generously made his primary source material on Lucas and other worker plans available. As well as versions of the original Lucas plans, the collection includes materials from manufacturing firms GEC Trafford, Parsons, Ernest Scraggs, Dunlop and Clarke Chapman.

6 Knight, Rosa and Schor (2013) proposed reduced working hours on climate grounds, without ignoring possible rebound effects of more leisure, such as the 'lights into flights' Tesco advertisements (Chitnis *et al.* 2013).

7 This discussion should not be confused with the agreements some unions made to accept short-time working, with the resulting loss of pay traded for promises of job security in some workplaces, which were not related to climate objectives.

References

Babiker, M. and Eckaus, R. (2007) 'Unemployment Effects of Climate Policy', *Environmental Science and Policy*, 10: 600–9.

Barry, J. (2013) 'Trade Unions and the Transition from "Actually Existing Unsustainability": From Economic Crisis to a New Political Economy Beyond

Growth'. In N. Räthzel and D. Uzzell (eds) *Trade Unions in the Green Economy: Working for the Environment*. London: Routledge.

Barry, R., Jenkins, T., Jones, E., King, C. and Wiltshire, V. (1998) *Green Job Creation in the UK*. London: Association for Energy Conservation, Friends of the Earth, GMB, UNISON.

Beynon, H. and Wainwright, H. (1979) *The Workers' Report on Vickers: The Vickers Shop Stewards' Combine Committee Report on Work, Wages, Rationalisation, Closure and Rank-and-file Organisation in a Multinational Company*. London: Pluto Press.

Bowen, A. (2012) '"Green" Growth, "Green" Jobs and Labor Markets', Policy Research Working Paper 5990, The World Bank Sustainable Development Network Office of the Chief Economist. Washington, DC: The World Bank.

Carter, N. (1997) 'Prospects: The Parties and the Environment in the UK'. In M. Jacobs (ed.) *Greening the Millennium? The New Politics of the Environment*. Oxford: Blackwell.

Chateau, J., Saint-Martin, A. and Manfredi, T., (2011) 'Employment Impacts of Climate Change Mitigation Policies in OECD: A General Equilibrium Perspective', Environment Working Paper No. 32. Paris: OECD.

Chitnis, M., Sorrell, S., Druckman, A., Firth, S. and Jackson, T. (2013) 'Turning Lights into Flights: Estimating Direct and Indirect Rebound Effects for UK Households', *Energy Policy*, 55: 234–50.

Coates, I. (2000) *Employment Implications of Environmental Policy*. TUSDAC Paper. London: DETR.

Cock, J. and Lambert, R. (2013) 'The Neo-liberal Global Economy and Nature: Re-defining the Trade Union Role'. In N. Räthzel and D. Uzzell (eds) *Trade Unions in the Green Economy: Working for the Environment*. London: Routledge.

Crowley, K. (1999) 'Jobs and Environment: The Double Dividend of Ecological Modernisation', *International Journal of Social Economics*, 26(7/8/9): 1013–26.

CSE (1977) *Workers' Power: A Socialist Report on the Power Plant and Energy Industries, Produced in Co-operation with AUEW-TASS*. Conference of Socialist Economists Energy Group. Liverpool: Big Flame Press.

DECC (2009) 'Strategy for Low-Carbon Businesses to Benefit British Jobs', press release, 15 July.

Doelfs, G. (2009) *Green Jobs in Germany and the UK: Conference Report. VIII. British-German Trade Union Forum, Frankfurt (Oder), 2–3 July 2009*. London: Anglo-German Foundation.

Dupressoir, S. (ed.) (2007) *Climate Change and Employment*, Brussels: ETUC.

ETUC (2004) *Climate Change: Avenues for Trade Union Action*. Brussels: ETUC.

Fankhauser, S., Sehlleier, F. and Stern, N. (2008) 'Climate Change, Innovation and Jobs', *Climate Policy*, 8(4): 421–9.

Felli, R. (2014) 'An Alternative Socio-Ecological Strategy? International Trade Unions' Engagement with Climate Change', *Review of International Political Economy*, 21(2): 372–98.

Flaxton, P. (2010) 'Work from Home Day: Smart, Green and Family Friendly', *Touchstone Blog*, 24 September.

Foster, D. (2010) 'BlueGreen Alliance: Building a Coalition for a Green Future in the United States', *International Journal of Labour Research*, 2(2): 233–44.

GCEC (2014) *Better Growth, Better Climate: The New Climate Economy Report: The Synthesis Report*. Washington, DC: The Global Commission on the Economy and Climate.

Gereluk, W. and Royer, L. (2001) *Sustainable Development of the Global Economy: A Trade Union Perspective*. Geneva: ILO.

Green, F. (2014) *This Time Is Different: The Prospects for an Effective Climate Agreement in Paris 2015*, Policy Paper, Centre for Climate Change Economics and Policy. Leeds: CCCEP.

Greenpeace International (1992) *Statement on Labour and the Environment. Prepared for XVth ICFTU World Congress 17–24 March 1992, Caracas, Venezuela*. Amsterdam: Greenpeace International.

Guivarch, C., Crassous, R., Sassi, O. and Hallegatte, S. (2011) 'The Costs of Climate Policies in a Second-best World with Labour Market Imperfections', *Climate Policy*, 11(1): 768–88.

Hackett, P. (1991) 'The UK Unions and the Environment'. In P. Schulte and J. Willman (eds) *The Environment. Challenges and Opportunities for Trades Unions*. London: Friedrich Ebert Foundation.

Hewett, C. and Foley, J. (2001) *Trade Union Sustainable Development Advisory Committee (TUSDAC), 2001. Employment Creation and Environmental Policy: A Literature Review*. A Report by Public Policy Research Associates Ltd. October. London: IPPR.

Horner, J. (1974) *Studies in Industrial Democracy*. London: Victor Gollancz.

ICEM (2001) *Labour and Climate Change: An ICEM Position*. Geneva: ICEM (International Federation of Chemical, Energy, Mine and General Workers Unions).

ICFTU (1997) *Climate Change and Jobs: Towards a Strategy for Sustainable Employment: Trade Union Statement to the Kyoto Conference (1–10 December 1997)*. Brussels: ICFTU.

——(1998) 'Getting Workers on Your Side Is Crucial to the Success of Programmes to Reduce Greenhouse Gases, Say the Unions', *ICFTU Online*, 11 November.

Interviewee Alpha (2007) Just Transition Project interview, 27 September 2007, conducted by London Metropolitan University, Working Lives Research Institute.

Interviewee Beta (2007) Just Transition Project interview, 5 October 2007, conducted by London Metropolitan University, Working Lives Research Institute.

Interviewee Delta (2007) Just Transition Project interview, 12 October 2007, conducted by London Metropolitan University, Working Lives Research Institute.

Interviewee Gamma (2007) Just Transition Project interview, 10 October 2007, conducted by London Metropolitan University, Working Lives Research Institute.

Interviewee Omega (2007) Just Transition Project interview, October 2007, conducted by London Metropolitan University, Working Lives Research Institute.

ITUC (2008) 'Labour Movement Gains Official Recognition at UN Climate Change Conference', press release, 3 December.

——(2009a) *Trade Unions and Climate Change: Equity, Justice & Solidarity in the Fight against Climate Change. Trade Union Statement to COP15, United Nations Framework Convention on Climate Change – UNFCCC, Copenhagen, Denmark (7–18 December, 2009)*. Brussels: ITUC.

——(2009b) 'Climate Change: Job Not Done in Copenhagen', press release, 21 December.

——(2011) 'Trade Unions at the Top of the World', press release, 27 May.

——(2012) *Growing Green and Decent Jobs: Summary*. Brussels: ITUC.

——(2014a) 'Sherpa Dorje Khatri Reported Killed in Everest Avalanche', press release, 18 April.

——(2014b) *Climate Change is a Trade Union Issue*. Brussels: ITUC.

——(2014c) *Workers & Climate Change. International Trade Union Confederation (ITUC) Contribution to the 20th Conference of the Parties to the UNFCCC 1–12 December, 2014 – Lima, Peru.* Brussels: ITUC.

Jacobs, M. (1995) *Green Jobs? The Employment Implications of Environmental Policy.* Brussels: WWF.

——(ed.) (1997) *Greening the Millennium? The New Politics of the Environment.* Oxford: Blackwell.

Jenkins, T. and McLaren, D. (1995) *Working Future? Jobs and the Environment.* London: Friends of the Earth.

Jones, V. 2008. *The Green Collar Economy.* New York: HarperCollins.

Kazis, R. and Grossman, R. (1982) *Fear at Work: Job Blackmail, Labor, and the Environment.* New York: Pilgrim Press.

Kinnersly, P. and Cooley, M. (1976) *Jobs and the Environment: Contributions to a Conference [held in 1975 by the Southeast London branches of the Socialist Environment and Resources Association and the Institute for Workers' Control].* London: SERA/IWC.

Knight, K., Rosa, E. and Schor, J. (2013) 'Could Working Less Reduce Pressures on the Environment? A Cross-National Panel Analysis of OECD Countries, 1970–2007', *Global Environmental Change,* 23(4): 691–700.

Kohler, B. (1996) *Sustainable Development: A Labor View – The Real Choice Is Not Jobs or Environment. It Is Both or Neither.* Presentation at the Persistent Organic Pollutants Conference, 5 December, Chicago, IL.

Kouri, R. and Clarke, A. (2012) 'Framing "Green Jobs" Discourse: Analysis of Popular Usage', *Sustainable Development,* online only (accessed 25 May 2013).

Krause, F., DeCanio, S., Hoerner, A. and Baer, P. (2003) 'Cutting Carbon Emission at a Profit. Part II: Impacts on U.S. Competitiveness and Jobs', *Contemporary Economic Policy,* 21(1): 90–105.

Lawn, P. (ed.) (2009) *Environment and Employment: A Reconciliation.* London: Routledge.

Leopold, L. (2007) *The Man who Hated Work but Loved Labor: The Life and Times of Tony Mazzocchi.* Vermont: Chelsea Green.

LRD (2007) *The Environment and Climate Change: A Guide for Union Reps.* London: LRD.

Neale, J. (ed.) (2009) *One Million Climate Jobs Now.* London: Campaign against Climate Change.

——(ed.) (2010) *One Million Climate Jobs: Solving the Economic and Environmental Crises.* London: Campaign against Climate Change.

——(ed.) (2014) *Time to Act: One Million Climate Jobs.* London: Campaign against Climate Change.

Nugent, J. (2011) 'Changing the Climate: Ecoliberalism, Green New Dealism, and the Struggle over Green Jobs in Canada', *Labor Studies Journal,* 36(1): 58–82.

OECD (1997) *Environmental Policies and Employment.* Paris: OECD.

Orion Innovations (2014) *Walking the Carbon Tightrope.* London: Orion Innovations.

Pagnamenta, R. (2009) 'Lord Mandelson's Claims of 880,000 "Green Jobs" in UK a Sham', *The Times,* 16 July.

Pearce, A. and Stilwell, F. (2008) 'Green-Collar Jobs: Employment Impacts of Climate Change Policies', *Journal of Australian Political Economy,* 62: 120–38.

Pearson, P. (2009a) 'US Labor Launches Centre for Green Jobs', *Touchstone Blog,* 9 February.

——(2009b) 'Message in a Bottle from a Small Island', *Touchstone Blog,* 30 March.

——(2009c) 'Just Transition: Getting the Message Across in Bonn', *Touchstone Blog*, 9 June.

——(2009d) 'Bonn Diary 2: Building a Union–NGO Coalition for Copenhagen', *Touchstone Blog*, 9 June.

——(2009e) 'Just Transition Forum: A Place at the Table', *Touchstone Blog*, 20 July.

——(2009f) 'Copenhagen Diary #6: Hopenhagen (really)', *Touchstone Blog*, 12 December.

——(2009g) 'Copenhagen Diary #7: Blah Blah Blah, Act Now!' *Touchstone Blog*, 13 December.

——(2010a) 'Carbon Diary: Robin Hood to Rescue Climate?' *Touchstone Blog*, 10 February.

——(2010b) 'Bonn Diary #3: Race to the Future', *Touchstone Blog*, 4 June.

——(2010c) 'Carbon Diary: Tough CO_2 Policies May Cost Jobs', *Touchstone Blog*, 26 July.

——(2010d) 'Cancun Diary #1: The Right To Be Heard', *Touchstone Blog*, 1 December.

——(2010e) 'Cancun Diary #3: Recapture Lost Ground', *Touchstone Blog*, 3 December.

——(2010f) 'Cancun Diary 4: UN Cuts Out Labour Rights', *Touchstone Blog*, 6 December.

——(2010g) 'Cancun Diary 7: Yes! Now for a Green Economy Council', *Touchstone Blog*, 12 December.

——(2011a) 'Durban Diary 2: Oil State Qatar to Host Next Climate Conference?' *Touchstone Blog*, 29 November.

——(2011b) 'Durban Diary 4: UN Returns to Just Transition', *Touchstone Blog*, 1 December.

——(2012a) 'Judith Reports from Rio+20: No Social Justice Without Environmental protection', *Touchstone Blog*, 20 June.

——(2012b) 'Building Our Low-Carbon Industries', *Touchstone Blog*, 25 July.

——(2013a) 'Bonn Diary 2: UN Opens Just Transition dialogue', *Touchstone Blog*, 5 June.

——(2013b) 'Green Jobs: No turning back', *Touchstone Blog*, 6 September 2013.

——(2013c) 'Warsaw Diary #3: UN's First Draft Is No Deal Without Just Transition', *Touchstone Blog*, 20 November.

——(2013d) 'Warsaw Final: Walking Out Is Not Our Way, But … ', *Touchstone Blog*, 25 November.

——(2014a) 'Budget 2014 Must Halt Overseas March of the Makers', *Touchstone Blog*, 17 February.

——(2014b) 'Carbon Time Is Running Out: Time to Change the Game?' *Touchstone Blog*, 17 September.

Porter, M. and van der Linde, C. (1995) 'Toward a New Conception of the Environment–Competitiveness Relationship', *Journal of Economic Perspectives*, 9(4): 97–118.

Räthzel, N., Uzzell, D. and Elliott, D. (2010) 'Can Trade Unions Become Environmental Innovators'? *Soundings*, 46: 76–87.

Rosemberg, A. (2010) 'Building a Just Transition: The Linkages between Climate Change and Employment', *International Journal of Labour Research*, 2(2): 125–61.

Rossman, P. (2013) 'Food Workers' Rights as a Path to a Low-Carbon Agriculture'. In N. Räthzel and D. Uzzell (eds) *Trade Unions in the Green Economy: Working for the Environment*. London: Routledge.

Sato, M., Neuhoff, K., Graichen, V., Schumacher, K. and Matthes, F. (2013) *Sectors Under Scrutiny: Evaluation of Indicators to Assess the Risk of Carbon Leakage in the UK and Germany*, CCCEP Working Paper 134. Leeds: CCCEP.

Scargill, A., Wise, A. and Cooley, M. (1978) *A Debate on Workers' Control*. Nottingham: Institute of Workers' Control.

Scott, M. (2014) *Climate Change: Implications for Employment. Key Findings from the Intergovernmental Panel on Climate Change, Fifth Assessment Report*. Brussels: ETUI.

Snell, D. and Fairbrother, P. (2010) 'Unions as Environmental Actors', *Transfer*, 16(3): 411–24.

——(2013) 'Just Transition and Labour Environmentalism in Australia'. In N. Räthzel and D. Uzzell (eds) *Trade Unions in the Green Economy: Working for the Environment*. London: Routledge.

Stanley, N. (2008) 'Green Jobs Are Good, and Unions Get It', *Touchstone Blog*, 23 October.

——(2009) 'The Climate Change Moment', *Touchstone Blog*, 17 July.

——(2010) 'Unions and Environmentalism – Uneasy Bedfellows?' *Touchstone Blog*, 8 March.

Sweeney, S. (2012) *Resist, Reclaim, Restructure: Unions and the Struggle for Energy Democracy*. New York: Cornell Global Labor Institute.

——(2014) 'Climate Change and the Great Inaction: New Trade Union Perspectives', Working Paper No. 2. New York: Trade Unions for Energy Democracy.

TUC (1990a) *Congress 1990: General Council Report*. London: TUC.

——(1990b) *Congress Report 1990*. London: TUC.

——(1990c) *Environmental Issues and Policy Implications: Towards the White Paper – Submission by the TUC*, April. London: TUC.

——(1991a) *Industry, Jobs and the Environmental Challenge: A Memorandum by the TUC to the National Economic Development Council, May 1991*. London: TUC.

——(1991b) *Employment and the Environment. Paper for the TUC Forum Work and Environment: The European Dimension*. London: TUC.

——(1996) *Trade Unions and the Environment: A Multi Stakeholder Initiative*. London: LRD.

——(1998a) *Congress 1998: General Council Report*. London: TUC.

——(1998b) *Environment, Sustainable Development and Multi-Stakeholders: The Implications of Kyoto – Conference Report*. London: TUC.

——(1999) *Note on DETR Paper 'Employment Implications of Environmental Policies', 25 March 1999*. London: TUC.

——(2008a) *Congress 2008: General Council Report*. London: TUC.

——(2008b) *Congress Report 2008*. London: TUC.

——(2008c) *A Green and Fair Future: For a Just Transition to a Low Carbon Economy. Touchstone Pamphlet*. London: TUC.

——(2008d) *International Development Matters, January 2008*. London: TUC.

——(2009a) *Congress 2009: General Council Report*. London: TUC.

——(2009b) *Congress Report 2009*. London: TUC.

——(2009c) *Green Jobs and Skills: Memorandum Submitted by the TUC to the Environmental Audit Committee, 30 June 2009*. London: TUC.

——(2010a) *Congress 2010: General Council Report*. London: TUC.

——(2010b) *Congress Report 2010*. London: TUC.

——(2010c) *Environmental Audit Committee Inquiry: Green Investment Bank – TUC Submission, 14 October 2010*. London: TUC.

——(2011a) *Congress 2011: General Council Report*. London: TUC.

——(2011b) *Congress Report 2011*. London: TUC.

——(2012) *Building Our Low-Carbon Industries*. London: TUC.

——(2014a) *Congress 2014: General Council Report.* London: TUC.

——(2014b) *Briefing Note: Energy Intensive Industries, 11 September 2014.* London: TUC.

——(2014c) *TUC Briefing Note: Climate Change and a "Just Transition",* November 2014. London: TUC.

Tudor, O. (2010) 'Robin Hood Goes Green: How FTTs Can Save the Planet', *Touchstone Blog,* 30 November.

TUSDAC (2003) *Submission to 'Learning the Sustainability Lesson', 3 March 2003.* London: TUSDAC.

——(2007) *Trade Unions at the UN Framework Convention on Climate Change (UNFCCC), 7–19 May 2007, Bonn.* London: TUSDAC.

UNEP (2007) *Labour and the Environment: A Natural Synergy.* Nairobi: United Nations Environment Programme.

——(2008) *Green Jobs: Towards Decent Work in a Sustainable, Low-Carbon World.* Nairobi: United Nations Environment Programme.

UNEP/Sustainlabour (2008) *Climate Change, its Consequences on Employment and Trade Union Action: A Training Manual for Workers and Trade Unions.* Nairobi: UNEP.

UNFCCC (2009) *Ideas and Proposals on Paragraph 1 of the Bali Action Plan.* Ad Hoc Working Group on Long-Term Cooperative Action under the Convention, Fourth Session, Poznań, 1–10 December 2008. Geneva: UNFCCC.

Uzzell, D. and Räthzel, N. (2013a) 'Introducing a New Field: Environmental Labour Studies'. In N. Räthzel and D. Uzzell (eds) *Trade Unions in the Green Economy: Working for the Environment.* London: Routledge.

——(2013b) 'Local Place and Global Space: Solidarity across Borders and the Question of the Environment'. In N. Räthzel and D. Uzzell (eds) *Trade Unions in the Green Economy: Working for the Environment.* London: Routledge.

Vallack, H., Timmis, A., Robinson, K., Sato, M., Kroon, P. and Plomp, A. (2011) *Technology Innovation for Energy Intensive Industry in the UK.* Birmingham: Centre for Low Carbon Futures.

Wainwright, H. and Elliott, D. (1982) *The Lucas Plan: A New Trade Unionism in the Making?* London: Allison & Busby.

Waters Wye Associates (2010) *The Cumulative Impact of Climate Change Policies on UK Energy Intensive Industries – Are Policies Effectively Focussed? A Summary Report for the Energy Intensive Users Group and the Trades Union Congress Summary Report. July 2010.* London: Waters Wye.

Young, J. (2003) 'Green-Collar Workers', *Sierra Magazine,* July/August.

4 Trade unions and climate politics in the UK

Introduction

This chapter brings the discussion down to the national scale and assesses various stances taken towards climate change by trade unions in the UK. It does so principally through the prism of the TUC. The chapter provides an overview of common trade union discourses and draws out some of the contradictions between different union framings, corresponding to the variable geometry of trade unionism identified by Hyman (2001). Why analyse TUC policy? The peak union body has been neglected by researchers, despite its important relations with other actors. There are a wide range of published and unpublished documents, statements, booklets, minutes and more recently blogs available to scholars for critical examination. The TUC regards itself as a key national institution in public life (Taylor 2000). Its multiple roles comprise 'a union policy "think tank", labour movement symbol, exemplar and guide for affiliates, federation to aid the reconciliation of union and other interests, possible coalition partner and supporter of affiliates' revival efforts' (Parker 2008: 563). The TUC has helped develop, albeit unevenly and cautiously, a workable consensus among UK unions on climate change. The TUC's roles make it a worthwhile site of study.[1]

The approach in this chapter is necessarily top-down, though it does not ignore a number of contradictions and tensions. The TUC's 1970 report on structure and development registered its 'perennial problem of reconciling the special interests of particular unions or groups of members with the general interests of the trade union movement and of deciding when which set of interests should prevail' (Taylor 2000: 13). For Heery (1998: 342, 356), though the TUC's strategy is to establish itself as the body that speaks 'on behalf of a broadly conceived labour interest', there is a contradiction between an 'attachment to social partnership and a commitment to campaigning and organising trade unionism, which is necessarily oppositional in its stance towards employers'. McIlroy (2000: 13) argues that the TUC pursues an 'insider strategy'. It accepts 'the rules of the game' for insiders, meaning that it is regarded (and regards itself) as a legitimate social actor with access to government.

The focus on the TUC suggests a number of questions: How do trade unions frame climate politics? To what extent have unions really engaged with (or accommodated to) the dominant climate politics? To what extent have unions as a movement articulated their own distinctive conception, based on a separate working-class interest? How does the TUC reconcile competing interests, discourses and framings? What are the limits of trade unions' framing? The first section examines union climate framing in terms of ecological modernisation. The second section examines the extent to which unions have reflected market, neoliberal discourses. While these framings have been dominant, the third section examines more explicitly class-focused stances.

Union climate policy and ecological modernisation

TUC climate policy is probably best characterised as following the ecological modernisation approach. A number of common themes from the ecological modernisation literature are found in the TUC's framing of climate issues: an emphasis on state intervention to deal with recognised market failures; support for target-setting and other non-market forms of regulation; an emphasis on science and technology; a focus on social justice and on social integration; and the conception of unions as a legitimate stakeholder partner deserving of a place in national (and international) policy-making. This is drawn out by examining the origins and development of TUC policy on climate change. Although there were pressures in other directions too – notably from the market and from class – understanding TUC climate policy initially through ecological modernisation provides the best starting point to evaluate its behaviour.

Origins: climate change within a 'balanced energy policy'

In the early 1970s, trade unions began to engage with the burgeoning environment movement. Probably the earliest significant reference to climate change in the TUC literature came from John Davoll, Director of the Conservation Society, who warned a TUC Workers and the Environment conference in July 1972: 'Your carbon dioxide and burning of fossil fuels changes the composition of the atmosphere and raises the possibility of changing global temperature' (TUC 1972: 46). Historically, the TUC has supported the 'balanced' development of all energy sources – a formulation that encapsulated a series of ecological modernisation themes around state intervention, technological solutions and multi-stakeholder interests. This 'balanced energy policy', formulated just before the first oil price hike and reaffirmed subsequently, also assimilated climate change during the mid-1980s.[2] An early mention of climate change can be found in an internal TUC document, *Acid Deposition and Power Station Emission Control (Draft)*, 19 July 1985. The report stated, 'There is also much concern, in another context, about the so-called "greenhouse effect", which has been variously traced to emissions of carbon dioxide, methane, ozone, chlorofluorocarbons, nitrous oxide and certain rare gases' (TUC 1985: 1–2). This paragraph was also used in *Acid Deposition and Power Station Emission Control: A Statement from the TUC Energy and Social Insurance and Industrial Welfare Committees* (TUC 1986), the first TUC public policy statement that mentions global warming.[3]

Another early reference came during acrimonious discussions over nuclear power, when leaders of the miners' and firefighters' unions advocated phasing out nuclear energy and were opposed by larger unions organised in the energy sector. In 1987, a TUC General Council report *Nuclear Energy* highlighted 'a particular concern, on which too little is yet known, must be the so-called "greenhouse effect", whereby carbon dioxide emissions from all fossil fuel burning is thought to be causing long-term changes to the world's climate, which could have catastrophic consequences' (TUC 1987: 44). A further report, *Nuclear Power and Energy Policy*, expressed the scientific uncertainty at the time. It stated:

> In the longer term, all fossil [fuel] burning involves emission of carbon dioxide (CO_2), which is associated with the possible 'greenhouse effect', whereby some of the sun's rays hitting the earth are unable to be reflected back into space, so causing a rise in the temperature of our atmosphere.

It concluded: 'Too little is still known about the greenhouse effect to be sure of its causes and consequences, but it is giving rise to concern in many countries' (TUC 1988b: 13).

In 1988, climate change burst into the spotlight politically, particularly after the US drought and NASA scientist James Hansen's testimony to the US Congress. This was also the year climate change was discussed publicly for the first time at TUC Congress, though it was hardly an auspicious beginning. Global warming was raised during another fractious debate between advocates and opponents of nuclear power. Bill Brett of the IPMS union spoke on behalf of members who had brought climate science to public attention, as well as members in the nuclear industry. He called for 'a greater research and development impact on the problems created by acid rain and, perhaps more seriously, the greenhouse effect' (TUC 1988a: 548). He moved an amendment to a motion on nuclear energy on 7 September 1988, which stated:

> Congress expresses its concern about the substantial environmental impact of non-nuclear energy and calls upon the government to commit substantial resources to research into the growing problems of 'acid rain', the 'greenhouse effect' and the environmental impact of tidal barrage schemes.
>
> (TUC 1988a: 681)

Other contributions focused on the contentious issue of the phasing out of UK nuclear reactors rather than climate change. Both the amendment and the motion were defeated in the stalemate.

Nevertheless climate change came back as part of an environment motion to the 1989 Congress, where the gathering recognised 'the now incontrovertible evidence that global warming, acid rain and the depletion of the ozone layer together pose a major threat to the survival of humanity' (TUC 1989a: 582). The motion was passed with much hyperbole, with Brett warning that 'if we do not do something about the greenhouse effect it will end civilisation' (ibid.: 385). Congress endorsed the TUC's *Towards a Charter for the Environment* (1989b: 10), which called for governments to implement United Nations targets for a 20 per cent reduction in global CO_2 emissions by 2005, compared to 1988 levels. The TUC established an Environmental Action Group, consisting of prominent general secretaries and other officials to investigate the issues further (Hackett 1992).

However, the connections between climate change and other trade union matters remained fraught, as an exchange during the energy policy debate the following day made clear (TUC 1989a: 482–3). Gordon Bellard (EMA) argued provocatively that, 'The increased awareness of the effects on the environment through the burning of fossil fuel, acid rain and the so-called greenhouse effect, has cast doubt on the increased use of coal as a major source of energy production.' Arthur Scargill (NUM) responded vociferously that emissions targets could still be met while retaining the existing coal industry and opposing nuclear power.

At the 1990 Congress, the General Council produced a *Report on the Environment* and delegates discussed the first separate motion devoted to climate change. The resolution recognised 'the enormous threat to the people of the world from the effects of "global warming"', stating that, 'It would seem that unless immediate action is taken to reduce the emission of numerous industrial gases into the atmosphere, millions of people around the world face catastrophe within the next ten to twenty years' (TUC 1990a: 560–1). The resolution recognised that the newly-established IPCC, whose reports on global warming it predicted 'will have profound implications for industry'. Congress resolved to set up a special climatic working group that would 'examine how, with the minimum damage to jobs and the standard of life, progress can be made towards reducing the threat of the devastating consequences of global warming'. The motion, moved by Diana Warwick from the AUT university teachers' union, called for 'steep cuts in emissions of carbon dioxide and other greenhouse gases'. The Thatcher government had proposed a target to stabilise 1990 emission levels by 2005, which Jimmy Knapp (NUR) said many in the unions regarded as 'too modest' (ibid.: 353–5).

Having grasped the rudimentary science, trade union leaders appear to have baulked at the political consequences of following through consistently on climate policy. In particular, they began to perceive that the effects of climate politics on jobs and workers' living standards might be quite stark.

The climate group was never constituted. Facing another Conservative government and with the onset of recession in 1992, as well as the pit closures crisis and further decline in membership, unions appeared to recoil from the challenge. This was illustrated by their response to the Labour Party's *In Trust for Tomorrow*, which emphasised sustainable development and renewable energy and called for a moratorium on road building (Labour Party 1994). At the 1994 Labour conference, 'the powerful TGWU and AEEU voted against accepting and GMB abstaining, as union leaders expressed concern about jobs in the open-cast mining, nuclear energy and road-building industries' (Carter 1997: 196). For several years afterwards, union climate politics in the UK fell into abeyance.

Trade union climate policy under Labour governments

The election of the Labour government in 1997 gave a significant spur to TUC framing of its climate policy in ecological modernisation terms. In December 1997 after the Kyoto Protocol, Prime Minister Tony Blair called business and trade unions leaders to a Green Summit and asked them to help combat the threat of climate change. One of the fruits of this insider status was the formation of the Trade Union Sustainable Development Advisory Committee (TUSDAC) on 6 July 1998. Its terms of reference included 'to provide a trade union perspective on the employment consequences of climate change, and the response to it' (TUC 1998: 153–4). TUSDAC was precisely the kind of government-stakeholder vehicle propagated by ecological modernisation thinkers.[4]

Perhaps the best illustration of the TUC's ecological modernisation approach was its support for the Labour government's third term climate policies. Environment Secretary David Miliband addressed Congress in September 2006 and appealed for trade union engagement with climate change in ecological modernist terms (TUC 2006b: 79). He also spoke to the TUC General Council in April 2007 in support of the Climate Change Bill, stressing the important role unions could play in addressing issues related to the environment and climate change (TUC 2007a: 62).[5]

TUC General Secretary Brendan Barber welcomed the Climate Change Bill when it was first read in Parliament (TUC 2007c). The Bill was discussed at the TUC's On Target? conference in June 2007 (TUC 2007e). Going further than the government's proposed 60 per cent target for CO_2 emissions reductions by 2050, union officials argued 'for a tougher 80 per cent reduction target, in line with the latest scientific evidence' (TUC 2007a: 65; 2007d). The Bill proposed an expert climate change committee to advise government on progress towards targets and a mandatory annual report to Parliament on progress. The TUC Congress in 2008 endorsed the Bill, including amendments on adaptation to climate change. The TUC called on the government 'to provide stakeholder representation on the Committee on Climate Change, or set up a similar tripartite body' and lobbied for a distinct trade union role and employee engagement (TUC 2008a: 75). TUC officials and representatives from the Unison public services union worked with NGOs to lobby MPs, adding their weight to demands for a higher long-term target to curb emissions. While it did not gain further representative rights, the TUC 'secured funding from the Carbon Trust to develop a Green-Workplaces project to build capacity within the trade union movement to address climate change and energy issues in the workplace' (TUC 2007a: 65, see Chapter 5 for a detailed discussion of this).

The TUC's approach to adaptation also had clear ecological modernisation undertones. Congress called on the government to develop and implement climate change adaptation strategies (TUC 2005: 25). Work on developing a distinctive union approach began with a seminar for affiliates in November 2007, where 'speakers from TUSDAC, the UK Climate Impacts Programme and the Association of British Insurers examined the impacts of climate change and some of the adaptation options'. In April 2009, the TUC published a report by AEA consultants, *Changing Work in a Changing Climate* (TUC 2009e), which recommended government guidance on adapting workplaces to deal with the impacts of climate change. It argued that employers should be encouraged to adapt buildings so staff could work securely and comfortably, renewing a long-standing health demand for a maximum indoor workplace temperature, above which employees would not be expected to work.

The report also cited the Fire Brigade Union's (FBU) demand for a statutory duty on fire and rescue services to respond to flooding, as evidence of unions adapting policy to climate risks – in this case, after the 2007 floods (FBU 2008; 2010). An important distinction was made between inward-looking and outward-facing adaptation. The study found that 'a number of employers were beginning to think seriously about the impacts of climate change and adaptation in an outward-facing manner: that is, looking at impacts on their business planning, markets and services'. However, very few were also looking at inward-looking adaptation: 'the need to look at impacts on workers and engage with them to develop adaptation measures that are workable, fair and sustainable in the longer term'. The TUC was given representation on Defra's adaptation partnership board alongside employers' organisations and NGOs.

Another illustration of the ecological modernisation framing of its climate policy was TUC support for state intervention to shape the low-carbon economy. Congress 2005 called for the government 'to develop a green industrial strategy, embracing the employment, training and research aspects of a new energy policy' (TUC 2006a: 78). In the 2009 Budget submission (TUC 2009c: 5), TUC officials called for £25 billion public investment, including a green public works programme. TUC policy officer Philip Pearson called the TUC's package 'a stimulating two-thirds pure green', with proposals for green manufacturing and renewable energy, a green rail stimulus, making the UK 'a leader in low-carbon vehicles and action on home insulation'. The TUC also called for a range of 'environmentally-neutral labour market support programmes' (Pearson 2009b).

At its Green Growth conference in April 2009, the TUC published its *Unlocking Green Enterprise* pamphlet, which called for a more state-interventionist green industrial strategy (TUC 2009d). TUC Congress welcomed the Labour government's low-carbon industrial strategy, published in July 2009, arguing that 'in order to make progress during the economic slowdown, an active industrialism approach was necessary, including government intervention around regulation, procurement and funding mechanisms' (TUC 2009a: 72–3). The General Council enthused about the planned 'Forum for Just Transition' made up of unions, business and government to advise on climate change policy to oversee the low-carbon industrial strategy.[6] In addition, TUC leaders welcomed the announcement in the March 2010 Budget of a £2 billion Green Investment Bank, with a mandate to invest in the low-carbon sector, considering new energy and transport projects in particular, and focusing initially on offshore wind generation. TUC policy officer Tim Page blogged that 'surely the days of laissez-faire industrial policy, when only the "market" decided what was in the country's economic interests, are well and truly behind us?' (Page 2010). Such technological optimism was short-lived: the policy and the Forum were jettisoned by the Conservative–Liberal Democrat Coalition government two months later.

Union support for carbon capture and storage (CCS) during this period was part of the balanced energy policy and epitomised the dominant ecological modernisation approach.[7] Energy union leaders and TUC officials have long promoted 'clean coal', though there was early recognition that 'there is unlikely ever to be completely clean combustion of fossil fuels' (TUC 1988b: 13). In the context of climate change, the NUM expressed its view that 'the Kyoto sacrifice in the UK has been made almost entirely by the mining communities, and they have little to show for it' (NUM 2004: 4). The union's leaders argued that CCS meant 'coal need not be black, it can be green' (NUM 2007: 3).

The TUC wholeheartedly supported CCS in strongly ecological modernisation terms, with an eye for a market opportunity. From 2002, when the first Congress resolution was moved by Sue Ferns from Prospect (TUC 2002: 200), support for CCS has stretched across the broad spectrum of union leaders within the 'balanced energy policy' consensus. Pearson (2009a) articulated the union case for CCS clearly in these terms. Rejecting charges of greenwash, he argued that unions' focus was not just on the capture of CO_2 from the UK's fossil fuel plants. Rather, CCS was described as essential if the increase in CO_2 emissions from rapidly developing economies such as China, India and other nations reliant on coal was to be reduced. Historic responsibility for CO_2 emissions lay with the developed world, so 'if developing countries need "space" to grow their economies, then we have to provide the means for a low-carbon future' (ibid.). Pearson also expressed a wider perspective, believing that successful CCS in coal-fired power stations could be extended to steel manufacture, chemicals, paper and pulp manufacture and other energy-intensive sectors. This was not to be dismissed lightly, with 60 per cent of global CO_2 from fossil fuels originating from power stations and energy-intensive industries like steel, cement and aluminium. A critical argument concerned the tens of thousands of workers in those plants. Shutting them all down was unrealistic, whereas cap-and-trade strategies could be used 'to stimulate the application of low-carbon technologies in their place – through CCS, ultra-low-carbon steel making, and other technological changes' (ibid.).

In 2006, the TUC established the Clean Coal Task Group, a joint industry, unions and government advisory body to progress its CCS policy. It published *A Framework for Clean Coal in Britain* articulating the policies needed to successfully develop clean coal-fired power generation plant, linked to carbon capture technologies, and to secure a long-term future for UK-mined coal (CCTG 2006). As its *Roadmap for Coal* put it, this scenario reflected 'the aligned interests between employers, unions and the government to support the transition of these key industries to a low carbon economy' (CCTG 2012: 5, 18).

A test case for TUC policy was the proposed new coal-fired power station at Kingsnorth in Kent, which energy firm EON planned to build on the site of its existing plant. The proposal was opposed by environmental organisations and was the site of the Climate Camp in August 2008 (Schlembach 2011). In an eye-catching intervention, Arthur Scargill made a rare public appearance at the camp, declaring that 'coal isn't the climate enemy, it's the solution' (Scargill 2008). TUC and unions with members on the site supported both the building of the new plant and its inclusion in the government's CCS competition. TUC leaders stated publicly that new power stations like the Kingsnorth project were '20 per cent cleaner than existing coal-fired plants and will be 80–90 per cent cleaner once carbon capture and storage is added' (TUC 2008f: 1). Pearson blogged just after the Climate Camp:

> We have supported Kingsnorth, unabated yes, but with the potential to become the UK's first clean coal plant. But the government hasn't yet mandated CCS for coal, now or at a known future date. Nor has it set out a policy framework to secure clean coal and gas stations for the future.

Pragmatically, they pointed out that if Kingsnorth did not proceed, it would mean extending the life of the older polluting fleet. The union position was conditional on the plant being 'capture-ready' (Pearson 2008a).

In 2009, EON shelved the plans to build the new plant and a year later withdrew from the competition to build a CCS demonstration plant at Kingsnorth. The union response was bitter. Pearson blogged that EON's announcement would 'accelerate gas dependency, despite the recession … [and]

delay the UK's carbon capture technology platform'. He argued for 'a middle way to ensure that CCS is built in the UK, with at least four UK-based full size clean coal power plants with CCS going ahead, within a defined and urgent timetable together with full financial support' (Pearson 2009d). CCS is a technological fix in ecological modernisation terms, but not a fantasy technology, given that its basic components were already in use across the energy industry. But union leaders supporting CCS did not call for a moratorium on new coal-fired power station until CCS was developed.

A final illustration of TUC framing on climate change that fits closely with ecological modernisation is the emphasis on union partnership with employers and government. This was clear from the initial grounding of union environmental work in a less confrontational approach to employment relations. An early TUC memorandum stated that active trade union involvement in environmental protection at the workplace level 'requires a new approach, based on partnership, cooperation and joint working. The traditional adversarial approach to industrial relations is not sufficient and may undermine environmental protection' (TUC 1991b: 9–10). This partnership approach was evident with the creation of TUSDAC. The TUC General Council report argued that TUSDAC formed the basis for a partnership or multi-stakeholder approach based on the 'interested parties' concept (TUC 1998: 152–3).

The renewed emphasis on government climate action in the Labour administration's third term prompted the TUC to renew its multi-stakeholder approach. A TUSDAC paper on the UK climate change programme stated that 'the social partners should work closely together in key sectors, such as energy and transport, to help achieve the government's climate change targets' (TUSDAC 2005c: 2). However, the committee was initially disappointed that the government's climate change review lacked 'a coherent vision of how the social partners are to work together successfully to achieve the government's challenging climate change targets' (TUSDAC 2005a: 4). Congress called for the government 'to work with the TUC on the development and implementation of climate change mitigation and adaptation strategies'. These must include 'clear expectation of employers that they work in partnership with trade unions on this agenda' (TUC 2005: 25).

Similarly, the TUC welcomed the publication of the Stern Review in these terms. Barber said: 'This review shows that immediate action against climate change could boost the economy ... [and] also benefit British business and create jobs' (TUC 2006e: 1). The day after the Stern Review was published, ministers argued at a TUSDAC policy group meeting that it was 'the route map for the post-carbon consensus'. The TUC response was to offer 'a partnership approach on climate change' (TUSDAC 2006: 3). Although the partnership envisaged by the TUC was never consummated with the Labour government nor with employers' organisations, the intention to engage with a wide range of social actors with climate change was articulated by leading trade union bodies.

Trade union climate policy under the Coalition government

The May 2010 general election brought the Conservative–Liberal Democrat Coalition government to power, changing the context for union climate politics in the UK. Before he became prime minister, David Cameron made the environment a signature issue, complete with huskies, cycling to work, a home wind turbine and a new party logo. His message was 'vote blue, go green'. Although Cameron's primary aim was to detoxify the image of the Conservatives as a 'nasty party', critics argue that his manoeuvres also pushed the Labour government to accelerate its climate policies (Carter 2009). The Coalition agreement pledged 'a full programme of measures to fulfil our joint ambitions for a low carbon and eco-friendly economy', while Cameron told DECC civil servants that he wanted his administration to be 'the greenest government ever' (EAC 2014: 7).

TUC leaders initially took the Coalition government's promises in good faith, perceiving elements of continuity with the ecological modernisation approach of the previous Labour government. They offered partnership on climate change – even to a government that was making swingeing austerity cuts – based on the discourse of the green economy, green growth and green jobs. The TUC's Alliances for Green Growth conference on 11 October 2010, addressed by the new Climate Minister Chris Huhne, was dominated by proposals for alliances between unions, employers and the government in the energy-intensive industries, green industries, over green skills and a new global climate treaty. TUC officials applauded Huhne's comment at the conference that 'we can only achieve the transition [to a low-carbon economy] if we work in partnership. Unions and business, each has a stake in this agenda' (Pearson 2010c). The TUC was awarded places on the government's Green Economy Council, which officials argued had 'taken over where the forum [for a just transition] left off in some ways' (Pearson 2011a). In January 2011, the TUC affiliated to the Aldersgate Group, a high-level group of leaders from business, politics and society concerned with sustainable economy issues (TUC 2011a: 72–3).

Disappointment set in within the first year of the new government, with early signs of a lurch by the coalition towards the more neoliberal pole of climate politics. Within the first year of the Coalition government, union leaders were critical of the impact of austerity on climate matters. They were swift to condemn the cancelling of a multi-million-pound loan to Sheffield Forgemasters. The new plant would have helped re-establish Sheffield as 'a centre of high quality steelmaking, not just for nuclear components but for any major specialist steels for low carbon industries – wind turbine components' (Pearson 2010b). A Prospect (2011) publication, *Is This the Lightest Green Government Ever?*, criticised the government for cuts to marine energy and forest research, for job losses resulting from government decisions at Bombardier train manufacturers, Eaga home insulation and to 350 solar companies after cuts to feed-in tariffs. It also complained about the axing of funding to the Carbon Trust and the Energy Saving Trust, the closure of the Sustainable Development Commission and the Royal Commission on Environmental Pollution, and the threat to 275 environmental laws posed by the Red Tape Challenge (ibid.: 2–3).

In fact, TUC leaders identified a strategic retreat early in the Coalition governement's term. Officials seized on a speech in which Chancellor George Osborne blamed environmental regulations for piling costs on the energy bills of households and companies. He claimed: 'We're not going to save the planet by putting our country out of business.' Rather, Britain would cut its carbon emissions 'no slower but also no faster than our fellow countries in Europe' (Pearson 2011b). Worse, Osborne's Budget in 2012 signalled a new dash for gas as part of a renaissance for fossil fuels. The Chancellor announced a £3 billion allowance for deep oil and gas field exploration off the Shetlands (with another allowance for small fields), backed by a new gas generation strategy to secure investment in gas-fired power stations (Pearson 2012b). TUC officials complained that of the £9 billion in energy subsidies, fossil fuels received three times the levels of ongoing subsidies of renewables (Pearson 2013h).

The retreat on climate policy was reinforced about the appointment of Owen Paterson as Environment Secretary in September 2012. TUC officials joined the chorus of NGO voices demanding to know whether Paterson was a climate sceptic (Pearson 2012f). The suspicion was reinforced when he downgraded flooding from Defra's top-line priorities and presided over the swingeing cuts to the department's adaptation staff (Pearson 2014d). And it was confirmed soon after Paterson was sacked from the government, when he called for the Climate Change Act to be scrapped (Hope 2014). As austerity eviscerated central government budgets, unions drew out the dire consequences for climate policy. Defra cut the number of civil servants working on adaptation to climate change from over 30 officials to just six (Pearson 2013d). Swingeing cuts, alongside the downgrading of flooding under Paterson, led unions to dub Defra the 'Department Evading Flood Risk Assessments'. During the winter floods of 2013–14, Prospect's Deputy General Secretary Leslie Manasseh called for an immediate moratorium on job cuts in the Environment Agency, as did FBU General Secretary Matt Wrack with regard to firefighter job losses (Pearson 2014a; 2014c).

When the Coalition government finally published its much-vaunted Energy Bill in November 2012, newly-elected TUC General Secretary Frances O'Grady said: 'We are a step closer to having renewable power at the heart of the UK's energy policy' and welcomed the additional support for the UK's energy-intensive industries (Pearson 2012h). However, the TUC argued that the Energy Bill should have included a binding 2030 target for power sector decarbonisation, 'to reduce the political risk currently associated with long-term UK industrial investment'. Consistent with its ecological modernisation approach, the TUC backed an (unsuccessful) amendment to that effect together with over 80 business and environmental organisations (TUC 2013a: 22). The government's 'compromise' was to take powers to introduce the target, without planning to use them until 2016 (Pearson 2013e). There was similar disenchantment with the way the Coalition government introduced the Green Investment Bank, which the TUC welcomed in principle. The key test was whether the bank would be able to 'borrow from the capital markets and enjoy a state guarantee'. Although the legislation contained an enabling power for state guarantee, the government provided up to only £3 billion of initial public support. By contrast, the German KfW state bank was investing 25 times as much each year in green investments (Pearson 2012e). In its first year the Green Investment Bank claimed it had created 3,500 jobs in wind and biomass projects (Pearson 2014e).

The biggest disappointment for trade unions came with the Coalition government's home energy efficiency scheme in England, dubbed the Green Deal, which replaced Labour's Warm Front programme. The Green Deal was based on private finance, and cut financial help to vulnerable households by two-thirds and triggered hundreds of redundancies in the insulation industry. In climate terms, unions believed it would take years to deliver emissions reductions and green jobs (TUC 2011a: 71). The TUC chastised government when only four people signed up to the Green Deal in its first six months (Pearson 2013f). Despite a government relaunch of the private loan scheme in May 2013, with ministers promising 10,000 'Green Deals' completed in the first year, the take-up remained poor (Pearson 2014b). Towards the end of 2014, fewer than 5,000 Green deals had been signed and the finance company providing the loans faced collapse, after it became clear it needed 60,000 deals a year just to break even (Rees 2014).

During the Coalition government, TUC leaders became increasingly exasperated with the continued demise of the indigenous coal industry in the UK, together with the lack of progress on CCS. The closures of Maltby colliery in Yorkshire, Daw Mill in Warwickshire after a devastating fire, Thoreseby in Nottinghamshire and Kellingley in Yorkshire were met with calls for state aid, including nationalisation, but to no avail (Pearson 2013c; 2014g). The NUM decided to invest £4 million in the last remaining deep mine in Britain, the employee-owned Hatfield colliery in Yorkshire, with a commercial loan to provide bridging funds to open new coalfaces and protect 500 jobs. NUM national secretary Chris Kitchen acknowledged this action is 'an unprecedented step for the union but reinforces its commitment to the deep coal mining industry in the UK' (Pearson 2014h). Conservatives anxious to perpetuate the legacy of Margaret Thatcher certainly got their way with the UK coal industry, regarding its future as a commercial matter and leaving the industry to the caprice of the market.

A more serious climate setback was the stalled progress on CCS. First, TUC leaders and trade unions in the power sector reacted with dismay to the Westminster government's decision to cancel the first commercial carbon capture project at Longannet, a coal-fired power station in Fife,

Scotland (Pearson 2011c). Second, ministers decided not to shortlist the Don Valley Power Project in Yorkshire for the UK's £1 billion CCS, despite it being the top ranked project in a parallel process run by the European Commission and potentially operational by 2016 (Pearson 2012g). Third, TUC officials seized on leaked Cabinet papers, which appeared to show that just £200 million had been set aside until 2015 for the supposed £1 billion CCS competition (Pearson 2013b).

The TUC's response was consistent with its ecological modernisation approach of partnership with industry bodies over aligned interests. To strengthen the case for CCS in the UK, the CCTG and the Carbon Capture and Storage Association (CCSA) commissioned a joint study of the economic and employment, as well as environmental, benefits of CCS technology (TUC 2013a: 23). The TUC and CCSA jointly published *The Economic Benefits of CCS in the UK*, which highlighted international evidence for CCS contributing 17 per cent of the necessary global emissions reductions in 2050 (from coal, gas and heavy industry users), and delivering 14 per cent of the cumulative emissions reductions needed between 2015 and 2050. The report pointed to the first actual power plant CCS installation at Boundary Dam in Canada (due to go into commercial operation) and to the jobs potential of CCS directly once rolled out internationally, and for energy-intensive industries (CCSA/TUC 2014: 4, 6, 9). Domestically, the union officials continued to promote CCS projects. In July 2014, the TUC hosted the relaunch of the Humber Area CCS partnership at a meeting in Leeds, with contributions from key local firms (Pearson 2014f). However, the TUC view was not accepted unanimously across the unions in Britain. Gordon Rowntree (PCS) told the 2013 Congress that although his union supported the development of CCS, it was 'an unproven technology' and did not 'eliminate the problem of CO_2 generation, but quite literally buries the problem' (TUC 2013b: 69). Despite union encouragement, the Coalition government was unwilling to create the conditions for a CCS industry in the UK.

Overall, the union verdict on the Coalition government's climate credentials was scathing. Jacque Hatfield (Community) told the September 2011 TUC Congress that the Coalition government's claims to be the greenest government ever was 'fast becoming the biggest sham ever' (TUC 2011b: 38). The following year, Chris Baugh (PCS) said the greenest government ever pledge was 'on a par with, "We are all in this together" as one of the most fraudulent claims ever made by leading senior British politicians' (TUC 2012b: 36–7). For unions, it became clear very quickly that blue and yellow had not produced green (Pearson 2013a). Instead, the Coalition government's climate policy resembled a rather putrid mélange.

Unions and neoliberal climate policy

Although much of the TUC framing of climate change was expressed in ecological modernisation language, other stances were articulated in more neoliberal terms. As discussed in Chapter 2, there are areas of symbiosis between the two main conceptions of climate politics and this is reflected in union discourses. The latter accommodation was clearest with respect to market instruments such as the European Union's Emissions Trading Scheme (EU ETS) and with the Heathrow airport expansion.

The TUC and EU ETS

Emissions trading has generally been the centrepiece of market-based, neoliberal responses to climate change. Emissions trading was proposed early in the development of climate politics and TUC officials expressed some reservations at the time. The TUC's submission to the 1990 *White Paper on the Environment* stated that 'some countries will find it extremely expensive and difficult to comply with permit standards'. It warned of the danger of a free-rider problem, which could 'hinder agreement on new targets, as countries with high compliance costs will be concerned at the impact on their domestic industries'. However, the TUC also saw the advantages of traded permits between governments. This could mean 'some of the industrialised countries, at the moment some of the biggest contributors to greenhouse gases, purchasing permits from less developed countries'. This would allow 'the industrialised world to ease the cost of transition towards less polluting production and could provide developing countries with valuable foreign exchange to protect their own environment and develop clean industrial technologies'. The TUC submission warned that the practicalities of such a scheme would have to be worked out, and 'two key considerations would be the need for effective monitoring and resistance to lobbying by industrial interests for the issuing of more permits' (TUC 1990b: 14).

TUC leaders contributed to government consultations on the various phases of EU ETS. In July 2004, TUSDAC debated the likely impact of the first phase of emissions trading on manufacturing, electricity generation, coal-fired generation, renewables and nuclear, with particular emphasis on the employment impacts (TUC 2004a: 64). The committee discussed a paper from the ISTC steel union, which argued that the way EU ETS was being introduced 'is causing the steel unions and other unions with involvement in manufacturing and electricity generation some problems'. It warned of the possible closure of the Corus plant on Teesside. The ISTC paper argued in market terms that 'the British steel industry and manufacturing generally will be put at a competitive disadvantage to the rest of the EU because of the unduly rigorous way British ministers are approaching their commitments' (ISTC 2004: 1–2). Subsequently, Congress noted that 'there is considerable uncertainty about the implications of the EU Emissions Trading Scheme for prices, investment and employment' (TUC 2004b: 25).

The renewed priority given to climate change during the third term of the Labour government convinced many union officials to back EU ETS and use it for both environmental and industrial objectives. TUSDAC's assessment of Phase II recognised 'the central importance of the ETS in reaching the UK's Kyoto-plus commitments' (TUSDAC 2005b) and that the scheme was 'seen to be an effective market mechanism for participating member states'. It argued that development and offsetting projects should be subject to rigorous standards and 'independent evidence of employee engagement' (ibid.: 1–3). Union leaders also suggested that proposals for new entrant power plants under Phase II would 'act as a disincentive to invest in clean coal technology allied to carbon capture, and have a negative impact on investment in the UK' (TUC 2006d: 2–3). TUC leaders and officials gave critical support for the central market mechanism for tackling climate change.

The high-level TUC view was pragmatic: EU ETS was better than no action by government and employers on climate change. They therefore sought to push through the market mechanism to win some bargaining gains. EU ETS was 'the most significant attempt by any nation, or set of nations, to impose an effective limit on greenhouse gas emissions' and 'by a long stretch the government's most effective market-based initiative to deliver cuts in carbon emissions through carbon pricing' (TUSDAC 2007). The TUC supported 'the auctioning of a higher percentage of allowances, particularly for the power generation sector, to avoid distortion of the carbon price' (ibid.: 1–2).

The TUC's assessment of Phase III stated that EU ETS was 'central to our shift to a low-carbon future' (TUC 2008d). It also claimed that the success of the scheme was 'vital in securing a stable long-term policy framework, cutting greenhouse gas emissions and securing quality jobs and investment'. However, based on experience to date, TUC officials were concerned about 'the effectiveness of this approach and about the scope for market manipulation' (ibid.). It urged the government to create 'a joint ETS policy-making forum with industry and trade unions to secure the scheme's huge potential environmental, economic and social benefits', an observatory to monitor and report on the industrial and employment impacts of the EU ETS in carbon-sensitive industries, and for auction revenues to establish a just transition fund supporting the rapid shift to low-carbon economic growth (ibid.:1–2, 9, 13).

These proposals were not taken up either by the EU or the British government. However, earlier sectional tensions resurfaced within the TUC discussions. As Phase III approached, the General Council argued that energy-intensive sectors were concerned 'over the exposure of these sectors to international competition from nations not covered by carbon reduction policies' (TUC 2008a). Unions in the sector called for impact assessments on such industries and for 'a long-term policy framework capable of securing a realistic price for carbon to stimulate investment in low-carbon technologies' (ibid.: 74). At Congress, the Community union demanded 'an EU-wide import adjustment system for energy-intensive industries', to avoid the problem of carbon leakage and the negative impact on the competitiveness. As Community General Secretary Michael Leahy put it, 'If the trading of emissions is not set up effectively, we run the risk of losing more than our manufacturing base. However, it is not only jobs that will be lost; it will almost certainly be the chance to reduce carbon emissions' (TUC 2008b: 20, 128).

TUC officials continued to support EU ETS during the Coalition government, proposing a series of measures to help sustain a meaningful market price for carbon while meeting other goals. The TUC supported the principle of a carbon tax to create a carbon price floor (TUC 2011a: 73). It argued that the billions of pounds of revenue from auctioning ETS permits and from the carbon price floor tax should be hypothecated to tackle issues such as fuel poverty (Pearson 2012d). The TUC and a number of unions along with 140 other major organisations supported the Energy Bill Revolution campaign, which aimed to persuade government to invest the new carbon taxes in home insulation, leading to a 'win–win' boost to the economy of lower emissions, more jobs and lower energy bills (TUC 2013a: 23). It pointed to the French, Estonian, and Australian governments, which were recycling some of their carbon revenues back to consumers through insulation measures and, in Australia, compensatory welfare benefit increases (Pearson 2013g).

The TUC and other market instruments

The Climate Change Levy (CCL) was described as 'an eclectic energy tax rather than a carbon tax concern'. Because of 'traditional political allegiances' between the Labour Party and trade unions, it was designed so that 'the carbon-intensive coal industry could not be damaged further' (Pearce 2006: 155). Union discourse on the levy was indeed openly sectional and largely within the bounds of neoliberal market policy. Participants at an early discussion feared that trade unions would be used as 'cannon fodder' between employers and the government (TUSDAC 1999: 3). John Edmonds told Congress, 'If you look closely, you will see that the trades unions were not involved at any stage … the current negotiations between industry and government exclude the trades unions entirely. This is both stupid and dangerous' (TUC 1999). He said that unless government learned some hard lessons from the experience of the levy, 'they run the risk of turning us from enthusiastic allies into rather resentful opponents. It is the duty of friends to give timely warnings, and that is what I give today' (ibid.: 61–2).

Many of the contributions to the discussion at Congress echoed business concerns (TUC 1999: 62–5). Edmonds said: 'It looks as though the levy will hit much of manufacturing industry like a body blow, and this is the wrong time to put further pressure on manufacturing industry.' David Boyle (GMB) argued that 'there is a real danger that the Climate Change Levy will destroy jobs – British jobs – without making any improvement in the global climate'. He added: 'We say to the government, what is the point in achieving clean air at the expense of industrial wastelands?' Allan Card (AEEU) quoted from a business report, which estimated that over 150,000 jobs could be lost over the following decade as a result of the levy. The General Council's assessment a year later expressed some satisfaction with the outcome of lobbying by employers and unions. It stated that concerns about the impact of the levy on competitiveness were 'alleviated by the announcement in the pre-Budget report of greater discounts for intensive users and other changes in the way in which the levy will be charged' (TUC 2000: 92). After the government implemented the modified levy in 2001, the General Council accepted that the changes had met its principal concerns on jobs (TUC 2001: 67).[8]

Another illustration of unions working through market mechanisms was the Carbon Reduction Commitment (CRC). The CRC was a market-based instrument arising from the Climate Change Act to create a CO_2 cap-and-trade scheme involving 20,000 of the largest public and private sector organisations in the UK – central government departments, local authorities, hospitals, prisons, schools, universities, shops, hotels and banks (TUC 2010b). The General Council supported the CRC because it provided 'a major opportunity to encourage and develop active, pro-environmental employee behaviours at work' (TUC 2009f: 2). TUC officials argued that it provided affiliated unions with further opportunities to deliver emissions reductions through social partnership.

TUC officials successfully lobbied the government for 'employee engagement' to be added to the criteria for compliance. This would mean energy management training offered to the majority of employees in the organisation, active employee working groups on energy management reporting to senior management to take forward emissions reduction initiatives and 'where an independent trade union is recognised for collective bargaining purposes, energy management issues are considered in these joint discussions and members actively take forward initiatives to reduce the organisation's carbon emissions' (Pearson 2009c). Climate Minister Ed Miliband wrote to the TUC, agreeing that:

> [E]mployee engagement will be vital in achieving the kind of behaviour change that CRC seeks to generate. I am therefore pleased to say that we will be including a tick box as you suggest, which will form part of the voluntary information that organisations submit alongside their annual emissions data.
>
> (Miliband 2009)

The TUC and the PCS civil service union published guidance on the scheme when it came into force in April 2010 (Pearson 2010a).

However, it proved to be a pyrrhic concession, after the Conservative–Liberal Democrat Coalition government first transformed the CRC into a green tax and an administrative burden, before coming close to abolishing it altogether (Pearson 2012a). In his omnishambles Budget in 2012, Chancellor

George Osborne backed by Business Secretary Vince Cable assured large service sector retailers and hoteliers that the Coalition government would scrap the CRC if he couldn't secure major savings (Pearson 2012b). Nevertheless, the Treasury appeared content to receive almost £1 billion in revenue from the CRC (Pearson 2014d). Fiscal and commercial considerations trumped climate concerns.

Union support for aviation expansion

Aviation expansion provides another example where some union leaders adopted sectional occupational concerns on climate matters. Aviation is for some the symbol of modernity, an exotic expression of freedom. In the quarter of a century after 1981, international air passenger aviation increased threefold and UK aviation numbers increased fourfold. Airlines travelling to or from the UK accounted for almost 10 per cent of global passenger flights. Go-for-growth aviation expansionism has been an integral part of the neo-liberal political economy, with the privatisation of British Airways and the British Airports Authority (BAA), low-cost scheduled airlines, together with the construction of new runways and terminals (Walker and Cook 2009). This expansionism continued under Labour, with official approval for a fifth terminal and third runway at Heathrow.

However, aviation is also recognised as an environmental hazard and increasingly as a driver of climate change, particularly because of the impact of radiative forcing. Aviation will take up an increasing part of the carbon budget if airport expansion proceeds (Anderson *et al.* 2006). The government's own figures for Heathrow predict an increase in flights between 2020 and 2080 and an additional three million tonnes of CO_2 every year would be generated. It estimates the 'social cost' of these emissions is around £4.8 billion (DfT 2007: 138). The contradiction was sometimes evaded by the oxymoronic expression 'sustainable aviation' (Howarth and Griggs 2006).

The TUC and key unions organising at Heathrow (TGWU and Amicus – later Unite, GMB and BALPA) are highly visible advocates of expansion. The TUC leadership supported proposals for a third runway from the beginning, in line with its long-standing position supporting expansion of the aviation industry in general, subject to limited environmental qualifications. The formal decision on the third runway at Heathrow was taken by the TUC's Executive Committee in November 2002 and expressed in the TUC's response to the Department for Transport consultation, which called for three new runways in London including at Heathrow and Stansted (TUC 2003b).

Congress 2003 stated that 'a viable air transport industry is vital for growth and jobs', directly creating 180,000 jobs and 'sustaining hundreds of thousands more in tourism and related industries' (TUC 2003a: 12). The TUC took a high-profile role in other pro-expansion campaigns, such as Future Heathrow, Freedom to Fly and Flying Matters. Future Heathrow included the TUC, Amicus and TGWU, GMB and BALPA, along with the major airlines, the CBI and other business organisations. At the height of lobbying for a third runway, Brendan Barber spoke alongside BA, Virgin and BAA in support of expansion, claiming that 'aviation supports around 500,000 jobs in the UK' (Future Heathrow 2007).

The TUC and the aviation unions welcomed the Labour government's go-ahead for the third runway at Heathrow in January 2009. GMB official Charlie King bluntly expressed support for expansion at Congress (TUC 2009b: 127). He said those who campaigned against a third runway at Heathrow

> do not understand how long-haul aviation works, do not understand about the problems of the economy and keeping an aviation-base in the UK for long haul, and are not concerned about the number of job losses that would occur if we did not do it.

After the Conservative–Liberal Democrat Coalition government halted plans for the third runway in 2010, the TUC wrote to ministers criticising the decision, warning that 'Heathrow currently employs 72,000 people and supports many more jobs' (TUC 2010a: 71).

Union support for Heathrow expansion was very much couched towards the labour market opportunities it would bring, and the climate implications were also filtered through market mechanisms. At the beginning of government's consultation process, the TUC proposed 'the introduction of a tradable emissions quota system across all industries', to ensure that 'greenhouse gas emissions targets are met' (TUC 2003b: 1). In the early Congress debate on aviation, Jim McAuslan (BALPA) said on the environmental impact, the industry was 'not beyond reproach', but 'greenhouse gases should be down to international and domestic regulation' (TUC 2003a: 131–3).

In public, unions recognised that climate change was a 'third factor', in addition to noise and air quality, that had entered the Heathrow debate. When the go-ahead was announced in January 2009, Barber said: 'We therefore expect the government to ... ensure that CO_2 emissions from aviation growth are consistent with the UK's new carbon budgets' (TUC 2009h: 1). The TUC concluded that the inclusion of aviation in the EU ETS would address climate concerns, alongside the industry's efforts to increase the fuel efficiency of its aircraft and reduce energy consumption in its buildings (TUC 2006c: 43–4). The General Council supported the proposal to include aviation in the EU ETS. These arguments were developed in greater detail in specific publications produced by individual unions (BALPA 2007a, 2007b; GMB 2007; Unite 2009). Support for Heathrow was perhaps the most graphic example of 'accommodationist solidarity' – in this case, union support for neoliberal climate politics. However, as we shall see in the final section of this chapter, this view was contested by some other unions.

Unions, climate and working-class politics

The argument so far is that high-level TUC climate policy remains largely within the dominant framings, particularly between ecological modernisation and neoliberalism, or between social integration and the market. However, even with the examples discussed so far, there have been elements of class politics present, though sometimes expressed in sectional terms. TUC policy had a strong occupational and employment strand from the beginning. This was reflected even in the least climate-conscious positions taken on energy-intensive industries and on aviation. Second, even where it supported government climate policy, there were efforts to extend it to address workers' concerns, to widen worker representation and to open new fields of collective bargaining. This was evident with the Climate Change Levy, EU ETS and the CRC.

Third, unions took a critical stance on fossil fuel extraction and use. With CCS, unions pursued a long-term, strategic goal consistent with both climate concerns and existing members' interests, but also with workers as a wider social class in Britain and across the globe. Significantly, Congress voted to oppose the fracking method of gas extraction, based on the precautionary principle that many of the risks, such as fugitive methane emissions, had not been adequately quantified or controlled (TUC 2012b). This policy was reiterated in 2014, when Congress agreed to 'continue to consult TUC affiliates about a just transition to a low-carbon economy, including a moratorium on extreme energy such as shale gas extraction (fracking)'. Tam McFarlane (FBU), summing up the 2014 debate, pointed to the 160 anti-fracking organisations across the UK, arguing that unions should 'be on the side of people who are on the same political side as us' (TUC 2014). Both the Unite and PCS conferences in 2014 passed resolutions calling for a moratorium on fracking. However, there was considerable debate around the stance, with both motions yielding an 'explanation' from the TUC General Council that the position did not preclude support for the gas industry as a whole.

Fourth, the TUC's emphasis on adaptation showed that it understood the need to make climate politics as much about immediate issues affecting workers now, rather than simply a matter of targets and restructuring for the distant future. This 'bottom-up' approach implicitly challenged the dominant, top-down climate regime. Finally, trade union questioning of benefits and losses drew into sharper focus the distributional consequences of climate change and climate policy. This section looks at where unions began developing a more class-focused politics of climate.

Distribution and property relations

The class dimension partly turns on how far unions have challenged the dominant social relations of production, or through strategic interventions helped tip the balance of forces between labour and capital in workers' favour. Challenging the distributional effects of climate policy is a tentative first step towards making such an approach and there is some evidence of it in union texts. When the TUC first began to grapple with climate politics, it engaged with leading scholars on the issues. For example, on 17 June 1990, it held a TUC forum on Energy Policy 2000, with speakers including Dieter Helm. In January 1991, its energy committee was addressed by Scott Barrett, who advocated carbon taxes to combat global warming. The Energy Committee's report stated: 'Although accepting that revenues from a carbon tax could be used to offset other distortions in the market, we were not persuaded of the merits of such a tax' (TUC 1991a: 184–5). Unions also took up distributional issues arising out of climate policy under Labour. On taxation, a Touchstone pamphlet on just transition argued that indirect environmental taxation was regressive and required 'a progressive direct tax system running alongside it to ensure that the poorest do not contribute disproportionately to public funds' (TUC 2008c: 13).

A more substantial intervention was made about the windfall profits gained from the EU ETS. In 2008, the TUC's Budget submission called on the Chancellor to introduce a green windfall profits tax on energy companies and to use the proceeds to tackle fuel poverty, improve home insulation and on other environmental and job-creating initiatives (TUC 2008e: 1). The call for a profits tax was based on the calculation by Ofgem, the energy regulator, that the electricity industry would benefit from a windfall profit of around £9 billion from the free allocation of tradable emission permits over the four years of Phase II of the EU ETS. This is on top of a previous DTI estimate of £800 million a year in extra profits to 2007 from Phase I of the scheme. The demand was repeated at the TUC Congress (Pearson 2008b). Barber said the excess profits did not 'flow from investment, innovation or hard work but simply result from the way that carbon trading has been implemented across Europe'. While carbon trading 'has a crucial part to play in tackling climate change', these windfall profits will give it a bad name 'unless they are used to fund socially useful and green spending' (TUC 2008e: 1).

Similarly, unions took up the question of fuel poverty and the related matter of energy prices. Congress resolved 'to help those facing most difficulty from the downturn – particularly the growing numbers facing fuel poverty, including pensioners, and those suffering from the difficulties in the housing market and construction sectors' (TUC 2008b: 34). TUC officials highlighted the increasing numbers of people falling into fuel poverty, whether this was measured crudely as those households that spent more than 10 per cent of their income on fuel or through a 'low income/high cost' index. Under the old measure, fuel poverty rocketed by 2013 to over 5.1m households in England from a low point of 3.5m in 2010. DECC's redefinition of fuel poverty has reduced the number to 2.8m households – still a shocking figure (Pearson 2013g). The TUC estimated that government support to tackle fuel poverty was cut in half by the Coalition government (Pearson 2012c). With fuel poverty, some of the class dimensions of climate politics came into sharp relief.

Another challenge to the dominant climate framings, with stronger class connotations, were interventions aiming at the public ownership of industries and natural resources. There were consistent calls for integrated publicly-owned transport, notably of the railways and occasionally buses and aviation. Successive Congress resolutions tied together industrial arguments for public ownership and control with driving down carbon emissions (TUC 2007b: 14; 2008b: 22). Frances O'Grady reaffirmed 'TUC support for a publicly-owned and accountable railway' and welcomed 'the call to lobby for rail electrification' (TUC 2008b: 146–7). The TUC and unions made representations regarding the Coalition government's intent to privatise public forests and welcomed the conclusion that the Public Forest Estate was a national asset that should remain in public ownership (TUC 2012a: 68).

Demands for public ownership were less prominent with regard to the energy sector, but they have been articulated – usually in response to the imminent collapse of firms or sectors. At the 2002 Congress, a motion was passed that called for the privatised and later insolvent nuclear firm British Energy to be brought back into public ownership (TUC 2002: 32). More recently officials argued that the National Grid should come under public ownership (Pearson 2013j), while the FBU issued a pamphlet arguing that the big six energy firms should be brought under public ownership, to tackle the cost of living and climate crises simultaneously (FBU 2014). Congress opposed the privatisation of the coal industry and voted repeatedly for its renationalisation – most recently over the closure of Daw Mill (Pearson 2013c; TUC 1993: 503; 2005: 7). As we shall explore in more depth in Chapter 6, Congress also backed calls for 'publicly-owned wind turbine manufacturing capacity, including at the Vestas site' (TUC 2009b: 29). Although nationalisation was apparently considered by climate thinkers such as Dieter Helm as a 'politically contaminated' concept, it was amazingly popular with the public, with more than two-thirds polled supporting the energy firms to be run in the public sector and almost three-in-five in favour of rail nationalisation (Pearson 2013j).

Union opposition to Heathrow expansion

Although the majority of UK trade unions and the TUC favoured Heathrow expansion, there was also consistent opposition to the proposal, including from some significant Labour-affiliated unions, from transport unions, and some organising in the aviation sector. Unison opposed the expansion of Heathrow in favour of regional airports (where it had members). Unison's response to the government's consultation stated: 'Uncontrolled and unplanned airport growth and expansion can damage the environment … Aviation emissions, for example, are a small but growing proportion of total global emissions and contribute to climate change.' It added: 'The full environmental costs of aviation must be taken into account in any cost-benefit analysis of air travel and airport expansion' (Unison 2003: 5–6). Unison proposed an environmental tax on aviation fuel, related to engine efficiency in aircraft. Unison delegate Jean Geldart spoke against airport expansion at the 2003 Congress (TUC 2003a: 132).

Trade unions and their leaderships opposed to airport expansion were able to challenge arguments that equated more flights with more employment. The government's impact assessment showed slightly fewer people employed directly at Heathrow by 2030 with a third runway than there were at the time (DfT 2007). Without a further runway, it estimated on-site employment would fall by around 10,000. Even with a third runway, BAA and the airlines planned job cuts (Sewill 2009). Oppositional unions worked with activist campaigns to make the case for a high-speed rail link as an alternative to expansion. The RMT transport and energy union published the report, *Who Says There Is No Alternative?* compiled by campaigner John Stewart. The report estimated that over a third of flights from Heathrow were short-haul, that more than 20 per cent serve destinations already served by a viable rail alternative, and that 20 per cent more were to places where rail is the potential alternative. It claimed that 'a fast rail service which substituted for further expansion at Heathrow would result in significant environmental benefits … climate change emissions would not rise so fast. High-speed rail emits between eight and 11 times less CO_2 than air travel' (RMT 2008a: 9). At its launch, General Secretary Bob Crow said the report 'shows that high-speed rail can provide a win–win solution for the economy and the environment' (RMT 2008b). The report was backed by John McDonnell MP, chair of RMT's parliamentary group and a high-profile opponent of the third runway, whose constituency was affected by the proposed expansion.

The RMT, along with rail unions ASLEF and TSSA, Unison, Connect telecom union and the PCS (with members in air traffic control, BAA and the Civil Aviation Authority), sponsored an advertisement in *The Times* newspaper on 14 October 2008 opposing the Heathrow expansion. The advertisement stated: 'If the government pushes ahead with expanding our airports, including Heathrow, the UK will never be able to meet the new target of cutting emissions by at least 80 per cent by 2050 and play its part in fighting climate change.' When the Labour government announced the Heathrow expansion would go ahead, these unions argued that a third runway would make the airport the biggest source of carbon emissions in the country. Crow said that 'a modern high-speed, low-carbon and sustainable rail network would simply do away with the need for a third runway', while PCS Assistant General Secretary Chris Baugh said it would mean 'the government won't be able to meet the targets in the historic Climate Change Act'. He argued that the government should instead 'produce a new transport strategy for the UK focussed upon a publicly-owned high-speed rail network that will create jobs and contribute to the transition to a low-carbon economy and the fight against climate change' (PCS 2009). PCS delegate Sue Bond also challenged the General Council at the 2009 Congress, arguing that in the light of climate change and the possibility of alternative transport and employment opportunities, the TUC should reconsider its support for the expansion of Heathrow (TUC 2009b: 127). PCS reps in aviation subsequently contributed to a report, which explored the positive arguments for the public ownership of aviation, the use of aviation taxation (such as VAT exemption and Air Passenger Duty) and proposals for a 'Heath-wick' dual-hub linked to Gatwick by high-speed rail to protect existing jobs (Molloy and Sealey 2013).

These arguments were on stronger climate ground than the advocates of expansion and were also mindful of class dimensions. Some opponents may have had sectional grounds for opposing Heathrow expansion – to promote their own aviation members elsewhere or to support alternative modes like rail – but they cast this opposition in more universal class and climate terms. They did not ignore the legitimate concerns over aviation employment, but incorporated the impact of dangerous climate change on workers locally, nationally and internationally into their perspective.

Trade union mobilisation on climate change

Another, more independent and class-focused element of union climate politics during this period was the increasing importance of mobilising union members for protests going beyond existing government and international climate policy (or at least to push it further and faster). Pearson (2009e) reported that TUC representatives and other international trade unionists joined the mobilisations outside the Copenhagen talks in 2009. He described how 100,000 people marched 6 kilometres to the UN conference, 'arriving in darkness beneath the metro flyover, with a huge inflatable Greenpeace snowman hauled sideways to get under the bridge'. A massive green banner with the words 'Unions have solutions: Just transition' was spread across the width of the march and held by the Belgian unions in green builders' hats with stickers that said 'Union solidarity: Just transition'. In Copenhagen, unions organised a three-day series of workshops at the World of Work Pavilion, hosted by the LO Denmark union confederation. The TUC organised workshops on CCS and climate solidarity, while TUC delegates took part in events organised by international union bodies, PSI, IMF and ETUC. The trade union presence in Copenhagen and at other COPs, where links were forged between high-level representatives of unions both the Global North and the Global South, had positive elements of 'transformatory solidarity' highlighted by labour geographers.

Trade union involvement in international climate mobilisations continued, despite the vicissitudes of the COP gatherings. At the Durban climate conference in December 2011, some 20,000 people marched for climate justice and green jobs, led by the South African labour movement, while the following day 500 delegates attended a one million climate jobs conference (Pearson 2011d). At Rio+20, trade unionists joined some 50,000 people marching to demand government action on the environment and climate change (ITUC

2012). At the Doha climate talks the next year, 40 union delegates joined a march there under the (forbidden) ITUC banner: 'No World Cup in Qatar without labour rights' – the first opposition demonstration to take place in the state (Pearson 2012i). And at the Warsaw climate conference in 2013, unions joined NGOs in an organised walk-out, arguing that pledges to cut carbon emissions were slipping away, unions did not have 'a place at the table' and staying in would have given 'a false legitimacy to failing states' (Pearson 2013i). Perhaps most impressively, a range of unions joined the 300,000-strong climate demonstration in New York on 21 September 2014, with mobilisation across the globe in solidarity, including some 40,000 marching in London the same day for 'system change, not climate change' (Pearson 2014i).

In the UK, unions joined climate mobilisations, bringing their members, banners and slogans. The TUC decided for the first time to support the national climate march on 3 November 2006, organised by NGOs such as the Campaign against Climate Change. It continued to publicly support demonstrations during COP meetings, culminating in The Wave demonstrations in London and Glasgow on 5 December 2009, which attracted 50,000 people.[9] Between 2007 and 2009, three 'green camps' were run at Tolpuddle, which drew dozens of trade union environment reps for debate and training (SWTUC 2011: 14). The most ambitious initiative was the Jobs, Climate, Justice demonstration on 28 March 2009, during a G20 meeting in London. Union leaders made the initial moves, donated to the costs of the event and took responsibility for logistics. An estimated 35,000 people protested on the day (TUC 2009g: 1).

The TUC and its affiliates became more involved in wider climate coalitions in the UK. Congress passed a motion in support of Vestas workers, who had occupied their factory after the firm told them it would close (TUC 2009b: 28). The TUC also began to develop links with climate campaigns, participating in the Campaign against Climate Change trade union conferences and engaging with the Climate Alliance activist network. Union officials held meetings on climate change with NGO representatives from Greenpeace and the Tearfund. The TUC explored the idea of a 'third sector alliance', comprising trade unions, national voluntary organisations, local community groups and others – the closest it came to formulating a social movement conception of climate action (Scott 2009). It also hosted meetings with prominent climate activists, such as Naomi Klein and Bill McKibben. These interventions and mobilisations, though generally quite restrained, shifted some unions towards activity separate from government and employers, while coming closer to more militant advocates of class politics within unions themselves and to radical climate activists.

Conclusion

This overview confirms that at the highest levels, UK union climate framing was closest to ecological modernisation during this period. This was particularly clear in the TUC support for the Labour government's Climate Change Act, for carbon capture, for its 'balanced' energy and aviation policy, and for partnership. TUC leaders wanted a more active industrial strategy focused on the development of green technologies and believed the Labour government had been won over to that perspective in the last year of its administration. However, the election in 2010 and the subsequent Conservative–Liberal Democrat Coalition government put paid to trade union efforts to tie climate and economic crises together. Less prominent, but still significant TUC framings were located closer to employers and deployed neoliberal market arguments, in particular over EU ETS and Heathrow expansion. Issues such as employment were sometimes posed in narrow, sectional terms or more blatantly in neoliberal terms close to business.

The limited nature of some union and TUC climate framing in class terms is clear from the examples cited. A class-based climate approach would have involved unions retaining a high degree of political, ideological and organisational independence from both employers and the state. There is some evidence of this in TUC fiscal policy, public ownership of rail transport and with the mobilisation of union members for climate goals (including opposition to airport expansion). However, there are at least three further areas where such an approach was more pronounced. First, union conceptions of just transition and climate jobs have been more consistently class-focused; second, forms of climate representation at work have exhibited elements of working-class organisation; and, third, union involvement in the Vestas occupation indicated distinctive forms of working-class action. Without ignoring neoliberal and ecological modernisation framings, the following chapters explore these more explicit cases of working-class representation in union climate politics.

Notes

1 TUC policy is set at its annual Congress, which debates individual motions from affiliated unions and also votes on the General Council's annual report. TUC policy papers and submissions to government consultations are voted on by its Executive Committee and General Council, which are made up of senior union and TUC officials.
2 Walker and Cook (2009: 388) argued that the notion of balance 'is fundamental to all forms of ecological modernisation'.
3 Paul Hackett (1991: 17), the TUC's first environmental policy officer, argued that it had taken so long for trade unions to tackle issues such as climate change because 'the 1980s were, after all, an extremely difficult period for unions. Rising unemployment, massive industrial restructuring, falling membership, the assault on union organisation and the ascendency of free market policies preoccupied unions and left little scope for developing new priorities.'
4 The final *Climate Change: UK Programme 2000* document (DETR 2000: 45) stated:

> There is great potential for trade unions and their representatives to work in partnership with the government and businesses to address environmental issues and to promote initiatives in the workplace. Trade unions can help to

ensure employee support for new programmes that are aimed at reducing emissions.

A similar statement was included in the 2006 programme (Defra 2006: 60).
5 At the TUC's Going Green at Work conference, 15 March 2010, Climate Minister Ed Miliband posed union engagement with climate change in terms of equity with three dimensions: intergenerational justice; between developed and developing nations; but also more significantly 'at home', for example, with higher energy bills. He argued that this view of equity required a 'just transition' approach to resolving climate change.
6 The Forum for a Just Transition, formally announced by government at the TUC's Beyond the Crisis conference on 16 November 2009 by Business Minister Pat McFadden, met on two occasions (9 December 2009 and 10 March 2010). It was not convened by the Conservative–Liberal Democrat Coalition government (McFadden 2009).
7 See Scrase and Watson (2009), Herzog (2009) and DECC (2010) for UK government CCS policy and IPCC (2005) for CCS in international climate politics.
8 Subsequent research by Martin, de Preux and Wagner (2009: 3) did not find 'any statistically significant impacts of the tax on employment' and suggested that 'worries about adverse effects of the CCL on economic performance are unsubstantiated'. The CCL also provided funding for the Carbon Trust.
9 Although unions such as Unison and PCS were enthusiastic supporters of The Wave demonstration, and managed to get the organisers to add the call for a 'just transition' to the list of demands, not all TUC affiliates were so enthused, with Unite, Prospect and the NUM refusing to back the march because of its demand to 'Quit Dirty Coal'.

References

Anderson, K., Bows, A. and Upham, P. (2006) *Growth Scenarios for EU & UK aviation: Contradictions with Climate Policy*. Tyndall Centre for Climate Change Research Working Paper 84. Manchester: Tyndall Centre.
BALPA (2007a) *Aviation and the Environment: The Pilot's Perspective*. London: BALPA.
——(2007b) 'Global Warming: A Balanced Debate', *The Log*, June–July.
Carter, N. (1997) 'Prospects: The Parties and the Environment in the UK'. In M. Jacobs (ed.) *Greening the Millennium? The New Politics of the Environment*. Oxford: Blackwell.
——(2009) 'Vote Blue, Go Green? Cameron's Conservatives and the Environment', *Political Quarterly*, 80(2): 223–42.
CCSA/TUC (2014) *Economic Benefits of CCS in the UK*. London: TUC.
CCTG (2006) *A Framework for Clean Coal in Britain*, 7 June. London: TUC.
——(2012) *Roadmap for Coal*. London: TUC.
DECC (2010) *Clean Coal: An Industrial Strategy for the Development of Carbon Capture and Storage across the UK*, March. London: DECC.
Defra (2006) *Climate Change: The UK Programme*. London: The Stationery Office.
DETR (2000) *Climate Change: The UK Programme*. London: The Stationery Office.
DfT (2007) *Adding Capacity at Heathrow Airport: Public Consultation*. London: Department for Transport.
EAC (Environmental Audit Committee) (2014) *An Environmental Scorecard*, 10 September. London: The Stationery Office.
FBU (2008) *Lessons of the 2007 Floods: The FBU's Contribution to the Pitt Review*. Kingston-upon-Thames: FBU.

——(2010) *Climate Change: Key Issues for the Fire and Rescue Service*. Kingston-upon-Thames: FBU.

——(2014) *It's Time to Take Over the Big Energy Firms*. Kingston-upon-Thames: FBU.

Future Heathrow (2007) 'Future Heathrow Responds to Department of Transport Consultation', 22 November.

GMB (2007) *Response to DfT Consultation: Adding Capacity at Heathrow Airport*, November. London: GMB.

Hackett, P. (1991) 'The UK Unions and the Environment'. In P. Schulte and J. Willman (eds) *The Environment. Challenges and Opportunities for Trades Unions*. London: Friedrich Ebert Foundation.

——(1992) 'Developing a Trade Union Charter for the Environment'. In D. Owen (ed.) *Green Reporting: Accountancy and the Challenge of the Nineties*. London: Chapman & Hall.

Heery, E. (1998) 'Relaunch of the TUC', *British Journal of Industrial Relations*, 36(3): 339–60.

Herzog, H. (2009) 'Carbon Dioxide Capture and Storage'. In D. Helm and C. Hepburn (eds) *The Economics and Politics of Climate Change*. Oxford: Oxford University Press.

Hope, C. (2014) 'Scrap the Climate Change Act to Keep the Lights On, Says Owen Paterson', *The Telegraph*, 11 October.

Howarth, D. and Griggs, S. (2006) 'Metaphor, Catachresis and Equivalence: The Rhetoric of Freedom to Fly in the Struggle over Aviation Policy in the UK', *Policy and Society*, 25(2): 23–46.

Hyman, R. (2001) *Understanding European Trade Unionism: Between Market, Class and Society*. London: Sage.

IPCC (2005) *IPCC Special Report on Carbon Dioxide Capture and Storage*. Cambridge: Cambridge University Press.

ISTC (2004) 'European Union Emissions Trading Scheme', paper for TUSDAC, 1 July.

ITUC (2012) '50,000 People on the March for Concrete Actions in Rio+20', press release, 22 June.

Johns, R. (1998) 'Bridging the Gap between Class and Space: U.S. Worker Solidarity with Guatemala', *Economic Geography*, 74(3): 252–71.

Labour Party (1994) *In Trust for Tomorrow: Report of the Labour Party Policy Commission on the Environment*. London: The Labour Party.

Martin, R., de Preux, L. and Wagner, U. (2009) *The Impacts of the Climate Change Levy on Business: Evidence from Microdata*, Centre for Climate Change Economics and Policy, Working Paper No. 7. Leeds: CCCEP.

McFadden, P. (2009) 'Reshaping the UK Economy. Speech at the TUC "Beyond the Crisis" Conference', London, 16 November.

McIlroy, J. (2000) 'The New Politics of Pressure: The Trades Union Congress and New Labour in Government', *Industrial Relations Journal*, 31(1): 2–16.

Miliband, E. (2009) 'Letter to Frances O'Grady', 21 July.

Molloy, C. and Sealey, R. (2013) *PCS Aviation Review: Protecting Jobs – Protecting the Planet*. London: PCS.

NUM (2004) *For a Balanced, Diverse, Secure Energy Policy Based on Indigenous Fuel. Submission to the DTI Consultation on 'A Carbon Abatement Technologies Strategy for Fossil Fuel Power Generation'*. Barnsley: NUM.

——(2007) 'Leadership Comment', *The Miner*, June.

Page, T. (2010) 'Budget Boost for Green Industry', *Touchstone Blog*, 24 March.

Parker, J. (2008) 'The Trades Union Congress and Civil Alliance Building: Towards Social Movement Unionism?' *Employee Relations*, 30(5): 562–83.

PCS (2009) 'Anger over Heathrow Third Runway', press release, 14 January.

Pearce, D. (2006) 'The Political Economy of an Energy Tax: The United Kingdom's Climate Change Levy', *Energy Economics*, 28(2): 149–58.

Pearson, P. (2008a) 'Clean Coal, Kingsnorth and Hansen's Warning', *Touchstone Blog*, 5 September.

——(2008b) 'Making Good Use of Windfall Profits', *Touchstone Blog*, 5 September 2008

——(2009a) 'CCS – Taking Climate Change Seriously', *Touchstone Blog*, 27 February.

——(2009b) 'Budget Flights to Copenhagen', *Touchstone Blog*, 7 April.

——(2009c) 'New Support For Green Reps in Energy Savings "League Table"', *Touchstone Blog*, 7 October.

——(2009d) 'Kingsnorth Delayed – What's to Cheer About?' *Touchstone Blog*, 8 October.

——(2009e) 'Copenhagen Diary #7: Blah Blah Blah, Act Now!' *Touchstone Blog*, 13 December.

——(2010a) 'Carbon Diary: Greening Whitehall (and the Rest of the Service Sector)', *Touchstone Blog*, 31 March.

——(2010b) 'Budget Stalls, Green Ambitions Losing Pace', *Touchstone Blog*, 22 June.

——(2010c) 'Carbon Diary #6: Who What Where When and Why?' *Touchstone Blog*, 8 December.

——(2011a) 'Osborne's Green Bank Moment', *Touchstone Blog*, 11 March.

——(2011b) 'No-Growth Chancellor Blames Green Agenda', *Touchstone Blog*, 4 October.

——(2011c) 'Government Kills Off First Carbon Capture Project', *Touchstone Blog*, 19 October 2011

——(2011d) 'Durban Diary 6: What Will UK Ministers Bring to the Table?' *Touchstone Blog*, 5 December.

——(2012a) 'Will Budget 2012 Scrap More Green Policies'? *Touchstone Blog*, 13 March.

——(2012b) 'Forget the Green Economy, This Was a Budget for Oil and Gas', *Touchstone Blog*, 21 March.

——(2012c) 'Fuel Truth: 47 Per Cent Cut in Fuel Poverty Budget', *Touchstone Blog*, 13 April.

——(2012d) 'Cuts to Homes Energy Efficiency Drive Up Fuel Poverty', *Touchstone Blog*, 17 May.

——(2012e) 'Can a Hobbled Green Bank Reboot the Economy?' *Touchstone Blog*, 12 June.

——(2012f) '"Climate Change Is Not a Hoax" – Obama', *Touchstone Blog*, 7 September.

——(2012g) 'DECC Shortlist Surprises Carbon Capture Industry', *Touchstone Blog*, 31 October.

——(2012h) 'Energy Bill Needs 2030 Carbon Target', *Touchstone Blog*, 29 November.

——(2012i) 'Qatar Blog #2: No Just Transition Without Labour Rights', *Touchstone Blog*, 3 December.

——(2013a) 'Mid-Term Blues for Greens?' *Touchstone Blog*, 7 January.

——(2013b) 'Hidden Cuts Jeopardise CCS Industry', *Touchstone Blog*, 14 January.

——(2013c) 'Coal – Make an Opportunity Out of a Crisis', *Touchstone Blog*, 13 May.

——(2013d) 'Why UKIP Can't Get Its Facts Straight on Climate Change', *Touchstone Blog*, 17 May.

——(2013e) 'Mps Challenge "Green Quad" Renewables Deal', *Touchstone Blog*, 30 May.

——(2013f) 'Secure, Affordable, Low Carbon Energy?' *Touchstone Blog*, 28 June.

——(2013g) 'No Shale Gas Price Revolution', *Touchstone Blog*, 22 August.

——(2013h) 'Time to Look at All £9bn of Energy Policy Support', *Touchstone Blog*, 25 October.

——(2013i) 'Warsaw Final: Walking Out Is Not Our Way, But', *Touchstone Blog*, 25 November.

——(2013j) 'Public Demand Answers to Energy Omnishambles', *Touchstone Blog*, 27 November.

——(2014a) 'Defra (Department Evading Flood Risk Assessments)', *Touchstone Blog*, 7 January.

——(2014b) 'Mayday Call from Green Deal Flagship', *Touchstone Blog*, 21 January,

——(2014c) 'Budget for Flood Security', *Touchstone Blog*, 18 March.

——(2014d) 'Budget 2014: Is £7bn 6-Year Makers' Budget Enough?' *Touchstone Blog*, 19 March.

——(2014e) 'Good Week for the Green Economy', *Touchstone Blog*, 27 June.

——(2014f) 'Carbon Capture: White Rose Takes Yellow Jersey', *Touchstone Blog*, 8 July.

——(2014g) 'UK Or Russian Coal – That's the Question', *Touchstone Blog*, 4 August.

——(2014h) 'NUM Invests in Future for Hatfield Colliery With £4m Loan', *Touchstone Blog*, 16 September.

——(2014i) 'A Good Week for the Green Movement – And It's Only Wednesday', *Touchstone Blog*, 24 September.

Prospect (2011) *Is This the Lightest Green Government Ever?* London: Prospect.

Rees, J. (2014) 'The Energy Saving Bailout: Government Rescue to Save Troubled Green Deal Finance Firm from Disaster', *Mail on Sunday*, 9 November.

RMT (2008a) *Who Says There is No Alternative? An Assessment of the Potential of Rail to Cut Air Travel (with Particular Reference to Heathrow)*. Compiled for RMT by John Stewart, Chair of the Campaign for Better Transport. London: RMT.

——(2008b) 'High-Speed Rail "The Viable Alternative to Heathrow Expansion" Says RMT', press release, 24 June.

Scargill, A. (2008) 'Coal Isn't the Climate Enemy, Mr Monbiot. It's the Solution', *The Guardian*, 8 August.

Schlembach, R. (2011) 'How Do Radical Climate Movements Negotiate their Environmental and their Social Agendas? A Study of Debates within the Camp for Climate Action (UK)', *Critical Social Policy*, 31(2): 194–215.

Scott, F. (ed.) (2009) *Working on Change: the Trade Union Movement and Climate Change*. London: Green Alliance.

Scrase, I. and Watson, J. (2009) 'CCS in the UK: Squaring Coal Use with Climate Change?' In J. Meadowcroft and O. Langhelle (eds) *Caching the Carbon: The Politics and Policy of Carbon Capture and Storage*. Cheltenham: Edward Elgar.

Sewill, B. (2009) *Airport Jobs: False Hopes, Cruel Hoax*. London: Aviation Environment Federation.

SWTUC (2011) *Green Workplaces Project Report and Evaluation, 2008–2011*. Bristol: South West TUC.

Taylor, R. (2000) *The TUC: From the General Strike to New Unionism*. Basingstoke: Palgrave.

TGWU (2003) 'Heathrow Runway Must Be Sooner Not Later, Says T&G's Tony Woodley', 16 December.

TUC (1972) *Workers and the Environment: Report of a TUC Conference held at Congress House on July 6 1972*. London: TUC.

——(1985) 'Acid Deposition and Power Station Emission Control (Draft), 19 July 1985'. In TUC (1988c) *TUC Environment Policy File*. London: TUC.

——(1986) *Acid Deposition and Power Station Emission Control: A Statement from the TUC Energy and Social Insurance and Industrial Welfare Committees. June 1986*. London: TUC.

——(1987) *Nuclear Energy: General Council Report. August 1987*. London: TUC.

——(1988a) *Congress Report 1988*. London: TUC.

——(1988b) *Nuclear Power and Energy Policy. April 1988*. London: TUC.

——(1989a) *Congress Report 1989*. London: TUC.

——(1989b) *Towards a Charter for the Environment: General Council Statement to the 1989 Trade Union Congress*. London: TUC.

——(1990a) *Congress Report 1990*. London: TUC.

——(1990b) *Environmental Issues and Policy Implications: Towards the White Paper – Submission by the TUC, April*. London: TUC.

——(1991a) *Congress 1991: General Council Report*. London: TUC.

——(1991b) *Industry, Jobs and the Environmental Challenge: A Memorandum by the TUC to the National Economic Development Council, May 1991*. London: TUC.

——(1993) *Congress Report 1993*. London: TUC.

——(1998) *Congress 1998: General Council Report*. London: TUC.

——(1999) *Congress Report 1999*. London: TUC.

——(2000) *Congress 2000: General Council Report*. London: TUC.

——(2001) *Congress 2001: General Council Report*. London: TUC.

——(2002) *Congress Report 2002*. London: TUC.

——(2003a) *Congress Report 2003*. London: TUC.

——(2003b) 'Three New Runways in London and the South East before 2030', *press release*, 23 June 2003

——(2004a) *Congress 2004: General Council Report*. London: TUC.

——(2004b) *Congress Report 2004*. London: TUC.

——(2005) *Congress Report 2005*. London: TUC.

——(2006a) *Congress 2006: General Council Report*. London: TUC.

——(2006b) *Congress Report 2006*. London: TUC.

——(2006c) *A Sustainable Energy Policy: TUC Response to the Government Energy Review, 24 April 2006*. London: TUC.

——(2006d) *TUC Response to EU ETS Phase II Consultation: Disincentives against Clean Coal, October 2006*. London: TUC.

——(2006e) 'TUC on Stern Report on Climate Change', press release, 30 October 2006

——(2007a) *Congress 2007: General Council Report*. London: TUC.

——(2007b) *Congress Report 2007*. London: TUC.

——(2007c) 'TUC Comment on Climate Change Bill', press release, 13 March 2007

——(2007d) *TUC Submission to the Joint Committee on the Draft Climate Change Bill, 1 June 2007*. London: TUC.

——(2007e) *TUC Response to Climate Change Bill Consultation, 12 June 2007*. London: TUC.

——(2008a) *Congress 2008: General Council Report*. London: TUC.

——(2008b) *Congress Report 2008*. London: TUC.

——(2008c) *A Green and Fair Future: For a Just Transition to a Low Carbon Economy*. Touchstone Pamphlet. London: TUC.

——(2008d) *TUC Response: Defra Consultation on Phase III of EU Emissions Trading System*. London: TUC.

——(2008e) 'Windfall Energy Profit Tax Should Pay for Green Budget', *press release*, 27 February 2008

——(2008f) 'Employers and Unions Call for Urgent Government Action over Clean Coal', *press release*, 28 March 2008

——(2009a) *Congress 2009: General Council Report*. London: TUC.

——(2009b) *Congress Report 2009*. London: TUC.

——(2009c) *A Budget for Jobs and Green Growth: TUC Budget Submission 2009*. London: TUC.

——(2009d) *Unlocking Green Enterprise*. Touchstone Pamphlet. London: TUC.

——(2009e) *Changing Work in a Changing Climate*. AEA Consultants. London: TUC.

——(2009f) *TUC Response to the Consultation on the Draft Order to Implement the Carbon Reduction Commitment*. London: TUC.

——(2009g) 'G20 Must Seize Chance to "Put People First"', press release, 1 April.

——(2009h) 'TUC Welcomes Government Go-Ahead for Third Runway', press release, 15 January 2009

——(2010a) *Congress 2010: General Council Report*. London: TUC.

——(2010b) *Talk about Saving Energy: A TUC briefing on the New CRC Energy Efficiency Scheme, Spring 2010*. London: TUC.

——(2011a) *Congress 2011: General Council Report*, London: TUC.

——(2011b) *Congress Report 2011*. London: TUC.

——(2012a) *Congress 2012: General Council Report*, London: TUC.

——(2012b) *Congress Report 2012*. London: TUC

——(2013a) *Congress 2013: General Council Report*. London: TUC.

——(2013b) *Congress Report 2013*. London: TUC.

——(2014) *Congress Report 2014*. London: TUC.

TUSDAC (1999) 'Minutes for 4th Policy Group Meeting', 7 July.

——(2005a) *Review of the UK Climate Change Programme: A TUSDAC Response to the Government's Consultation paper*. London: TUSDAC.

——(2005b) *EU Emissions Trading Scheme: TUSDAC Response to Defra Consultation on the ETS Phase II*. London: TUSDAC.

——(2005c) 'Minutes of Working Group Meeting', 30 June.

——(2006) 'Minutes of Policy Group Meeting (26th)', 31 October.

——(2007) *A Long-Term EU Emissions Trading Scheme*, 4 December. London: TUSDAC.

Unison (2003) *Response to the Department for Transport Consultation Papers: Future Development of Air Transport in the UK*. London: Unison.

Unite (2009) *Sustainable Transport and the Environment, Transport and General Workers' Union Section, March*. London: Unite.

Walker, S. and Cook, M. (2009) 'The Contested Concept of Sustainable Aviation', *Sustainable Development*, 17(6): 378–90.

5 Workplace climate representation

Prisoners of neoliberalism or swords of climate justice?

Introduction

Trade union environmental representation in the workplace suggests a distinctive working-class contribution to climate mitigation and adaptation. Trade union activity is dismissed by neoliberal thinkers as simply market-distorting and by ecological modernists as just one 'partner' among many. However, a Marxist interpretation of climate political economy construes such activity as unique and innovative. During the first decade of the twenty-first century, trade union activism on climate change in workplaces across the UK increased significantly. The initiatives developed by trade union representatives in the UK deserve to be better known, yet they have hardly featured in research (Cox et al. 2012). This is in contrast to work in Australia (Snell and Fairbrother 2010; Markey et al. 2014), which highlights the role of 'climate heroes' or 'champions' – union representatives dedicated to promoting climate change at the workplace level.

This chapter uses union documents and surveys to evaluate this new form of working-class representation around climate change in the UK. The first section examines the growth of workplace trade union climate representation and asks how effective union reps are as actors reducing carbon emissions. It assesses whether this kind of representation is merely an adjunct of neoliberal climate politics. The second section evaluates the union Green Workplace projects in the context of ecological modernisation discourse and assesses the extent to which climate reps are partners with government and employers. The third section evaluates the significance of union reps for workers' climate action and whether they are a force for union renewal.

Trade union climate representation

The growth of trade union climate action in the workplace

Trade union environmental representation signifies a novel, working-class contribution to climate politics, based on the independent organisation and mobilisation of lay trade union activists and officials. The idea emerged as part of the surge of interest in environmental issues in general and concerns about climate change in particular.[1] The explicit demand for an environmental role for UK trade unions was first made in the late 1980s and it took the form of extending safety representation beyond the work environment. An early reference to this role was made in a TUC memorandum submitted to the Royal Commission on Environmental Pollution, which demanded 'the need to involve trade union representatives in decision making at the workplace about environmental protection policies' (TUC 1988: 118). The TUC's *Charter for the Environment* stated that trade unions needed to be more active regarding environmental pollution in the workplace (TUC 1989b: 12). At Congress, speakers (and the media) referred to 'green shop stewards' and 'green strikes' (TUC 1989a: 377; 1990: 351). Subsequently, Congress called for union reps to have statutory rights for inspection, information and training on environmental issues (TUC 1991a: 438; Benn 1992).

However, it was not until the first decade of the new century that trade union climate-related workplace activity in the UK really emerged and mushroomed into one of its most high-profile successes (TUC 2002). The remarkable progress made by unions on environmental issues in recent years is evident from union sources. In 2005, the TUC's *Greening the Workplace* report highlighted only a handful of union examples (TUSDAC 2005a). Yet surveys carried out by the Labour Research Department (LRD) in 2007, 2009 and 2012 indicated much more widespread activity. Surveys found thousands of union reps making a substantial contribution towards curbing carbon emissions across the UK (TUC 2009c: 1; 2012b).[2] Several unions (such as Unison, PCS, UCU and Prospect) established climate and environment networks involving hundreds of reps.

The LRD surveys found examples of union representatives engaged in a wide range of climate-related activity in the workplace, including mitigation and adaptation. Some union reps had been involved in discussions on substantial energy efficiency measures with their employers, such as the installation of solar panels and wind turbines, modifications to heating and ventilation systems, changes to IT and lighting use, as well as other energy consumption measures at work. Similarly, union reps reported engagement with workplace green travel plans, cycle to work schemes, public transport subsidies and remote working. A range of recycling and waste reduction measures as well as a green procurement policy were reported, indicating a variety of measures to bring about climate-related behavioural change in workplaces. Less evidence was found on climate change adaptation, particularly in tackling high temperatures during the summer months (such as changes to dress codes), or for adequate plans to respond to extreme weather events such as flooding and storms in the workplace. However, a *prime facie* case can be made that a significant layer of trade union officials, activists and representatives had begun to engage with the implications of climate change at work.

In 2006–7, union workplace climate activity became more visible with the TUC's Green Workplaces project, which aimed to raise awareness and build capacity 'within the British trade union movement to address climate change and energy issues in the workplace'. The project was launched at a conference through TUSDAC for workplace environmental reps marking World Environment Day on 5 June 2006, with backing from the Carbon Trust (TUC 2006a: 80). The six demonstration projects participating were at Corus, Friends Provident, Defra, Scottish Power, the British Museum and the TUC itself. The TUC's own evaluation of these initiatives found that they were 'union-led, and there was an unusually high level of engagement from both members and potential members'. During the year, 'around 500 reps were trained in energy saving skills' (TUC 2008b: 2–3). Two guides were produced: *Go Green at Work*, incorporating a model agreement and guidance for reps and officers, and the leaflet *How to Green Your Workplace*. These were used 'to update environment education programmes with a particular focus on climate change'. The projects provided 'considerable organising opportunities' and 'widened the bargaining agenda into an area of strong concern for workers of all ages' (TUC 2008a: 78). Unison held a national one-day environment conference for members and workplace representatives in the public sector on 17 January 2007, attended by over 100 delegates. Cover story articles on climate change appeared 'in approximately eight or more different trade union journals over the last year' (TUC 2008b: 12–13).

The success of the original Green Workplaces pilots helped the TUC secure funding for the Carbon Partnerships Project. The initiative aimed to train 500 workplace reps and develop energy efficiency partnerships, a carbon calculator and green union leaders (TUC 2007a: 66). A year later the General Council celebrated this new leadership role at a 'well-attended breakfast event' involving union general secretaries and Climate Minister Joan Ruddock in November 2007. Ruddock acknowledged 'the unique and valuable role of trade unions in raising awareness and mobilising people to help address the challenge of climate change' (TUC 2008a: 78).

Momentum was further spurred after the TUC secured funding from the government's Union Modernisation Fund (UMF) in 2007 to expand its work on environmental representation. This project aimed at 'developing new skills in the workplace and extending the union consultation agenda to include environmental and climate change issues' (TUC 2009a: 71). The TUC's own evaluation claimed that it had 'trained 97 environmental representatives, resulting in changes to workplace structures and the formation of environmental committees/forums' at British Telecom Adastral Park, Ipswich, Great Ormond Street Hospital for Children, Leicester City Council, the National Library of Scotland in Edinburgh, National Museums Liverpool, the National Union of Teachers (NUT) and United Utilities (ibid.). Those projects that established formal structures for union involvement were able to put in place a process that will enable 'greater staff consultation in the workplace by linking top-down management approaches to union-led bottom-up approaches' (TUC 2010d: 4, 31). Towards the end of the project, the General Council proudly claimed that it had produced a range of support materials and advice for union reps and officers, including the distribution of over 6,000 copies of its new environmental workbook, briefings on key topics and a monthly *Green Workplaces* newsletter. Over 9,000 copies of the TUC reps' handbook, *Go Green at Work*, had been requested by affiliates, 'reflecting the growing interest from union reps in including energy and environmental issues in the collective bargaining agenda' (TUC 2010a: 69). The joint TUC, CBI and Department for Business publication, *Reps in Action: How Workplaces Can Gain from Modern Union Representation*, lauded 'the considerable reduction in energy consumption attributed to an earlier Green Workplaces project at the British Museum', worth around £700,000 (BERR 2009: 8).[3]

By the second decade of the century, networks of union representatives acting on environmental and climate change issues had been established within a number of unions and between activists in different unions. Progress was registered by the 2009 union survey (TUC 2009c: 2). Some 1,301 union representatives and activists responded to the survey. TUSDAC and the TUC officials were delighted with the results, which had found 'a remarkable range of union-led initiatives to tackle climate change in the workplace, including over 200 joint management–union committees discussing climate-related issues, and 150 working parties covering environment/climate change issues' (ibid.). In June 2009, the TUC held its annual half-day conference to mark World Environment Day. The event launched *Unions and Climate Change: A Guide for Union Reps*, a booklet containing the results of the TUC survey and *Targeting Climate Change*, the TUC's new Unionlearn education workbook for union representatives.

Apart from the significant number of workplace committees discussing climate-related matters, the surveys also found that a small number of union reps in both the private and public sectors had negotiated agreements with their employers on environmental matters. Such agreements institutionalised the role of union reps and union members in reducing emissions. The 2009 survey reported that Unison, Prospect, Unite and GMB unions within the energy firm EDF had 'negotiated an international agreement on corporate responsibility, which includes commitments to tackle climate change'. Management at Western Power Distribution had agreed to expand the remit of the safety committee, to make it a safety, health and environment committee and to allow additional environment reps to sit on the body. The agreement included 'time off for training for the environment reps, as well as for existing safety reps, in recognition of the complexities of climate science and the rapidly developing government policy on the issue'. UCU had negotiated an agreement at South Thames College on environment reps. The survey reported that Unison and GMB reps at Bristol City Council were negotiating an agreement on facility time – thought to be the first full formal green reps agreement with any local authority in the UK (TUC 2009c: 30–2).

Two years on, the UMF project *GreenWorks* report noted that unions such as UCU and Unison produced their own environmental newsletters, while PCS, Prospect and Unison provided online resources to aid negotiations on greening the workplace. The TUC registered 'a growing number of requests for speakers and information on green issues at union conferences at events', including the Tolpuddle Green Camp. The Connect and NUT young teachers' conferences both had climate change as their main theme (TUC 2010d: 34). The TUC launched an online guide *Greener Deals: Negotiating on Environmental Issues at Work*, at a unionlearn conference (TUC 2010e). The guide included 13 case studies, highlighting the progress made by union reps on negotiating trade union involvement in workplace environmental management (TUC 2010a: 69).

The UMF project report stated that after nearly five years of frenzied voluntary activity by union environment reps, the workplace initiatives had reached a tipping point. The TUC's development model, 'based on capacity building in demonstration projects, with training courses, training materials, and other support activities' (TUC 2010d) helped to set standards and ensure 'the spontaneous development of many other green workplace projects throughout the UK' (ibid.). TUC officials concluded that it was now possible to coordinate a network of union green reps and develop resources to 'exploit the true potential of workplace engagement in climate change' (ibid.: 5). Officials estimated that there were probably over one thousand union green workplace projects in the UK (Pearson 2011; TUC 2011a: 77). On 25 February 2011, union leaders launched the first UK online network for green union reps. Officials claimed that green reps play 'a crucial role in encouraging employers and staff to take part in environmental projects at work, cutting UK carbon emissions and boosting company profits' (TUC 2011d: 1).They reiterated the demand for 'giving reps basic legal rights to act on climate change issues in the workplace, statutory time off to perform their roles, and access to training, would go a long way to unleashing the untapped potential that exists among green reps in UK workplaces' (ibid.).

Although battered by the recession and austerity, many union reps clung tenaciously to their climate commitments. An LRD survey in 2012 received 1,200 responses and indicated further progress with advancing climate issues at work, while new case studies demonstrated continued appetite for climate action, despite a more difficult political and economic context. The survey cited numerous examples, including GMB reps at ASDA encouraging workers to close walk-in fridge and freezer doors when they are not in use; union reps at a weapons manufacturer successfully lobbying for the installation of showers for cyclists and parking spaces for car sharers; Community reps at Tata Steel negotiated the replacement of thousands of light fittings with energy-efficient tubes; PCS reps at Defra regulated the office temperature during the winter months, with windows having been resealed, and heat from the canteen re-used to heat the building; and CWU reps at mail distributor Parcelforce encouraging the firm's management to buy greener vehicles (TUC 2012a). Progress was also registered in six case studies for the TUC publication *The Union Effect* at Allianz Insurance, Defra (York), EDF Energy, Furzedown Low Carbon Zone: a community project based on a further education college, Great Ormond Street Hospital and The Port of Felixstowe (TUC 2014d: 6). It seemed that the time for climate reps had finally arrived.

How effective are union reps at taking climate measures?

How effective are union reps as actors reducing carbon emissions? A Euro-foundation report by Vitols *et al.* (2011: 52), while largely supportive of the 'remarkably positive development' of union environmental representation across Europe, nevertheless argued that 'the actual impact of the projects aiming to green the economy, implemented by social partners, is barely measurable'. They described the projects as 'still very recent initiatives and lack a final evaluation' (ibid.). This argument cannot be sustained today once the UK experience is examined: on the contrary, tangible and quantifiable outcomes were recorded in a range of projects. The first Green Workplaces projects indicated quite specific amounts of carbon emissions reduced by their activity – and the evaluation provided the conversion equations to enable reps in other workplaces to calculate their contributions. The project evaluation report estimated the carbon savings from Green Workplaces Phase 1 of 465 tonnes of CO_2, with a further projected saving of 2,744 tonnes of CO_2 (TUC 2008b: 12). Although the UMF project did not attempt to quantify the carbon savings it had overseen, the National Library of Scotland did pledge to a 30 per cent cut in carbon emissions over the next five years through the Carbon Trust's Carbonlite programme and joined the 10:10 campaign – 10 per cent emissions reductions by 2010 (TUC 2010d: 19).

The TUC's *Greener Deals* publication (TUC 2010e) claimed that BECTU reps had saved nearly a £1,000 a year in reduced energy costs at the Princess Theatre in Torquay. At Bristol City Council, training was expected to deliver fuel savings of at least £350 every year for each diesel van covering at least 25,000 miles in a year. At Guys Marsh Prison, Shaftesbury, the anaerobic digestion plant that reps had campaigned for saved around £1,500 a month. Worcestershire County Council introduced a remote-controlled energy system at the suggestion of GMB reps, which helped reduce energy costs by at least 15 per cent every year (TUC 2010e: 18–19, 23, 30). The TUC's *Green Workplaces News* bulletin reported further successes. The most outstanding was a project called JUPITER (Join Us People in Tackling Energy Reduction) at ABInBev's Magor brewery in South Wales, where 'a union-led energy saving project' had cut carbon emissions 'by a massive 40 per cent within two years' (TUC 2011c: 1).

All six case studies in *The Union Effect* sought to measure progress towards their targets and can point to considerable successes. At Allianz Insurance, CO_2 emissions per employee have fallen by 55 per cent since

2006. In the Furzedown Low Carbon Zone, 900 energy saving advice visits to local homes took place. At the Port of Felixstowe, nitrous oxide levels fell by an average 10 per cent over five years, while sulphur dioxide levels were reduced by 80 per cent. This does not mean that progress has been universal and linear. Not all the targets set have been achieved and, with no legal basis for union involvement in environmental issues and no legal obligation on employers to consult unions on the issue, 'enthusiasm, both among management and union members has sometimes waned' (TUC 2014d: 6–7).

The difficulties with quantifying emissions at a workplace level should not be underestimated, particularly when transport is included. Ultimate responsibility for these figures did not rest with union reps – only employers had the necessary data to produce adequate estimates and they were not obliged in law to disclose their emissions. Perhaps the Green Workplaces projects and other examples were Potemkin villages, unrepresentative of most workplaces? Undoubtedly unions put forward the best examples they could find. But the wide range of possible activities highlighted by the surveys suggested that, at the very least, union environmental reps were more widespread than had been anticipated, and could demonstrate the potential power and interest to instigate significant emissions reductions. If a handful of climate reps could have a larger ripple effect on scores and even hundreds of employees, particularly in larger workplaces, thousands of reps could make a substantial contribution, given the opportunity.

Pensioners or prisoners of neoliberalism?

Union environmental representation made great strides during the first decade of the new millennium. But how far was the work of environmental reps independent of the government and employers? To what extent were they captive of other interests? In a wide-ranging assessment of the structural and contextual situation trade unions faced under Labour, John McIlroy (2009: 195) summed up the accommodation of union leaderships in succinct fashion. In practice, 'the majority of British trade union leaders have adapted to neoliberalism'. They were 'prisoners and pensioners of neoliberalism, sometimes reluctant prisoners – over employment legislation – sometimes enthusiastic pensioners – over training and the funds that go with it'. Although McIlroy did not examine the newly-emerging environment reps, his tantalising thesis does raise the question of whether union environment representatives also became pensioners and prisoners of neoliberalism. Swaffield and Bell (2012) and Lewis and Juravle (2010) found that non-union 'climate champions' in the UK constructed the process of social change in neoliberal terms. Was this also the case for union environment reps?

The strong 'pensioners' thesis could be expressed as follows: union environmental rep projects were fuelled from government coffers, creating an artificial involvement in climate matters that would not have taken place without such funding. Evidence of government financial support certainly exists. TUSDAC is a joint government–unions body, with Defra contributing staff time for policy and working group meetings, as well as funding for ad-hoc projects such as Climate Solidarity (the latter was closed down prematurely by the Conservative–Liberal Democrat Coalition government in 2010). The Carbon Trust, established and funded as a result of the Climate Change Levy, also provided finance, including for Caroline Molloy to be seconded from the TGWU to the TUC to take responsibility for the first pilot Green Workplaces projects. The TUC secured further funding from the Carbon Trust for the Carbon Partnership projects. The next phase of Green Workplaces projects was funded by a UMF grant, which paid for the secondment of Sarah Pearce from Unison to the TUC, while the South West project was part-funded by the Regional Development Agency. Government-funded Unionlearn also contributed finance for training and related materials.

However, the argument about 'pensioners' can be readily discarded, at least with respect to environmental representation. If creating environmental representatives was a project supported by Labour, then in government it never provided sufficient financial backing and failed to take the opportunity to institutionalise them when it had the power to. The more likely explanation is that Labour ministers were anxious to avoid legislating because of resistance from employers' bodies, and that funding was much more of a sop to union leaders to continue with voluntary initiatives instead. Government money for union environmental representation probably did not exceed a million pounds over the decade, a fraction of the input from unions themselves. The government contribution to unions hardly compares favourably to the financial support provided directly and indirectly to employers and their organisations on the environment and climate change over the same period. At best, the funds gave the TUC additional capacity to oversee and coordinate activity promoted by affiliated unions. Individual unions and the TUC self-funded full-time and part-time posts for officials to attend events and produce briefing papers. The costs of conferences, seminars and other collective gatherings were borne by the unions themselves, even where they were attended by government, business and NGOs' personnel. The government money went to the top of the trade union movement, paying for temporary extra staff. Very little went directly to workplace union reps, though some trickled down in the form of publications and free conferences. In the main, the activities of union environmental reps were undertaken free of charge from central government's point of view: it was either during work time (in which case employers were effectively paying) or conducted outside of normal working hours voluntarily by the reps themselves. The charge that environmental reps were pensioners of the neoliberal state does not stand up to scrutiny.

If environment reps were not pensioners of neoliberalism, then there appears to be more traction with the weaker thesis, namely that they were nevertheless captives of Labour approach and therefore 'prisoners' of neoliberal climate politics. To some extent 'in some of the projects researched, the state played a major role' (Vitols *et al.* 2011: 53). Most union leaders and TUC officials often did support the Labour government's climate politics, though there was still some disagreement over energy and transport policy. Unions were also cognisant of the political context of their demands, supporting government initiatives such as the Carbon Reduction Commitment to widen the scope for involvement of union reps.

However, union environmental representation was never Labour government policy between 1997 and 2010. The initiative and direction of environmental representation were set by union leaders, TUSDAC, union officials and by workplace reps, not by government. The demand for union environment reps came from the unions themselves, as did the specific proposal for a statutory basis for representation in the workplace and outside. Despite making the demand for over two decades and initiating the surge of activity in the new millennium, legal rights appeared no nearer to being implemented by Labour ministers towards the end of their administration than it had been at the beginning. In many respects, environmental representation was rather inconvenient to the government, since it stepped outside of the neoliberal paradigm of actors, which it centred largely on business leaders, managers and individuals only as consumers.[4] In fact central government had almost no direct role in any of the Green Workplaces projects.

Certainly the projects required what Sarah Pearce called 'senior management buy-in', because as voluntary projects they would simply have been obstructed by employers without their consent (TUC 2010b: 3). In these cases, it was often an existing part of the employment relations apparatus, such as a joint union–management consultative committee or safety committee, where discussions on the environment and climate change were raised and progressed. Employers such as Corus and Leicester City Council had pre-existing environment programmes, which union reps could appeal to as justification for their own involvement. In cases such as the British Museum, the York office of Defra, Great Ormond Street Hospital, the National Library of Scotland, National Museums, Liverpool and United Utilities, the original moves and instigation came from union reps in the workplace and were backed by central or regional union officials.

Even in firms such as BT with established environmental targets and 'carbon clubs', pressure for further workplace involvement came from reps, often responding to materials put out by their individual unions. As Andrew Cassy, Prospect (formerly Connect), union environment rep at BT's Adastral Park, put it:

> I have found the union support and resources invaluable for my own personal development and awareness on environmental matters, which has directly fed into my employment activities. The full range of union resources has been used, from online information feeds, training events,

local, national and even international conferences, green camps and booklets through to local branch representation and support.

(TUC 2010d: 12)

This was confirmed by the three LRD surveys, where some reps who later joined Green Workplaces projects reported that their activities stretched back a number of years before government money was made available.

Union environment reps were not 'prisoners' of Labour climate politics in the sense of carrying out the government's bidding in workplaces. The only real sense in which union environmental representation was 'imprisoned' by the Labour government was the way in which ministers dangled the promise to examine statutory rights if sufficient evidence was accumulated. In fact, ministers stuck to the neoliberal approach, to the exclusion of legal changes, in order to placate employers' organisations. Defra Minister David Miliband told Congress in 2006 that he welcomed the TUC's commitment 'to create a thousand climate change champions in the workplace'. However, when asked about rights for reps on the environment, he evaded the question by arguing 'this is a way to serve the interests of employees and the interests of the company or the organisation at the same time' (TUC 2006b: 78, 80). David Miliband was asked the question again at Unison's Green Your Workplace conference in January 2007 and at the TUC's On Target? climate conference in June 2007. In both cases he said he would wait for the government's consultation on workplace representatives' facilities and facility time to 'see the case for it'.

The Labour government's response to this consultation decided it was 'premature' to consider providing distinct time-off rights to environmental representatives. The government said it 'appreciated' the arguments to put environmental representatives on a statutory footing and that like union learning representatives, this type of representative was 'an exciting feature of modern trade unionism'. The response concluded that 'their development is still in its infancy, and it is not yet certain whether there is a real and sustained demand among union members for them to function at their workplaces'. However, it made available UMF funding 'to co-finance innovative projects by trade unions to nurture and develop these categories of representatives' (BERR 2007: 4–5, 13). The emphasis on voluntary agreements instead of statutory rights for environmental reps was continued by the next Environment Secretary Hilary Benn. Speaking at the TUC's climate change conference on 16 June 2008, he praised the 'real commitment and enthusiasm' for their 'bottom-up union and employee led action', but did not commit on statutory rights (TUC 2009d: 35).[5]

The ground appeared to shift slightly in 2009, in light of growing evidence of the activities of union environment reps and examples of workers making green demands around jobs. Ed Miliband spoke at Congress in September 2009. The pressure was heightened by the presence of workers from the recent Vestas wind turbine plant occupation (see Chapter 6). Miliband paid 'tribute to the green reps throughout the country who are doing such a fantastic job'. He said the 'low-carbon revolution' could not be done by government alone, it needed 'people to make it happen, and all round this country trade union green reps are showing the way to the low-carbon future that we want'. Asked about legal rights for environmental workplace reps, he replied: 'I certainly have not said that we are ruling out putting environmental reps on a statutory footing and I have a role in the next manifesto, so I think that is a very live and important issue for the next manifesto and I think it is something that trade unions and I need to discuss' (TUC 2009b: 124–5). Asked about green reps' legal rights at the TUC Going Green at Work conference, on 15 March 2010, Ed Miliband said he was 'sympathetic' and that 'there should be more of them'. However, the pledge did not make the manifesto and did not feature in subsequent Labour climate policy.

Green reps and ecological modernisation

Although union climate representation at work was an independent, working-class approach juxtaposed to neoliberal framing, there is nevertheless evidence of accommodation to ecological modernisation discourses. Labour governments were prepared to grant some high-level trade union officials some insider access on climate matters, without extending legal collective rights at work. The Labour government view was expressed in jocular fashion at a special TUC conference about the implications of Kyoto on 27 October 1998. Asked by TGWU official Alan Dalton about extending safety reps' rights to the environment, Deputy Prime Minister John Prescott replied:

> So we will certainly have a look at the environmental points, it's an interesting one. I could see all the difficulties and I can see all the cracks that have been made about it, as you and I can, you know – half your day as safety rep, the other half of your day on the environment, do you ever work for anybody?
>
> (TUC 1998: 5–6)

This section probes the rationale behind union green workplace activity.

The Nattrass Report

The lack of traction with Blair's Labour government over legal environmental rights for union representatives forced trade unions to adopt a different approach, which was to flower as climate change became a more high-profile issue during the administration's third term. The turning point was cemented by an independent report to TUSDAC in 1999 by former safety inspector Stuart Nattrass, who questioned the earlier emphasis on extending safety reps' rights and suggested a way forward more suited to the existing political context and the tastes of ministers. Nattrass (1999: 17, 9) asked the hard question: How strong is the case for statutory rights for time off for environmental training for union representatives? He found that 'virtually no one outside union circles accepted the validity of the case, even in organisations with successful voluntary arrangements'. Employers and civil servants saw 'no need for environmental representatives as regards the workplace environment, because health and safety representatives cover it'. They told him the workforce is 'one of many stakeholders in the external environment and could not see why they alone should have legal representation'. Union attempts in the early 1990s to energise a green works campaign had been misrepresented as 'a back-door way of gaining recognition or influence and ran into the sand'.

Nattrass (ibid.: 4) examined potential strategies for the future and outlined two main options. The first was to continue to propagate the case for legal rights to appoint representatives. His report questioned 'whether such rights would be effective without a general duty on employers to adopt a systematic approach to environmental management' (ibid.). Since virtually no one outside union circles accepted the case for legal rights, 'unions would have to demonstrate their willingness to meet the substantial training costs that would arise'. He proposed a second option, without abandoning the eventual goal of legal rights. This strategy would 'concentrate on taking advantage of opportunities to become more involved on a voluntary basis'. The report suggested 'it might be possible to apply to the DTI partnership fund for financial support for projects on a sector basis, or to work up case studies and guidance on environmental partnerships, or for projects between unions and particular employers' (ibid.).

TUC leaders debated the key issues raised by Nattrass, resolving that environmental representatives should be constituted separately from safety reps. They decided that the most compelling argument to advance legal rights would be to point to successes where employers had conceded union involvement in environmental matters voluntarily – such examples would add to the case for legal rights. A key element of such a strategy would be 'collecting and publicising best practice case studies' (TUC 2000b: 2). The General Council retained its policy calling for an environment law placing general duties on employers to protect the environment, including the requirement to consult with unions, because it felt that voluntary measures would only have traction with better employers. On the issue of existing or new forms of representation, 'unions were divided and the TUC adopted the view that the duty on employers should be to consult unions, leaving them to decide how best this could be achieved' (TUC 2000a). However, it agreed to develop voluntary projects to demonstrate the relevance of union involvement (ibid.: 93). The Nattrass report was thus a watershed in the union approach to environmental representation, which turned in classic ecological modernisation terms towards voluntary partnership activity to build up the evidence base for separate environmental representation. Increasingly too, the more modestly-endowed union learning reps rather than safety reps became the model.

This approach was consolidated by the Warwick Agreement between affiliated unions and Labour in July 2004. The Labour Party promised to review facilities, rights and time-off for union representatives, if unions helped to secure its election the following year. TUSDAC argued that the government should support 'the development of new representative roles – which will both add value in the workplace and may be more attractive to potential representatives than traditional steward's roles' (TUSDAC 2005b: 4). The committee proposed 'a flexible approach to tackling sustainability at work – shop stewards may take the lead, or health and safety reps or environment reps'. And the committee (if not all individual unions) explicitly broke with the old approach, stating, 'we are not convinced that environmental issues should be "ghettoised" as a safety reps' function' (TUSDAC 2006: 1).

The new strategy was most fully articulated in the TUC's response to the DTI consultation on facility time in 2007. The response restated that 'there is a strong case for government to support unions to develop the role of environmental and equality representatives, and to place the functions of these new forms of representative on a statutory footing' (TUC 2007b). TUC officials argued that if 'union environmental representatives were able to access paid time-off to undertake training and carry out duties related to the role, government would hand a significant boost to "green" UK workplaces' (ibid.: 10–11). Environmental representatives should be 'entitled to paid time off to attend a minimum 10 days of accredited training in the 12 months immediately following their election/appointment'. They should also be entitled to

> reasonable paid time off for relevant training and updating on TUC or union courses in relation to their responsibilities; be appointed or elected by recognised independent trade unions; have the right to reasonable paid time off to carry out their functions; and have a right to information from the employer to assist them in their duties.
>
> (2007b: 4, 13)

TUSDAC sought the amendment of the ACAS Code of Practice, *Time Off for Trade Union Duties and Activities*, 'to recognise the role of union reps in consultations on sustainable production and consumption' (TUSDAC 2007: 7).

The approach also began to win support in wider circles, in particular from environmental organisations.[6] Tony Juniper, Executive Director of Friends of the Earth, wrote to Brendan Barber expressing his support for the campaign. He wrote: 'It concerns Friends of the Earth that trade union and environmental representatives have trouble being released to deal with environmental matters or attend training courses.' He added, 'That is why I would like to add Friends of the Earth's voice to your call for the government to give stronger rights for workplace environmental representatives by amendments to the ACAS code of practice' (LRD 2007a). Similarly, the Campaign against Climate Change endorsed the demand, agreeing to establish a trade union group, which organised conferences of union environment representatives and climate activists in 2008, 2009, 2010, 2013 and 2014.[7]

Voluntary initiatives

Most unions and the TUC employed the language of ecological modernisation to explain the benefits of union environment reps for employers and the government. This was more than a tactical or presentational decision: it reflected a widely held belief within the top echelons of UK trade unions that environmental and climate matters were more universal than traditional concerns and joint working for co-benefits was a genuine possibility. This approach was clearly articulated early in a *Memorandum by the TUC to the National Economic Development Council*, which insisted that 'active trade union involvement in environmental protection at the workplace level requires a new approach, based on partnership, cooperation and joint working' (TUC 1991b). The 'traditional adversarial approach' to employment relations was 'not sufficient and may undermine environmental protection'. The submission registered that 'a new approach carries extra responsibilities and obligations on trade unions. Such obligations must be balanced by the establishment in law or through collective agreement, fundamental rights for workers' (ibid.: 9–10).

The ecological modernisation discourse of co-benefits for both employers and workers in tackling climate change at work was evident in the Green Workplaces projects. The aims of the first Green Workplaces project included 'practical engagement of workers and management in six schemes at workplace level, to secure measurable energy savings in the short term' and 'longer-term Framework Agreements' (TUC 2008b: 4). The Carbon Partnerships Project aimed to 'enable unions to work with employers in the private, public and voluntary sectors to cut carbon' (TUC 2007a: 66). Frances O'Grady argued that 'partnership working with unions can deliver spectacular results for employers ... Greening our workplaces is all about unions, workers and managers working together towards a common cause' (TUC 2010c: 1–2).

Co-benefits were an explicit objective of the UMF projects in 2008–10. The General Council claimed that green projects 'can have a positive, transformational impact on industrial relations' and pledged to 'work intensively with affiliates and employers over a two-year period to develop best practice in up to 15 workplace environmental projects in key sectors' (TUC 2008a: 77). The TUC's UMF evaluation report stated that union involvement 'can lead to business benefits through improved environmental performance' (TUC 2010d: 5). It claimed the projects showed the potential for 'transformational change' through activities such as:

enhancing union understanding of energy efficiency and cutting carbon emissions as a key business practice, expanding union experience of partnership working with management on a key business goal, increasing the capacity of union officials to extend the consultation agenda to include new and emerging issues relating to the environment, sustained engagement and dialogue between employees and management on environmental issues that will help to transform employees' understanding of the workplace as a focus of action on climate change and help to secure lasting changes to union–management relations.

(TUC 2010d: 8)

In the UMF evaluation for government, Sarah Pearce claimed that each pilot project was established upon 'a principle of cooperation between management and unions' (BIS 2010). She pointed to the 'mutual appreciation of the material impact that these projects can have on reducing carbon emissions has fostered improved industrial relations', because the projects expanded union experience of 'a key business goal: carbon reduction' (ibid.: 10). TUC officials lauded the way unions had managed to progress projects in the context of a recession, budget cuts and job losses, providing 'an insight into the potential for these projects to sustain dialogue within the workplace at times when industrial relations are potentially strained'. Discussions on largely non-adversarial topics, such as energy efficiency, offered an opportunity to maintain lines of communication on all sides (TUC 2010d: 30).

Some participants in the Green Workplaces projects from the union and management side also saw relations as non-adversarial and working towards common goals. Workers at Leicester City Council argued that the project meant 'we can break away from a traditional union approach – more organic, less autocratic'. Similarly, the sustainability manager at United Utilities stated that climate change is 'changing the rules and I think that extends to industrial relations'. Green reps would be enthused, empowered and willing to convince colleagues to take action 'whether the formal structure exists or not' (ibid.: 17, 25–26). The government's review endorsed a carefully prescribed role for environmental reps within this paradigm. It said that the role of the environmental rep was 'to gather information about their specific department and help managers and fellow work colleagues to "get the green message", through identifying how each area could make efficiency savings'. The environmental rep initiative had 'further solidified the relations between management and unions, and employees felt engaged in the decision-making processes relating to the environment' (BERR 2009: 8). This sounded like the ecological modernisation discourse that influenced other areas of Labour policy.

Voluntary initiatives continued during the Coalition government and despite its austerity. UCATT reps played a leading role in Wakefield District Housing in support of an ambitious homes energy efficiency programme, in the social housing sector where it is perhaps needed most (Pearson 2011). PCS reps at Guys Marsh Prison in Dorset helped to develop the first anaerobic digestion plant, turning all the prison's food waste into energy (TUC 2011b). Community union within Tata Steel Europe (previously Corus) aimed to have environmental representatives at all of Tata UK's operations 'in order to work with the company to reduce its carbon footprint'. This had already happened at the 20" Pipe Mill in Hartlepool (TUC 2013a). At Babcock's site at Rosyth, another six Prospect environment reps were reported to have received training. Recognition of reps, time off and setting up an environment committee were agreed in principle by management. Prospect also secured 11 new environment reps at Babcock's Devonport Royal Dockyard (TUC 2013b). Even in the depths of recession and in the midst of attacks on the right to organise, union reps persevered, with some continuing to gain concessions.

Despite the impact of austerity, new agreements were won. Plymouth City Council signed a Joint Trade Unions Greener Workspace Agreement with the unions Unite, Unison and the GMB to 'introduce a Green Workplaces Scheme to encourage council staff to work with their managers to reduce carbon, encourage sustainability and save money'. The union facilities agreement providing time off for reps was updated to recognise support for the work of green reps (Pearson 2014a). After the last local elections, the new council leader made 100 pledges aimed at making Plymouth a greener city. TUC official Rob Garrett said: 'Plymouth FC fans are nicknamed the "Green Army", but this new agreement means that Plymouth's real Green Army is the council and the thousands of staff that work for them' (Hatch 2014). Stockport Council also signed an agreement with Stockport Unison to support existing efforts on the part of both management and union to respond to climate change and reduce carbon emissions. Don Naylor, Unison branch environment officer at Stockport Council, said:

> Within the branch, we recognise the full range of contemporary environmental and climate issues, their threats and, yes, how trade unions are well placed to offer some solutions. These are no longer fringe issues; they are beginning to have major impacts globally, often affecting the poorest and most vulnerable.
>
> (TUC 2014c)

The deal agrees resource time for union green reps to carry out their role and to attend meetings with management on workplace environmental issues (Pearson 2014b).

Partnership

Some incisive critiques of union environmental representation claim that it was bound politically and ideologically to government and employers, not just by a common ecological discourse but also by the self-limiting doctrine of partnership. Martin Wicks argued that trade union activists needed to 'wake up' if they wanted to influence whether or how environmental reps are introduced (Wicks 2007). This was because the TUC's conception of how to tackle the environmental crisis and the role of reps in that context 'is rooted in its partnership philosophy and the idea that "globalisation" can be "made to work for everybody"' (ibid.). As he put it, 'without too great an exaggeration, the TUC approach could be described as "unions and employers – working together to save the planet"' (ibid.). Wicks criticised TUSDAC for accepting 'the framework of government policy, the belief that market mechanisms can resolve the environmental crisis'. Tackling environmental issues 'will not be done on the basis of "harmonious" industrial relations. It will require a struggle', he argued. He was also sceptical about whether the introduction of environmental reps would attract many young people (ibid.: 8).

There is little doubt about the commitment of the TUC and the majority union leaderships to partnership during this period. John McIlroy and Gary Daniels (2009: 149) argue that even the rhetorical rejection of the term partnership by 'awkward squad' leaders did not negate the practice of their unions collaborating with employers and the Labour government, rather than using mobilisation strategies. The TUC took the advice of Stuart Nattrass to apply to the government's partnership fund for financial support for environmental partnerships. Perhaps the most graphic endorsement of this approach was the joint government, TUC and CBI document, *How Workplaces Can Gain from Modern Union Representation* (BERR 2009). Barber wrote after the second TUC survey that 'greening the workplace pays off, not just in environmental terms but also in business benefits' (TUC 2012c: 3). TUC officials argued that 'the green shift in the labour movement is also reflected in the new alliances emerging around green issues like the feed in tariff or green growth. Unions are now working closely with a number of environmental organisations and businesses taking on the low carbon challenge' (Pearson 2011). At the Port of Felixstowe, Unite's green workplace rep Kevin Rogers also had the role of assisting in communication with the workforce on environmental issues (TUC 2014d: 44). Rogers said that he had demonstrated 'how a non-confrontational dialogue can be progressed between the trade union and management through constructive joint working' (Rogers 2012).

However, the extent of partnership over environmental reps should not be exaggerated. Although the veneer of partnership was glossed over the model projects, the actual activity more closely resembled the organising approach. As Vitols *et al.* (2011: 16, 19) commented, unions and employer associations 'interact much less in the UK's system of industrial relations than in other EU countries'. The UK is characterised by 'conflictual relations between unions and employer associations, and a general neoliberal context focusing on voluntarism'. Employers' associations in the UK were 'not involved in the projects and do not see a need to be involved'. The reason for their lack of participation was that 'the project is seen as a trade union matter and the relationship between trade unions and employers in the British system of industrial relations is generally conflictual rather than cooperative' (ibid.). However, some employers saw it as 'a good idea, since one of the aims of the projects is to help reduce costs' (ibid.). In short, while some employers clearly welcomed the opportunity to work with unions for common environmental objectives, others saw the intervention of unions as at best an unhelpful distraction, or worse as an unwanted encroachment on their own sphere of decision-making.

Perhaps union environment reps were just unconsciously doing the employers' bidding on green issues? The limits of partnership in this field were graphically illustrated by events at United Utilities (UU). Sarah Pearce reported that 'to promote a partnership approach', a presentation was given by United Utilities' head of sustainability and the TUC project manager to the joint management–union forum in January 2009. After further joint meetings to design training for union reps and stewards, the company shared lists of its carbon champions with the unions and mapping of union reps began. However, the company soon went through a period of restructuring and job losses directly affected key managers involved in the Green Workplaces project. In the circumstances, the launch was postponed at the company's request (TUC 2010d: 25). In her otherwise strongly pro-partnership evaluation of the project, Pearce was moved to warn about the dangers of union environmental reps and managers becoming 'green police' (TUC 2010e). She argued that union green reps 'can come under pressure to police staff behaviour, to use more of the stick approach and less of the carrot' (ibid.). Individual actions, such as turning off photocopiers at night, 'are all worthwhile, as a first step forward. But many other changes may be necessary. Employers must be tasked with the duty to reduce the workplace carbon footprint' (ibid.). As well as asking each staff member to turn their computer off, 'it makes economic and environmental sense to invest in technology to automate energy saving processes. That's why green issues need to feature on the collective bargaining agenda' (ibid.: 13–14). The point is well made, but it brings out one of the crucial limitations of the ecological modernisation approach many trade union leaders took during this period.

Union environmental representatives: a force for climate action?

There are multifaceted class dimensions to workplace environmental representation, in terms of organisation, control and ideology. The very fact of trade union organisation in the workplace, on climate change or any other issue, was an anathema to neoliberal framing, which regards collective organisation by workers as an impediment to the free functioning of markets. At the most basic level, trade union workplace climate activity was independent of other actors, in at least three senses: first, often it was instigated by unions and their members of their own volition; second, sometimes it was coun-terposed to the immediate employer, or the government and indeed to NGOs; and third, in some sense, it asserted workers' unique interests. This section explores the extent to which union workplace climate action was independent of the dominant actors and hegemonic framings.

Workers' climate action

Climate action in the workplace instigated by union reps was a unique form of climate mobilisation, implicitly independent of other actors. Even less adversarial union reps tended to go beyond the parameters laid down by government and employers. The most far-reaching incursion into what would normally be considered management's territory were agreements over environmental matters, such as those at Bristol, Plymouth and Stockport Councils, Western Power Distribution and South Thames College, which gave union reps partial suzerainty over environmental decisions, with at least the possibility of consultation and implicitly of veto. The most thorough-going agreements also allowed for time during working hours to progress environmental issues, for workers in general and union reps in particular. Discussing environmental matters on joint union–management committees has similar effects, extending the union role to partially encroach on aspects of the work process, for example, by taking part in audits and inspections of the workplace and then making recommendations for change. At a lower level, the use of meetings, conferences, fairs, DVD showings, 'Question Time' panels and other educational events during work time and on work premises also implicitly challenged the frontiers of control (TUC 2009c).

At Allianz and the Port of Felixstowe, the reduction in their carbon foot-print and other improvements was 'primarily driven by management, with unions playing a willing role in winning employee support'. However, at Furzedown, it was 'the unions who have been the instigators of the whole attempt to develop environmental awareness in the community and pro-moting sustainability skills among students' (TUC 2014d). Similarly at Defra (York), unions 'played a central role' – for example, in auditing the work-place. At Great Ormond Street Hospital, 'unions and management have worked together over a long period' – though the hospital's Unison branch instigated the Green Workplace project. Finally, at EDF Energy, the climate change commitment arose from a corporate social responsibility agreement signed with the unions at international level (ibid.: 7, 21, 36).

There is an important distinction between the kind of independent activity that was undertaken with apparently common goals in mind (perhaps where employers and managers were not living up to their commitments or per-ceived interests), and independent activity over different goals and indeed in conflict with employers and managers. For example, LRD research high-lighted the Unison green group at Arun District Council, which took green initiatives while working together with local managers. A long-standing

Unison member volunteered to become the union branch environment offi-cer and recruited four other enthusiasts, who called themselves Sustainable Working and You (SWAY). SWAY received backing from the council's chief executive for their first campaign on energy saving in offices, using free posters ordered from the Carbon Trust. They also organised an energy saving quiz with prizes donated by the Unison branch and local firms such as Body Shop, and a car-sharing questionnaire to promote the existing scheme. In another transport campaign, the union green group persuaded the council to fund, and a local bike shop to discount, cycles for a bike pool. This has enabled some staff to commute between sites by bike. The union received good publicity in the local paper for the scheme. It went on to build a group of green champions, with a recruitment campaign to have a union green rep in every department. They produced a green champions' hand-book, published newsletters and used the intranet to inform and cajole. In doing so, the high profile of SWAY strengthened the union (LRD 2009: 29).

However, independent activity of this kind still relied upon willing parti-cipants on both sides. In other cases, union environment reps undertook independent activity because of divergent goals from employers. The 2009 TUC survey found that three in five (60 per cent) of union reps said their employer had not distributed the benefits of climate change savings to their workforce or to other energy initiatives, while only 7 per cent had received some financial incentives for engaging in environmental activity. While some union reps were able to point to tangible improvements in their pay and conditions arising from green improvements, others suggested that their employers were simply pocketing the financial gains of carbon emissions reductions. A Prospect rep in one ministry summed this up in pithy fashion: 'No bonuses, just a rollicking if you leave kit turned on!' GMB reps at one large engineering firm said the gains accrued to the company only, while Unison reps in a water company reported 'nothing to benefit the worker'. Within one government department, PCS reps reported that there were 'no bonuses or no time off for going green. All pay is subject to work-related performance management pay, but the green issue has not been taken on board. This has been raised a number of times during pay negotiations' (TUC 2009c: 24–5). Concerns about the distribution of gains and losses between workers and employers suggest deeper conflicts of interest over climate politics.

Disagreements crystallised over car parking. The 2009 TUC survey found that in central government, local government, the health service and higher education, some employers introduced parking charges, parking restrictions or removed car allowances, often justified as 'green measures', while failing to provide alternatives. UCU reps in further education expressed this ter-sely: 'Who can use the limited car parking? This has not helped climate change, but has created problems for staff and students for whom public transport cannot help.' They added, 'Not everyone who can use public transport, walk or cycle will or can always do so and not everyone can access public transport and [some] live too far away (for good reasons) to walk or cycle' (ibid.: 36).

Further evidence of divergent interests between union environment reps and their employers on the climate issues came from the TUC survey, which illustrated the problems some of these representatives had and how they often had to struggle against the wishes of their managers to gain an environmental voice at work. Raw comments from reps about proposals made to management on environmental issues included: 'drew a blank', 'rejected', 'ignored', 'refused to implement', 'blocked', 'request not acknowledged', 'declined', 'dismissed', 'no action taken', 'cancelled due to budget restrictions' and 'nothing happened'. In some cases there was 'no buy-in from senior management. Seen as troublemaking'! Management were 'not interested in ideas' and 'don't think it's a priority'. There was a lack of effective consultation, 'lip service – no real commitment'. Another reports that 'the company says it is interested in climate change, but when proposals are put forward by union reps, they are rejected allegedly on cost grounds every time' (ibid.: 35).

These problems were identified even in workplaces that took part in the Green Workplaces projects – those where there was significant management consent for union green initiatives. Reps at Leicester City Council reported 'very limited piecemeal actions, which seem to be more of a token measure', while at Bristol City Council a rep reported that 'very little has been done to adapt my workplace', explaining how workplace temperatures were not regulated, wasting money, burning carbon and making people uncomfortable. At Defra, some reps were unable to get facility time off for an ordinary members' training session, though this was agreed later on, after the problem had been passed up the management chain. Some 15 per cent of reps reported that they had other difficulties in taking up climate change in the workplace, while about 4 per cent said they had been refused time off to attend union training on climate change and environment. Almost three-quarters (73 per cent) of the reps said they did not have facility time for environmental work (ibid.: 36, 39).

The TUC surveys asked about action taken independently by union reps and members in their workplaces. The 2009 survey found that union reps have sometimes taken unilateral action and helped deliver step changes in workplaces, with almost a quarter (23 per cent) of reps saying they had taken independent action (ibid.: 26). This figure may appear to be too small, or simply capture activity such as agreements and committees that were over and above simple engagement with employers' and managers' schemes. Nevertheless, it suggests that union environment reps saw their own activity as something arising from their union and members' interests, rather than just from common interests. Employment relations on climate issues were not uniformly harmonious, but subject to the pressures of consent and coercion. To write environmental reps off as merely a new form of class collaboration would be to miss some important antagonistic aspects of the activity.

Climate representation and union renewal

Vitols *et al.* (2011: 12) argue that trade unions should not be conceived as akin to environmental NGOs. These authors rejected the argument that unions have constructed an environmental role for themselves, one that can help to shape a new sense of union purpose. Rather, they believed that 'the direct interests of employees are largely restricted to such issues as maintaining jobs and social security. Environmental action is something additional to these interests and, until now, has been less pronounced' (ibid.). By contrast, Snell and Fairbrother (2010) and Markey, McIvor and Wright (2014) argued that climate change provides possibilities for unions to renew themselves with a fresh sense of purpose, through the way they organise and through the forms of solidarity they develop to address climate matters.

The UK evidence offers some support for the latter view. Steve Crawshaw, Unison chair of Bristol City Council's green reps committee, said: 'I've had new union members tell me that they only joined the union because they wanted to become a green rep.' He added, 'There has been a far greater appetite amongst rank and file members to get involved with tackling environmental issues than there is for the other traditional trade union work areas. We have no problem recruiting green reps and even had a waiting list initially' (TUC 2010e: 19, 3). There was further evidence from the LRD surveys, which found that union reps who wanted to do environmental work used whatever convenient forms of representation were available to enable them to be effective. Just over half (55 per cent) of respondents were union reps or stewards, while one in five were safety reps. Less than 10 per cent defined themselves solely as environment reps (TUC 2009c: 2, 32; 2012c). However, reps made use of existing structures to negotiate collectively with management, with the joint management–union health and safety committee being the most popular forum for discussing climate-related issues and around a third of the reps taking part in some sort of organised structure.

Of course progress was not linear and many reps faced difficulties. This is illustrated by the experience of union reps at Great Ormond Street Hospital, one of the second wave of Green Workplaces Projects. In recent years 'staff changes have taken their toll' on both management and union sides, while 'the effectiveness of the Joint Environment Committee had fallen away'. For a time, reps felt management were less engaged, while some staff reps left the workplace and were not replaced on the committee. The TUC also had less capacity to provide support after funding came to an end in 2012 (TUC 2014d: 37–8).

Union environmental reps also practised forms of climate solidarity, with other unionised and non-union workers in the UK, and with other workers across the globe affected by climate change. As we saw in Chapters 3 and 4, union environmental reps deliberate on a wide range of climate-related politics in relation to energy, transport and other questions far outside of their immediate work experience. This included support for international, national and local action to combat climate change. And as we will show in Chapter 6, union environmental reps took up support for the Vestas workers, even where their own industries were remote from wind turbine manufacture. Finally, it should be clear that the range of activities union environmental reps engaged in went beyond their own narrow pay and conditions, though these of course had an environmental dimension. One TUC survey asked about their concern for climate change in the context of the economic downturn, which had begun the year before. A very high proportion (44 per cent) said they were more concerned with climate change this year compared with a year ago, while another half (50 per cent) said their concern was about the same. It concluded that 'the sustained interest of union reps in tackling climate change is one of the most remarkable findings of the survey' (TUC 2009c: 26). A subsequent union survey found that nearly 38 per cent of respondents were more still concerned about the environment and climate change than a year before; and 57 per cent said their concern was about the same (TUC 2012c: 34).

Workplace climate representation has also resonated globally, as part of international labour movement renewal. The ETUC launched a Green Workplaces Network, providing training to enable workers to fully engage in these matters with management and promote the extension of information, consultation and participation on environmental performance, energy and resource efficiency. It has produced a European Green Workplaces Handbook and held a European conference in October 2012 involving 100 delegates (TUC 2012b). Belgian trade unions joined a network of environmental organisations and youth movements in the Belgian Climate Coalition, to launch the 'Jobs4Climate' campaign. The coalition calls for worker education and training programmes, and research and development strategies to exist alongside these new opportunities (TUC 2014a).

In 2004, Spanish union federations CC.OO and UGT signed a social dialogue agreement with the Spanish government and employers organisations to jointly implement the commitments and consequences of the Kyoto Protocol (Morales 2006: 25). The agreement aimed to 'prevent, avoid or reduce the potentially adverse social effects that could result from compliance with the Kyoto Protocol, in particular those related to competitiveness and employment' (ibid.). It created an obligation for 'dialogue tables' within seven industrial sectors (ICFTU 2004: 8; 2005: 6). In some regions, such as Navarre in Spain, environmental delegates are designated by tripartite agreement. The delegate can visit businesses to help workers exercise their right to be informed, and to contribute to reducing or eliminating environmental impacts in their workplaces. Collective agreements have been signed with the General Chemical Industry Convention and at the Michelin Company (Nieto 2007: 35).

Workers' climate representation has resonated in other parts of the international labour movement. A Green Workplaces pilot project led by the US communications union IUE-CWA won a Champions for Change Award for its work in training union members to identify energy efficiencies in

manufacturing companies (Pearson 2012). In 2005, the CGT union confederation signed an agreement with the national government of Argentina
to jointly implement agreed measures to address environmental issues,
including the Clean Development Mechanism (ICFTU 2005: 3). Unions in
Peru, CATP, CUT and CGTP, organised a people's summit and trade union-
related events to coincide with COP20 in Lima, according to Luis Isarra
from the Peruvian water union FENTAP (TUC 2014b). Trade union representatives continue to participate in formal climate gatherings as well as
bottom-up mobilisations, at global to workplace scales.

The limits of workers' climate representation

Vitols *et al.* (2011: 22) argue that there is a problem with a union-led project
'when the collective actor representing employees is missing in organisations
because they are not unionised'. In such organisations, 'the prerequisite for
interaction is missing and hence projects are unlikely to be implemented'
(ibid.). UK unions certainly believed that their role had to be revitalised and
expanded if they were to contribute significantly to tackling climate change.
Barber wrote in his Foreword to the 2009 survey:

> Unions are 21st century organisations, relevant to the most vital con-
> cerns of our members and the public. Playing our full part in the fight to
> prevent dangerous climate change is an important part of union renewal,
> bringing new reps into the movement and engaging with the fundamental
> questions of our age.
>
> (TUC 2009c: 2)

This recognised that unions were now starting from a smaller base.

First, with overall union density down from its historic peak of 50 per
cent in 1979 to around half that figure by 2010, UK unions had certainly
been weakened during the neoliberal period. However, the concentration of
trade unionists in the public sector and in larger workplaces (including
among the large energy and transport firms that were big polluters) also
offered the prospect of 'low hanging fruit' – making emissions reductions at
work when the government centrally or locally was the employer or in strategically important basic industries. Second, the relative size of this potential
'carbon army' should not be underestimated. Union representatives still
constituted a major resource. Even the government recognised that there were
still approximately 200,000 workers who acted as lay union representatives. This
was a far larger layer of activists than any of the environmental NGOs, with
far greater connectivity and reach to other workers (BERR 2009: 2). As climate campaigners Haydn Young put it, union reps are vital 'connectors', who
are 'respected, passionate and are important because of the influence that they
have' (SWTUC 2011: 15). At best, the objection adds to the case for loosening
the shackles on unions and giving environmental reps statutory powers.

Vitols *et al.* (2011: 22) highlighted another limitation of climate representation, namely that 'many workplaces can only be "greened" to a limited extent'. Major changes, such as 'fundamental alterations in production processes, or reviewing a company product that might be harmful to the environment, are difficult to change' (ibid.). If this objection means that for now production decisions are in the hands of capital, then it is irrefutable. However, it does not follow that action by other actors is futile. Organised labour is a collective actor with a historic tradition of pushing capital into modifying production relations, such as the shorter working week and better safety conditions. Workers and their union reps have exercised partial control over production, sometimes through institutionalised structures, but at other times more informally. To rule out this power as a possible workplace climate strategy would be premature in light of the experience of environmental reps during the period.

Conclusion

Union climate representation came of age during the first decade of the twenty-first century. Trade union environmental representatives emerged from the more long-standing health and safety representation role, but became defined as a separate function for many different reps as climate politics entered the mainstream. By 2010, a significant breakthrough had been made in the number of union representatives who saw themselves as carrying out an environmental role, whatever formal position they held within union structures. Denied formal, legally defined responsibilities, trade union environmental reps adapted pragmatically, using whatever structures were available, as stewards, safety or learning reps as well as permanent or ad hoc committees, to put climate questions on the workplace bargaining agenda. They proved capable of instigating, directing and supporting significant reductions in workplace carbon emissions (and probably saving millions of pounds) through agreements, committees and events.

Trade union climate representation was initiated by individual unions and supported by the TUC. Although the TUC was a recipient of some government funding, union environmental reps were not a government-backed enterprise. On the contrary, Labour ministers consistently opposed placing union reps' environmental functions on a statutory footing, while supporting their voluntary initiatives. Therefore, union environmental reps cannot be characterised as pensioners or prisoners of neoliberalism. The partnership approach propagated by some unions and the TUC meant that union environment reps often carried out activities inconsistent with government and their employers' objectives on climate-related issues. But few were captive of government or employers' interests and in significant cases, they took up climate issues, even when obstructed by these other actors.

Union climate representation was a radical new direction for trade unionism, expressing both the specific interests of working people on climate change as well as embracing a general interest beyond the immediate workplace context. These union reps did engage in bargaining about the distribution of losses and gains from environmental issues, but they also proposed and supported the introduction of measures with no immediate, sectional benefit to themselves or their members. Union environmental representation offered a genuinely novel contribution to climate politics during this period, suggesting perhaps a surprising potential avenue for sustained action as climate politics became more prominent.

Notes

1 Rikards called for 'legislation to enable a co-ordination of all trade union and management efforts to combat industrial pollution' at the 1972 TUC Environment Conference (TUC 1972: 39).
2 The author was employed by Labour Research Department (LRD) during the period and carried out an environmental reps survey in 2007 and the subsequent 2009 TUC survey. The role also meant speaking to key union actors, attending TUSDAC and providing input into TUC and other union publications and events. The 2007 survey (LRD 2007a) received 677 responses and found a 'real appetite' among union reps for work on environmental and climate issues. The following survey (TUC 2009c) received 1,301 responses, while a further survey received 1,208 responses (TUC 2012c: 5). These surveys were self-selecting and not a representative sample of union reps' activity. Therefore care has to be taken with quantitative generalisation from the results. However. these surveys were indicative of a range of union reps' attitudes, behaviours and activities and recorded some interesting qualitative comments and assessments made by these representatives.
3 Overlapping with the national projects, the TUC in the South-West of England started its own Green Workplaces project in 2008. When the project finished in 2010, the evaluation report claimed that it had 'briefed over 920 individuals on its work and on why climate change is a trade union issue' (SWTUC 2011: 8).
4 An amusing example took place at a TUSDAC meeting in 2007, when Defra officials presented their plans for 'environmental engagement'. This showed a triangle, consisting of government, business and individuals/society. When asked by somewhat irritated participants about the omission of unions, Defra officials first suggested it was with employers, before conceding that in fact unions were in all three.
5 This was in sharp contrast to earlier Labour Party promises. John Edmonds (TUC 1991a: 438) told TUC Congress in 1991 that,

> We want in environmental issues the right to inspect, the right to information and the right to training. I am delighted to say that the Labour Party shares our belief in green rights and argues that these green rights for employees should apply in every European Community state.

Labour's policy statement, *An Earthly Chance*, stated that 'trade unions should have the right for time off to receive training in environmental matters' (Labour Party 1990: 13). Labour's statement, *In Trust for Tomorrow*, retreated from the earlier enthusiasm, but pledged that a Labour government would 'introduce a statutory obligation for companies to consult their workforce over environmental issues, in just the same way as they currently have to consult on health and safety matters; indeed, the two areas are often hard to distinguish'. It would also 'introduce protection for "whistleblowers" who reveal that a company is breaking environmental laws' and give employees 'the right to refuse work that will lead to environmental damage in contravention of regulatory requirements' (Labour Party 1994: 51–2).

6 The Green Party of England and Wales supported statutory trade union environmental rights at its conference in September 2008 and included the demand in its election manifesto in 2010 (Green Party 2008; 2010).

7 The author was a workshop speaker in support of statutory rights for trade union environment representatives at the 9 February 2008 and 7 March 2009 Campaign against Climate Change trade union conferences. The Campaign against Climate Change organised further conferences for union reps on 13 March 2010, 8 June 2013 and 20 September 2014.

References

Benn, H. (1992) 'Green Negotiating: The MSF Approach'. In D. Owen (ed.) *Green Reporting: Accountancy and the Challenge of the Nineties*. London: Chapman & Hall.

BERR (2007) *Workplace Representatives: A Review of their Facilities and Facility Time: Government Response to Public Consultation*. London: BERR.

——(2009) *How Workplaces Can Gain From Modern Union Representation*, May. London: BERR.

BIS (2010) *Green Workplaces: Greening the Work Environment, Union Modernisation Fund. July 2010*. London: Department for Business, Innovation and Skills.

Cox, A, Higgins, T., Gloster, R., Foley, B. and Darnton, A. (2012) *The Impact of Workplace Initiatives on Low Carbon Behaviours*. Edinburgh: Scottish Government.

ETUC (2012) *Green Workplaces: A Guide for Union Representatives*. Brussels: ETUC.

Green Party (2008) 'Greens Back TUC in Call for Environmental Reps', press release, 9 September.

——(2010) *Fair Is Worth Fighting For: Green Party General Election Manifesto 2010*. London: Green Party.

Hatch, K. (2014) 'Plymouth Council Staff Become the City's New "Green Army" – and Get Green Reps Facilities', *Green Workplaces News*, May.

ICFTU (2004) *Securing Consensus through Social & Employment Transition for Climate Change: Trade Union Statement to COP10, Buenos Aires, Argentina, (6–17 December, 2004)*. Brussels: ICFTU.

——(2005) *Preventing Disruption & Enhancing Community Cohesion Social & Employment Transition for Climate Change Trade Union Statement to COP11/MOP14 Montréal, Canada (29 November–9 December, 2005)*. Brussels: ICFTU.

Labour Party (1990) *An Earthly Chance. Labour's Programme for a Cleaner, Greener Britain, a Safer, Sustainable Planet. NEC Statement*. London: The Labour Party.

——(1994) *In Trust for Tomorrow: Report of the Labour Party Policy Commission on the Environment*. London: The Labour Party.

LRD (2007a) *The Environment and Climate Change: A Guide for Union Reps*, June. London: LRD.

——(2007b) 'Unions Seek More Green Involvement', *Labour Research*, June.

——(2009) 'Climate Change and the Workplace', *Workplace Report*, June.

Lewis, A. and Juravle, C. (2010) 'Morals, Markets and Sustainable Investments: A Qualitative Study of "Champions"', *Journal of Business Ethics*, 93(3): 483–94.

Markey, R., McIvor, J. and Wright, C. (2014) *Climate Change and the Australian Workplace. Final Report for the Australian Department of Industry on State of Knowledge on Climate Change, Work and Employment*. Sydney: Centre for Workforce Futures, Macquarie University.

McIlroy, J. (2009) 'Under Stress but Still Enduring: The Contentious Alliance in the Age of Tony Blair and Gordon Brown'. In G. Daniels and J. McIlroy (eds) *Trade Unions in a Neoliberal World: British Trade Unions under New Labour*. London: Routledge.

McIlroy, J. and Daniels, G. (2009) 'An Anatomy of British Trade Unionism since 1997: Organization, Structure and Factionalism'. In G. Daniels and J. McIlroy (eds) *Trade Unions in a Neoliberal World: British Trade Unions under New Labour*. London: Routledge.

Morales, J. (2006) *Labour and Environment: Some Experiences of Spanish Trade Unions in Environment*. Madrid: CC.OO.

Nattrass, S. (1999) *Union Workplace Involvement in Environmental Issues: Report to the Trade Union Sustainable Development Advisory Committee, October 1999*. London: TUC.

Nieto, J. (2007) 'The Trade Union Movement and Environmental Participation: Shaping the Change, Renewing Trade Unionism'. In UNEP, *Labour and the Environment: A Natural Synergy*. Nairobi: UNEP.

Pearson, P. (2011) 'ACAS' Green Blind Spot'? *Touchstone Blog*, 13 September.

——(2012) 'President Obama Award for US Greenworkplace Project'! *Touchstone Blog*, 17 April.

——(2014a) 'Green Reps at Work Gaining More Support', *Touchstone Blog*, 28 May.

——(2014b) 'Good Week for the Green Economy', *Touchstone Blog*, 27 June.

Rogers, K. (2012) 'Greening the Workplace at Port of Felixstowe', *Stronger Unions Blog*, 30 October.

Snell, D. and Fairbrother, P. (2010) 'Unions as Environmental Actors', *Transfer: European Review of Labour and Research*, 16(3): 411–24.

Swaffield, J. and Bell, D. (2012) 'Can "Climate Champions" Save the Planet? A Critical Reflection on Neoliberal Social Change', *Environmental Politics*, 21(2): 248–67.

SWTUC (2011) *Green Workplaces Project Report and Evaluation, 2008–2011*, March. Bristol: South West TUC.

TUC (1972) *Workers and the Environment: Report of a TUC Conference Held at Congress House on July 6 1972*. London: TUC.

——(1988) *Congress 1988: General Council Report*. London: TUC.

——(1989a) *Congress Report 1989*. London: TUC.

——(1989b) *Towards a Charter for the Environment: General Council Statement to the 1989 Trade Union Congress*. London: TUC.

——(1990) *Congress Report 1990*. London: TUC.

——(1991a) *Congress Report 1991*. London: TUC.

——(1991b) *Industry, Jobs and the Environmental Challenge: A Memorandum by the TUC to the National Economic Development Council, May 1991*. London: TUC.

——(1998) *Environment, Sustainable Development and Multi-Stakeholders: The Implications of Kyoto – Conference Report*. London: TUC.

——(2000a) *Congress 2000: General Council Report*. London: TUC.

——(2000b) 'Trade Union Involvement in Environmental Decision Making at Enterprise Level', *TUC Mail*, January.

——(2002) *TUC Environment Survey*. London: Prospect.

——(2006a) *Congress 2006: General Council Report*. London: TUC.

——(2006b) *Congress Report 2006*. London: TUC.

——(2007a) *Congress 2007: General Council Report*. London: TUC.

——(2007b) *Workplace Representatives: A Review of their Facilities and Facility Time: TUC Response to the DTI Consultation Document*. March. London: TUC.

——(2008a) *Congress 2008: General Council Report*. London: TUC.

——(2008b) *TUC Green Workplaces Project 2006–07: Objectives and Outcomes Report*. London: TUC.

——(2009a) *Congress 2009: General Council Report*. London: TUC.

——(2009b) *Congress Report 2009*. London: TUC.

——(2009c) *Unions and Climate Change*. London: LRD.

——(2009d) *Targeting Climate Change: A TUC Education Workbook for Trade Unionists, June*. London: TUC.

——(2010a) *Congress 2010: General Council Report*. London: TUC.

——(2010b) *GreenWorkplaces News. February*. London: TUC.

——(2010c) *Green Workplaces News. March*. London: TUC.

——(2010d) *GreenWorks: TUC Green Workplaces Project Report 2008–10. March*. London: TUC.

——(2010e) *Greener Deals: Negotiating Environmental Issues at Work*. London: TUC.

——(2011a) *Congress 2011: General Council Report*. London: TUC.

——(2011b) 'UK's Leading Green Workplaces to Share Secrets of Success at TUC Climate Conference', *Green Workplaces News*, June.

——(2011c) *Green Workplaces News. June*. London: TUC.

——(2011d) 'First UK Online Network for Green Union Reps Goes Live', press release, 25 February.

——(2012a) 'Unions Are Making a Green Difference at Work', press release, 2 July.

——(2012b) 'European GreenWorkplaces Conference: Team GB Shine at Brussels Conference', *Green Workplaces Newsletter*, October.

——(2012c) *Green Unions at Work 2012*. London: LRD.

——(2013a) 'Community Reps Get Active at Tata Steel's Pipe Mill in Hartlepool', *Green Workplaces News*, January.

——(2013b) 'New Green Reps Gain Facility Time at Babcock International', *Green Workplaces News*, December.

——(2014a) 'Belgian Climate Coalition Launches Jobs4Climate Campaign', *Green Workplaces News*, May.

——(2014b) 'Unions Fight for Sustainability and Justice in Peru', *Green Workplaces News*, May.

——(2014c) 'Stockport UNISON Secures Agreement on Climate Change and the Environment', *Green Workplaces News*, June.

——(2014d) *The Union Effect: Greening the Workplace*. London: TUC.

TUSDAC (2005a) *Greening the Workplace: A Report by the TUSDAC Unions, June 2005*. London: TUSDAC.

——(2005b) *Facilities, Rights and Time-Off for Union Representatives*. London: TUSDAC.

——(2006) *Trade Union Representatives: Rights and Responsibilities, TUSDAC Policy Group, 30 March 2006*. London: TUSDAC.

——(2007) *Workplace Environmental Representatives: Their Facilities and Facility Time. March*. London: TUSDAC.

Vitols, K., Schütze, K., Mestre, A., Chavanet, S., Marquant, S., Poupard, J-F. and Jakubowski, A. (2011) *Industrial Relations and Sustainability: The Role of Social Partners in the Transition Towards a Green Economy, European Foundation for the Improvement of Living and Working Conditions, 29 June 2011*. Dublin: Eurofound.

Wicks, M. (2007) 'Environmental Workplace Reps?' *Solidarity Magazine*, 20, June–August.

6   The Vestas occupation and climate politics

Introduction

In July–August 2009, the contemporary confluence of trade unionism and climate activism reached its high point, when Vestas wind turbine manufacturing workers occupied their factory on the Isle of Wight. Although the occupation did not ultimately keep the plant open, the protest gave rise to innovative acts of climate solidarity and put the firm and government's climate politics under the spotlight. The Vestas occupation raises a number of interesting political questions beyond the narrative, impact and outcome of the immediate events. It was also a good example of a struggle where social media played a significant role.[1]

The Vestas occupation represents perhaps the best contemporary UK example to date of working-class climate politics and the potential for climate solidarity, an experience that challenges the dominant paradigms of neoliberalism and ecological modernisation. The first section examines the reasons given to justify the occupation and discusses why it took place. The second section assesses the significance of the Vestas occupation for various climate actors, including renewable capital, government ministers, environmentalists and the trade union movement. The third section examines whether the Vestas struggle heralded the beginning of a new alliance of social movements or a more profound fusion.

Vestas: class and climate change

The Vestas occupation reconstructed

The Isle of Wight is for the most part staunchly Conservative, with very little history of class struggle or climate activism. Patrick Rolfe, one of the young socialist climate activists who helped spark the Vestas events, recounted that at the time of these events, the island had one Labour councillor, no branch of any left group and an inactive Green Party (Rolfe 2009b). Yet on Monday 20 July 2009, a group of around 20 workers occupied the St Cross Vestas factory. One participant, Ian Terry said: 'At one point we had about 50 people ready to occupy. But we were rushed into going in.' Another occupier Mike Godley said that they originally planned to go into work with leaflets announcing the occupation on the Tuesday, but were 'grassed up' (SWP 2009e).[2]

Workers outside the plant organised swiftly to meet the threats made by the company and the police to end the occupation. As several hundred workers milled around on 21 July, RMT transport and energy union officials were crucial in helping the outside workers to get organised. One of the committee members brought his camper van to the site and it became the committee office. The main spokespeople were two workers from the factory, Steve Stotesbury and Sean McDonagh. They also organised a 'families and community committee' to support the workers (Thomas 2009a).

The occupation immediately faced threats, which took a variety of forms. The Isle of Wight-based *VentnorBlog* reported that one of the occupying workers, Sebastian Sikora, had seen police inside the building dressed in riot gear (Perry 2009q). Vestas management threatened to send private security personnel to storm the premises to evict the workers, warning that if they did not leave the building they would be arrested, sacked and lose their redundancy payments (Perry 2009t). Vestas management offered food to the occupiers – but only on the condition that they left the building and wouldn't go back in again (Perry 2009r). Workers occupying the building responded by making a new banner – 'Starved to saved green jobs' (Perry 2009s). Vestas worker Doug Green waited four hours to deliver food to the occupying workers, but was not permitted to take it in. The blockade was overcome by what became known as the 'mass pasty trespass', when 20 people walked past police and private security to deliver supplies (Sophielle 2009). Later Vestas management took control of food deliveries, but complained that they were not running a Michelin restaurant. But RMT General Secretary Bob Crow criticised the 'starvation rations', pointing out that workers 'fighting for their livelihoods and for the future of turbine manufacture in England' were being treated 'far worse than the prisoners just up the road at Parkhurst who are legally entitled to three square meals a day' (RMT 2009d).

A week after the occupation began, Vestas managers escalated the dispute. First, *The Guardian* reported on 28 July how managers sent the remaining occupiers a nasty surprise with a slice of pizza: letters telling workers they had been sacked with immediate effect and without compensation (Walker, P. 2009). On 29 July, the firm went to court to evict them. However, Vestas had failed to serve the notices properly and the judge adjourned the case for a week, handing the workers and their supporters (much to their delight) a further opportunity to spread their message (Perry 2009c; 2009u). Mike Godley said that before the occupation, management had not completed all the one-to-one consultations. Some workers were not happy with the settlements being offered and the majority had refused to sign. The prolonged occupation meant all workers (except the 11 still inside) continued to receive full pay until the extended consultation period ended (on 12 August). Some workers benefited particularly in another respect, as they qualified for an extra week or two weeks redundancy money, when previously they had fallen just a few days shy of the threshold for enhanced payments (Perry 2009d).

On 4 August, Vestas bosses finally won their possession order in court. Of the remaining ten workers (one had already left due to ill-health), four walked out a few hours after the verdict. The remaining six departed on Friday 7 August, some 18 days after they first had occupied the building (Perry 2009h). Some exits were spectacular. Ian Terry and Mark Flower abseiled down the side of the building, while Jaymie Rigby jumped 30ft from the balcony (Perry 2009i). Although there was a brief trespass of the grounds on 8 August by around 200 people, the occupation was over. On 14 August Vestas paid the outstanding wages and redundancy money into the bank accounts of the majority of workers (Foster 2009b). On 22 September, police cleared the 'camp' at the marine gate of the factory, so the remaining blades could be removed (Perry 2009m).

The occupation justified

Why did Vestas workers occupy their workplace when they did? How did the workers justify their actions? Was it simply to protest at their redundancy, or the terms of it – or was there something wider involved, including climate change? Hyman (2010: 5) notes that Vestas was the last of a spurt of workplace occupations in Britain and Ireland during 2009, with sit-ins at the Waterford Crystal factory, Visteon car parts manufacturer and Prisme Packaging. Gall (2011: 613–14) examines the motivation, objectives and outcomes of these occupations comparatively, bringing out some of the special features of the Vestas occupation. In general, the foundations for occupation are aspects of consciousness, whereby collective anger leads to the collective hope of resolution through collective action. Gall argues that the general stimuli to occupy are: first, the collectivised experience of compulsory redundancy; second, the immediate and unforeseen nature of redundancy; third, the loss of deferred wages and compensation; fourth, some pre-existing collective organisation and, finally, a positive demonstration effect. Each of these reasons can be understood on the terrain of working-class politics.

The economic, geographical, political and employment relations contexts help to explain what drove some workers to take militant action in July–August 2009 and to galvanise others to solidarity with them. Vestas was then the largest wind turbine manufacturer in the world. The firm emerged to command 40 per cent of global market share by the end of the 1990s (Ryland 2010). Its balance sheet certainly appeared healthy. In 2008, revenue reached €6 billion (£5.6 billion) and operating profits for the year were €668 million (£620 million), 51 per cent higher than the previous year. Globally,

Vestas employed over 20,000 workers, almost double the numbers contracted just three years previously (Vestas 2009: 6–7).

At the beginning of 2009, Vestas employed over 600 workers on three sites in England. Around 500 were employed at the St Cross factory in Newport on the Isle of Wight manufacturing wind turbines, while 50 were employed at a separate research and development facility on the island and another 100 were employed at a distribution site in Southampton. The St Cross facility was a purpose-built, deliberate location. Workers skilled at making strong and light yachts, famously sailed during Cowes Week on the Isle of Wight, had adapted those skills to produce distinctive onshore wood composite wind turbines, which Vestas believed it could sell in Europe and North America. The firm also developed prototype blades from reinforced plastic and carbon fibre (Marsh 2001: 19). After Vestas merged with NEC Micon in 2004, the St Cross facility became part of Vestas Blades UK, 'forging ahead' with the development of its new 49m blade (Marsh 2006: 52).

The economic climate also appeared conducive to the firm's continued growth. Despite the global economic downturn in 2007, the firm made plans to expand towards what it called the triple 15 – which meant 15 per cent operating profits and €15 billion revenue by 2015. It was confident that a global climate agreement expected in Copenhagen in 2009 would produce profitable opportunities for wind turbine manufacturers. The European Union had set ambitious targets for 20 per cent emissions reductions and 20 per cent of energy from renewables by 2020. Vestas management was also encouraged by Labour government announcements of an imminent 'low-carbon industrial revolution' and a more interventionist strategy of support for green industries, a change of emphasis welcomed by TUC leaders.

Therefore the closure announcement came as a considerable shock to workers at the factory. There is little doubt that Vestas workers were motivated to act by the prospect of imminent redundancy and concerns about compensation. The 'Statement from a Vestas worker' placed on the *Save Vestas Blog* (SVB) – the semi-official website of the campaign, stated that workers were confident despite the recession that renewable energy jobs would be created, not lost. They were therefore 'horrified to find out that our jobs were moving to America', finding it 'hard to stomach as the government are getting away with claiming they are investing heavily in these types of industry' (SVB 2009a). Shortly after they occupied Vestas management offices in the building, one of the workers, Luke Paxton, told the *VentnorBlog* (Perry 2009b) that redundancy pay arrangements had been held up at the last minute and workers were very worried about their livelihoods.

Gall (2011: 617) recognises a distinctive feature of the Vestas occupation: 'a more overtly political dimension existed in the workers' motivation'. Many had been attracted to work at the plant because of the desire to produce green technologies for green energy. At a protest on 11 July, occupier Mark Smith said, 'I've been here seven years. Getting another job will mean moving my family off the island.' He urged people to 'join us and stand up for themselves and their jobs – and the environment, the planet. This is about the future for our kids' (Walker, T. 2009a). Mike Godley later told *The Guardian* it was crazy for ministers to make statements about green energy and green jobs and at the same time this factory was closing. He said it would be 'a tiny step financially to keep this factory open, but it would be a huge statement about the government's commitment to the green economy. Just as they could not afford to let the banks fail, they can't afford to let this fail. It's about the history of humanity' (Weaver and Morris 2009).

The synthesis of personal occupational interest with wider climate concerns was well summed up in the speaker notes used by the 'outside' workers to spread the message at meetings across the UK. The Vestas workers' notes said workers quickly realised that they were 'at the centre of a perfect storm', a golden opportunity to seize the factory and force the issues of 'green energy, massive job losses and corporate responsibility' into the international spotlight. They heralded the solidarity given as 'truly global, sweeping across the planet and uniting environmentalists, workers and union movements as one force'. The Vestas factory occupation combines 'two wills in one fight – for a cleaner, safer future [and] a future with jobs for all' (Morris 2009b). The climate aspect was still evident in statements made after the occupation had finished.

Ian Terry came to the island from London to get an environmentally friendly job. He said 'when I finally got in, I thought I'd done something special ... I was an environmental rep'. Similarly, Mike Godley added: 'Before the occupation, climate change wasn't big on my agenda. Paying the bills, providing for my family – that was my motivation. But now it's opened my eyes to the bigger picture' (SWP 2009e). Leanne Godley told journalists that the campaign 'has never been about one agenda. It is about saving the local economy with green jobs, fighting capitalism and helping climate change. This is what makes it so important' (Perry 2009j). These comments indicate elements of climate class consciousness, as set out in Chapter 2. However, these are mixed with ecological modernist reasons for action, centred on green technology.

Employment relations at the St Cross factory before the occupation were vexed. Workers told Patrick Rolfe that there was an unofficial but widely used 'three-strikes and out' policy: three small contraventions of the rules meant the sack. Workers reported management bullying if they called in sick and that they were only allowed to take the second half of a day off, never the first. The regional Unite official said his predecessor had approached management, who said they didn't want a union and so little effort was put into organising the plant. Just before the occupation, the Health and Safety Executive had successfully prosecuted Vestas after 13 employees suffered dermatitis caused by exposure to epoxy resin (TUC 2009b). Although some had joined Unite as individual members, there was no representative structure other than an ineffective works council. Unite did not have sufficient confidence to instigate statutory union recognition procedures. In a subsequent investigation, Gall (2011: 611) found that 'there was a very small degree of existing unionisation' at the St Cross plant before the occupation.

The wider employment relations context was also characterised by a handful of workplace occupations, including by workers at two Visteon car components plants in early 2009. This encouraged some at Vestas to believe that industrial action could improve terms. Visteon workers also showed a degree of climate consciousness, issuing a statement: 'Our skills – we can make anything in plastic – should be used to make increasingly needed parts for green products: bike and trailer parts, solar panels, turbines, recycling bins, etc.' (Neale 2010: 45). Visteon union reps also provided advice and guidance to some Vestas workers prior to the occupation, which acted as a catalyst for action.

Vestas was therefore somewhat peculiar, since previous union organisation was virtually non-existent. However, the intervention of socialist climate activists as well as the Visteon model as a 'demonstration effect' helped coalesce the collective will to occupy. The Vestas case highlights 'the supportive and conducive nature of political networks and communities of collectivism in constructing and mobilising actions' (Gall 2011: 619). There is substantial evidence to support this interpretation: in particular, socialist climate activists were pivotal role to galvanising Vestas workers to take action, raising political demands and advising on industrial tactics – in other words in raising specifically working-class politics.[3]

Rolfe described how socialist activists from Workers' Climate Action (WCA) and the Alliance for Workers' Liberty (AWL) visited the Isle of Wight on 15–18 June, because they had heard that the Vestas plant faced closure. He reported that after four days' work, they had 'a meeting set up, sponsored by Cowes Trades Council, to launch a campaign against the closure'. They made contact with trade union officials, Labour councillor Geoff Lumley and local environmental activists. They went to the factory at shift changes, 'talked to workers, and made contacts' (Rolfe 2009a). On 3 July, WCA and Cowes Trades Council held a public meeting, which was attended by around 100 people opposed to the closure of the plant. The activists reported that the room was 'packed with workers from the factory', as well as people from the wider community. By the end of the meeting, 'there were people seriously discussing the tactic of a factory occupation to save jobs and force much-needed investment in wind energy' (Rolfe 2009b).

Ed Maltby, another socialist activist involved and one of the speakers at the meeting, recalled that when workers started looking disgruntled and leaving in disgust after a speech by a Unite official, who only offered to help with signing on, he remembered something the Visteon speaker Ron Clark said about the importance of identifying potential leaders. Maltby went around taking numbers, making contacts, talking to workers about things that could be done next, like building up a telephone list and sounding out people on the shop floor. Maltby also explained the activists' motivation. They chose to intervene at Vestas because they saw 'workers' control as central to an agency for solving ecological crisis'. They drew analogies between 'capitalist environmental degradation and capitalist-workplace degradation of workers' bodies, we were able to respond intelligently to a lot of the issues raised ... [giving] the notion of workers' struggle as an agency real grip' (AWL 2009g).[4]

Dan Rawnsley, another key activist involved in leafleting the factory and organising the 3 July public meeting, recalled the assessment in early July that there seemed to be only a 20 per cent chance of an occupation taking place (Rawnsley 2009). Other reports in the socialist press suggested that the campaign against the closure had stepped up with mass leafleting and petitioning on 11 July (Walker, T. 2009b; Norman 2009). Some 50 people turned up in Newport in solidarity with the Vestas workers, with delegations from the RMT, Unison, and from Southampton, Plymouth and Ryde trade councils (SVB 2009b). Activists used a visit by Prince Charles to the island on 17 July to raise the public profile of the campaign, holding up banners and collecting more signatures (SVB 2009c).

Workers formed a committee and discussed plans for direct action. The demand was formulated for Vestas 'to hand over the plant to the government, and for the government to continue production by nationalising the plant under new management'. Vestas was also distinctive in terms of its more radical aims (AWL 2009a, 2009b). Although Vestas workers did not develop a sophisticated conception of workers' control, their demand for the government to nationalise the plant went further than the other occupations of that period. This challenge to property relations is further evidence that the Vestas occupation should be understood as a class struggle, as defined in Chapter 2.

The positive involvement of outsiders in terms of political ideology and organisation raises the question of whether socialist activists substituted for workers' leadership. Although Vestas management and some other local people suggested outside agitators had led the workers on, the participants themselves didn't see it that way. Mike Godley was specifically asked about it by journalists shortly after the occupation had finished. He made it very clear that 'the campaign has been no way "taken over" and continues to be driven by ex-Vestas workers'. He said the workers 'hugely appreciate the support that they've received from the outside groups and will continue to work with them to keep the fight going for more green jobs to be created on the Island' (Perry 2009l). Another Vestas worker, Tracey Yeates, summed up the interaction positively: 'What's made the difference? I suppose at the start it was because you, the activists from outside, showed us how we could do something. Then we had our own way of doing things. If everyone puts their own unique bit in, it makes a bigger picture, doesn't it?' (AWL 2009e).

The Vestas occupation and climate solidarity

One measure of the impact of the Vestas occupation was the wide range of solidarity it generated, on the Isle of Wight itself, in the rest of the UK and to a limited extent internationally too. Vestas workers and their supporters had already planned for public demonstrations and meetings before the occupation started. However, once the occupation had begun, a permanent camp was established outside the factory – on the 'magic roundabout' – which served as the base for solidarity activity on the island (SVB 2009d). There were regular meetings of supporters outside the Vestas factory twice a day – at 10.30 a.m. and 5 p.m., under a gazebo (SVB 2009f). Some of the activity was based around sustaining the occupiers inside the factory. The 'mass pasty trespass' on 22 July involved climate activists rushing the factory to deliver food to the occupying workers, and helped to break the blockade imposed by Vestas management. On 30 July, another stunt involved a group of people wearing costumes and laden with carrier bags disguised to look as though they were carrying food, squeezing through the fence and making a dash for the front door. Meanwhile, two others were hiding in adjacent bushes. They waited for the right moment of distraction, and then delivered the food (Perry 2009e). Other actions occurred at local benefit offices and at the local MP's constituency office (Perry 2009k).

Probably the most spectacular act of solidarity took place on the morning of the second court appearance, when Climate Camp activists and an RMT member occupied the roof of another Vestas site in East Cowes. They hung a banner saying 'Vestas Workers – Solidarity in Occupation. Save Green Jobs', which was on show to international sailors during Cowes Week (Perry 2009g). The final acts of solidarity took place to try to secure the redundancy payments for the 11 final occupiers. Some workers and supporters set up camp at the marine gate of the St Cross factory, to try to prevent Vestas management from removing the last remaining blades, which could only be moved by barge (AWL 2009f). This was briefly successful: for over a month after the occupation, the blades did not leave the plant (Godley and Morris 2009).

Solidarity with the Vestas occupation was not confined to the island – it was also evident in other parts of the UK and to a limited extent elsewhere. Vicki Morris, one of the socialists who maintained the *Save Vestas Blog*, reported that on 25 July and 28 July, activists protested outside Vestas' headquarters in Warrington (Morris 2009f). Messages of support were sent to Vestas workers, notably from others involved in workplace occupations and industrial disputes, such as the Visteon plants, the Lindsey Strike Committee and Thomas Cook (Morris 2009c; 2009d; 2009e). One telling intervention took place when Vestas workers challenged Ed Miliband at a public meeting of 600 people at Oxford Town Hall on 27 July. Vestas worker Dave Hughes addressed the meeting and challenged Miliband over failing to nationalise the firm (Dwyer 2009). On 31 July, Gerry Byrne organised a Save Vestas protest on the fourth plinth in Trafalgar Square, as part of Antony Gormley's *One and Other* art project, while Billy Bragg dedicated songs to the Vestas workers (SVB 2009e; Perry 2009f). The Campaign against Climate Change organised a number of lobbies, pickets and meetings around Vestas (Robinson 2009; Morris 2009g).

Imaginative direct action was a particularly notable feature of the solidarity protests around Vestas and targeted government bodies. On 3 August, solidarity activists 'donning red, black and green clothing to symbolise their diverse political viewpoints' glued themselves together outside DECC's offices in London. Molly Grayson told reporters that 'climate change has to be tackled and in a recession green jobs should be the last to go' (Brooks 2009c). Members of the Climate Rush campaign group chained themselves to Business Secretary Peter Mandelson's home on 10 August. Ellie Robson told journalists: 'If we're going to have a low-carbon Britain then we need our government to support these workers, rather than forcing the closure of their factory and the loss of their jobs' (Press Association 2009). Another dramatic act of solidarity came late in the campaign, when protesters scaled up cranes in Southampton docks that were to be used to lift the last remaining Vestas blades onto the barges (Perry 2009y).

Activists in at least 25 towns and cities across Britain organised solidarity on the first Vestas national day of action on 12 August, according to *Socialist Worker* (SWP 2009c; 2009d). WCA members occupied the offices of the South East England Development Agency in Guildford, Surrey (Morris 2009j). At least 12 Vestas support groups were established. WCA activists organised four Vestas-related workshops at the Climate Camp, which began in London on 26 August. These were on women and the miners' strike; climate change as a class issue; Visteon, Lindsey, Lucas and worker-led just transition; and the occupation itself (Morris 2009m; 2009n). Vestas workers toured the UK, speaking on a number of platforms. A second national day of action took place on 17 September, with events in at least eight cities (Brooks 2009d). Activists also reported that a teachers' pack had been produced (Terry 2009a).

Solidarity was not confined to the UK. Soon after the occupation began, the *Save Vestas Blog* posted messages of support received from across the globe, including from Chile, France, Germany, Greece, South Korea and the USA (Alex 2009; Morris 2009a; 2009i; 2009k). Potentially the most important act of solidarity came from Scandinavia. On 24 July, it was reported that more than 30 protesters had gathered outside Vestas' northern Europe headquarters in Malmö, Sweden (SWP 2009a). The company sent workers home and closed its office for the day in response. A week later, Vestas workers in Copenhagen sent a message of support to the occupation, which was read out to cheers on the Isle of Wight. The Danish workers said that the factory 'should be run under workers' control, as it is only workers who can' (SWP 2009b). Despite the end of the protests on the island, the closure of the factory became an issue at the Copenhagen climate summit (7–18 December 2009). WCA activists invaded a Vestas drinks reception, chanting slogans and handing out leaflets. Ian Terry spoke at the protest and at other meetings on the fringe of the summit (Rawnsley 2010).

Altogether, the climate solidarity that developed around the Vestas occupation was transformative, in the sense defined by labour geographers.

Vestas workers and their supporters confronted class relations beyond the confines of their particular locale. They did not seek privileges or special protection, but rather challenged existing relations of ownership and control. The class interests of the workers' continued employment coincided with the wider climate necessity to develop low-carbon renewable energy sources. This helps explain why this particular struggle resonated so widely at the time.

Trade union responses to the Vestas occupation

The trade union movement in the UK was historically supportive of the development of renewable energy, particularly because it promised thousands of skilled jobs. At the turn of the century, trade unionists welcomed Environment Minister Michael Meacher's announcement that some 300 wind farms would be in place by 2010 (TUSDAC 2001). The TUC's *Greening the Workplace* report forecast up to 30,000 new jobs in the UK's renewables sector in the following decade, though it recognised that 'the number of jobs secured depends on how much manufacturing takes place in the UK' (TUSDAC 2005a: 21). Although a workers' occupation might be expected to produce straightforward solidarity from the trade union movement, in fact, responses to the Vestas closure were far from homogeneous. Therefore, the occupation also provides a useful barometer of the depth and extent of union climate politics.

Unite: between class and the market

Unite, and its predecessor Amicus, was the only union organising among Vestas' manufacturing workers before the occupation. In 2004, Amicus members gained recognition at the Vestas plant in Scotland. Following an 11-month campaign, workers at Vestas Celtic Wind Technology, which manufactured wind turbines for Scottish Power and Powergen, voted overwhelmingly in favour of union recognition, which the union claimed was the first vote of its kind in the UK's emerging renewables sector. It claimed that political pressure on the Scottish Executive secured Vestas a special grant and financial incentives to set up Vestas Wind Technology in Campbeltown (TUSDAC 2005b: 8). Amicus said the recognition deal signalled that as traditional industries declined, the union was successful in 'gaining a foothold in the new cutting edge manufacturing sector'. Dougie Rooney, Amicus National Officer, promised that the union would be 'working with the management team to make the business a success'. The union wanted to see 'good conditions for our members and job security, and in return we will cooperate by agreement in increasing productivity' (Amicus 2004).

However, the recognition agreement did not extend to the Isle of Wight facility. By the time of the occupation, Unite had as few as 15 members at the St Cross facility and management were considered hostile to unions

(Rolfe 2009a). Phil Blair, a member of the stewards' committee, said: 'People who have tried to organise unions here have been penalised, basically – put under pressure, pulled up under other pretexts' (AWL 2009d). As Vestas worker, 'Matt', explained, the firm was 'extremely anti-union and some workers who have joined unions in the past have been singled out and fired on various grounds'. The nearest thing to a union was 'a consultation network imposed by European law, where supposedly elected representatives (but in reality hand-picked by management) attended meetings' (Morris 2009b). Unite had made only limited efforts to unionise the Isle of Wight facility. Ian Terry said he had spoken to a local Unite official to try to unionise the plant and 'was pretty much told in no uncertain terms that it wasn't going to be achieved' (Terry 2009b). By 2009, there was very little in the way of solid union membership, organisation or representation.

Three weeks after the redundancies were announced, Unite Deputy General Secretary Jack Dromey joined a TUC delegation to discuss Vestas with Ed Miliband on 19 May. At the meeting, Unite asked the Westminster government to follow the example of the Scottish Parliament, which had recently invested £10 million in the Skykon site. Dromey articulated the union's case in ecological modernisation terms, arguing that closure would be 'a disaster from the point of view of green jobs'. He added: 'The government talks about how green jobs will help the country climb out of the recession, so we hope they will take action to save England's only wind turbine manufacturing capacity to survive' (Unite 2009a). The union launched a campaign together with Friends of the Earth to save the factory. Unite's briefing asked Vestas to 'hold fire' until the government launched its renewables strategy, to give the government 'the chance to stimulate the domestic market for wind turbines, particularly in relation to onshore wind'. Alternatively, the government should 'consider whether the taxpayer would get better value for money and more secure jobs if the sites were taken into some form of municipal or public ownership' (Unite 2009b; 2009c). However, the campaign did not appear to gain much traction.

Local Unite officials spoke at the trades council meeting on 3 July, but advised Vestas workers simply to join the union, write to 'Lord Mandelson' and offered help with getting unemployment benefits. Activists dismissed local Unite officials as 'business unionists and social partnership bureaucrats' (Rolfe 2009b). Rawnsley said that in a meeting with Cowes Trades Council representatives and a regional Unite official, 'we raised the idea of holding a public meeting and were told we were "pissing in the wind"' (Rawnsley 2009). The lack of engagement locally was brought out by a Unite press release issued on the day the occupation began, which emphasised familiar market and ecological modernisation themes. The union stated that it was not too late to save the plants, urging the government to address blockages in the planning system, counter NIMBYism and thus increase demand for wind turbines. It added: 'We urge the government to match its green rhetoric with action to support green jobs, saving Vestas would send out a clear message that it is serious about saving the environment as well as supporting UK manufacturing' (Unite 2009d).

After the occupation began, Unite Assistant General Secretary Len McCluskey was quoted in *The Guardian* as saying that Vestas was 'the clearest case for government intervention we could wish to see: 700 industrial jobs are being put at risk because of market failure in a sector the government is desperate to see expand'. He said the workers were 'fighting for our economic and environmental future as well as their jobs' (Milne 2009). However, Unite was silent on the occupation itself and whether it backed the workers' actions. Unite executive member Tom Cashman visited the protest on 25 July to show his support. He told workers who had quit Unite to join RMT that 'the important thing is that you have a union, not an argument about which union it should be'. Even seasoned socialists were bemused by the union's poor showing, commenting that 'Unite is a notoriously bureaucratic union, but even for Unite, the union's performance here is exceptionally bad. Exactly why is still unclear' (Evans 2009). Unite officials attended the meeting with Climate Minister Joan Ruddock on 6 August. Dromey seconded the Vestas emergency motion at TUC Congress. Jerry Hicks tried to make it an issue in the Unite General Secretary election contest with McCluskey the following year. Hicks' election address stated that the union 'should have supported the occupation at Vestas on the Isle of Wight' (Unite 2010).

RMT: class and climate

The RMT led by Bob Crow had a reputation for industrial militancy and 'social movement unionism' (Darlington 2009: 84–5). Its leaders and reps approached the Vestas occupation as a class struggle and reacted accordingly. A day after workers took over the factory, the RMT leadership pledged full support to occupation and called on the government to 'nationalise the factory, protect the jobs and show that they are walking the talk when it comes to green and renewable energy' (RMT 2009a). Activists from the RMT joined the Vestas workers outside the factory soon after the occupation began. RMT Portsmouth officials Richard Howard and Mick Tosh, who organised the Portsmouth–Ryde ferry workers, played key roles early on. They managed to work their union facility time and holiday leave from work to be outside the factory for long periods. The local RMT reps' role was regarded by participants as a model of what good trade unionists should do, going to the aid of other workers and helping them organise, rather than seeing their job as only to look after the sectional interests of the workers already signed up to their union. The RMT activists were crucial in helping Vestas workers outside to elect a committee and get organised. Howard held an impromptu meeting and was able to get a committee of stewards elected, supplying RMT hi-vis vests. The difference was that the RMT was more democratic, its branches were more likely to have secretaries and activists 'ready to look beyond their narrow concerns, and full-time officials more responsive to the rank and file' (Evans 2009). As Mark Smith put it: 'I joined Unite before the occupation, purely in order to have legal assistance. But then Unite didn't turn up at all, for a long time, and when they did, they weren't that interested. Unite people had been told not to get involved.' By contrast, 'RMT did turn up, and have been a lot more militant. It's a question of the relation between what you say, and what you're actually willing to do' (AWL 2009e).

The RMT also put national resources into the struggle. Crow spoke at the 23 July rally and the union began to recruit Vestas workers, reportedly gaining 200 members in the first week (Perry 2009w). Crow argued that Vestas workers shouldn't be used like pieces of lemon, 'squeezing the juice out of them ... then tossing them to the side when they're not wanted any more'. He said the criminals were not the workers inside the building, but the company for wanting to shut down the works. He declared that if food wasn't allowed in, the RMT would arrange for a helicopter to fly over and drop food to those taking part in the sit-in (Perry 2009u). The RMT announced it would provide legal assistance to Vestas workers. Crow argued that the dispute brought together two crucial issues: protection from companies that abuse the law to hire and fire, and a world where the environmental sustainability is an absolute priority. The union demanded that the government intervene urgently. Crow chastised ministers for 'sheer hypocrisy' over 'public announcements on climate change while our only wind turbine factory faces the axe'. He said: 'If the government can nationalise the banks at the drop of a hat, there is no reason whatsoever why they can't nationalise Vestas' (RMT 2009b).

The RMT legal counsel helped postpone the eviction of the occupiers for an extra week at the court hearing on 29 July. The union reported another 'significant milestone' on 31 July, after Vestas held back the scheduled closure date of the facility and wrote to staff confirming that the consultation had been extended indefinitely. Union officials described the move by Vestas as a 'massive victory', allowing 'a serious opportunity to draw up a rescue package similar to the one supported by the Scottish Parliament earlier this year, which saved the Vestas factory in Kintyre'. Crow hailed the growing support for the Vestas campaign, which had 'fired the imagination of the labour and environmental movements all around the world' (RMT 2009c).

However, the RMT were unable to prevent the eviction order for a second time and to prolong the occupation further. With six remaining workers inside the factory on the eviction day, Crow told the workers involved in the occupation that they could hold their heads high and be 'proud of the brave fight they have put up for green jobs'. They had 'turned a local fight over a factory closure on the Isle of Wight into a global battle for the future of manufacturing in the renewable energy sector and that is an extraordinary achievement' (RMT 2009e). The RMT backed the national days of action in support of Vestas and successfully moved an emergency resolution at the

TUC Congress on the occupation. The union continued to represent ex-Vestas workers and supported efforts to launch the Sureblades firm to manufacture fully-recyclable micro-turbine blades (RMT 2010).

During the Vestas occupation, the RMT acted as a social movement trade union, in the sense explained in Chapter 2. Its organisation was generally democratic, using its resources and officials to mobilise its new members in militant fashion. It understood the power of the workplace occupation to maximise workers' economic leverage. The union was also politically independent of liberal and social democratic parties and set out a class perspective to cement the coalition that formed around the Vestas workers. It understood solidarity in the classic sense of 'an injury to one is an injury to all' and reached out to other workers in other unions, neighbourhood-based organisations and other social movements.

TUC: the limits of ecological modernisation

The TUC did not play a prominent role as the Vestas occupation unfolded. Rather it expressed its concerns in explicitly ecological modernisation terms. When the redundancies were announced, Brendan Barber told journalists that 'the loss of these jobs on the Isle of Wight would not only be a blow to the emerging green sector, but would also be a personal tragedy for the hundreds of workers affected locally' (Webb 2009a). Vestas was discussed at the TUSDAC working group meeting on 8 May, with a view to raising the matter with Ed Miliband. The TUC held the meeting with Miliband on 19 May, its first with the new minister. The TUSDAC working group meeting on 9 July 2009 also heard a brief report of the meeting with Miliband (TUSDAC 2009a). However, at the high-level policy group meeting with Defra Minister Hilary Benn on 13 July 2009, Vestas was not discussed (TUSDAC 2009b).

The TUC did not comment publicly on the occupation for ten days, although officials were active behind the scenes. Barber called for government help to halt the Vestas factory closure urging business, unions and government to 'get around the table' and secure a future for wind turbine manufacturing in the UK. He added that Ed Miliband had 'proved himself to be a champion of the green agenda and the drive to create new jobs' and asked him to 'go the extra mile for the 600 workers and the production facility'. He said: 'Everything must be done to look for positive alternatives', although the TUC did not specify what kind of alternative might be acceptable (TUC 2009c: 1). Barber also wrote to Miliband on 3 August. He argued that in the context of growing global urgency to cut carbon emissions, it would be difficult to find 'a more damning example of market failure, or of corporate inflexibility', than the Vestas case, which threatens the viability of existing UK-based green energy manufacturing and the livelihoods of a skilled workforce. He requested that Miliband press Vestas to halt its closure plan 'to give time for proper dialogue and for every possible alternative to be fully explored'. Barber asked the government to bring together business, unions and industry experts with a view to securing a future for wind turbine production in the UK (SVB 2009g). The TUC called for partnership when workers expected sharper criticism of employers and the government, coupled with active solidarity.

Congress 2009 was overshadowed by Vestas. On 16 September, Ed Miliband addressed the gathering and was repeatedly questioned about the government's stance on Vestas, joining a standing ovation for the Vestas workers' delegation in the hall (TUC 2009a: 126; Mulholland 2009). Congress passed an emergency resolution on Vestas and green jobs, which applauded 'the Vestas workforce and their families who courageously fought to save their jobs, including occupying the factory. Their principled stand to defend their community and to fight climate change is a tribute to the finest traditions of our movement' (TUC 2009a: 28). Alex Gordon for the RMT described Miliband's speech as 'replete with crocodile tears' for the job losses. He said the trade union movement had 'the power, the voice and the authority to call for green jobs to be union jobs and for union jobs to be publicly-owned jobs' and said the UK government had 'an absolute responsibility to nationalise the Vestas factory on the Isle of Wight'. Dromey told workers, 'Vestas may have walked away, but we will never abandon you.' He said workers 'will be remembered long after those who sacked them end up where they richly deserve to be – in the dustbin of history' (ibid.: 167). Vestas was still a point of reference at following Congresses.

Local trade union coordination across the Isle of Wight was not well organised before the occupation. The island had a county association of trade union councils and three trades councils in Newport, Ryde and Cowes. After the closure was announced but before the occupation, the county Trades Council, which claimed to represent 8,000 workers across the island, met with the local MP to discuss the matter (Brooks 2009a). Probably the Trades Council's most significant act was to support the public meeting on 3 July with Workers' Climate Action. It was this meeting that began to galvanise workers and their supporters to take action themselves to prevent the closure, rather than simply appealing to others to help them. Trades Council delegates took part in solidarity activity to support the workers' occupation. The occupation also had the effect, at least in the short term, of revitalising local trade union coordination, including the involvement of Vestas workers' representatives, with joint Trades Council meetings in October and November following the summer of protest (AWL 2009h).

Vestas workers received strong support from trade union representatives of many TUC-affiliated unions on the island (Perry 2009s). Local FBU and Unison reps collected funds for food in the first days of the occupation (Unison 2009a). PCS members, themselves facing redundancy at a local tax office, supported the Vestas workers (PCS 2009). There was also some support from national unions beyond the input from the RMT and from local union branches (Unison 2009b). Sally Hunt, UCU General Secretary, wrote to Ed Miliband on 27 July. PCS Assistant General Secretary Chris Baugh and 15 other union leaders signed a letter published in *The Guardian* on 1 August, urging Ed Miliband to intervene (Baugh *et al.* 2009). These efforts were important, but the high-level TUC response to Vestas is probably best characterised as 'accommodationist solidarity'. TUC leaders prioritised partnership at a time when the employer turned hostile and the government refused to step in to save the factory. Far from projecting a class vision and emphasising the class antagonisms involved, TUC leaders did not go beyond a weak ecological modernist expression of concern, which was hopelessly inadequate for the situation. In contrast, local trades councils and trade unionists enacted 'transformatory solidarity', in the best traditions of the labour movement.

The Vestas occupation and climate actors

The Vestas dispute can be understood as a significant metric for the state of climate politics in the UK in the first decade of the twenty-first century. It indicated how far various climate actors were able to deliver on promises to promote a low-carbon economy. This section examines the activities of key climate actors: capital, government, climate NGOs and trade unions, to evaluate their low-carbon credentials. In light of the events, it also assesses the implications of Vestas for employment relations theories and how far Vestas prefigured a new alliance of actors conducting climate politics.

The neoliberal climate politics of renewable capital

The closure of the Isle of Wight wind turbine manufacturing plant reflected particularly badly on its owners. Vestas Wind Systems A/S was the world's largest producer and exporter of wind turbines with production facilities in 11 countries (Ryland 2010). The year before the occupation, Vestas had a £6 billion order book (Vidal 2008). In early 2009, Vestas had a better-than-expected 51 per cent rise in its full-year operating profit and maintained its 2009 sales and profit forecasts (Macalister 2009a). On 22 April 2009, the British Wind Energy Association, the renewables industry lobbying body, argued that there were £10 billion 'shovel-ready' wind projects in the UK, which 'could lay the foundation for the green economy'. It estimated that there would be between 23,000 and 57,000 jobs in the UK wind industry by 2020, up from 4,800 employees at the time (BWEA 2009: 15). By 2014, the BWEA expected there would be at least 1,800 and at best over 3,000 wind turbine manufacturing jobs (SQWenergy 2008).

Yet less than a week after these optimistic predictions, Vestas Blades UK announced the probable closure of its manufacturing plant on the Isle of Wight, the only one in England.[5] Workers at the Isle of Wight plant were called to an early morning meeting on 28 April to be told that the firm was opening a 90-day consultation on redundancy (Perry 2009a). It left the reputation of the new green economy – never mind the prospects for the 600 workers at the Vestas plant – in tatters. As Andrew Simms put it a few days later, learning that a wind turbine maker was closing its factory was 'a bit like hearing that pharmaceutical companies are closing down the production of flu vaccines just as the alert for swine flu goes from level five to full pandemic' (Simms 2009). Announcing the closure, the firm appeared evasive and self-serving. In an interview with *The Guardian*, chief executive Ditlev Engel blamed NIMBYs, the planning application process, the government and the pound for the decision. He promised that Vestas would consult its workers. Engel said the firm was in 'constant dialogue' with the government and that no assistance had been offered to try to save the plant (Webb 2009b).

These claims were neither consistent nor coherent. Even Conservative Isle of Wight MP Andrew Turner told the House of Commons that Vestas was not cutting jobs because of the recession or because of a need to downsize; rather it had decided it would be more profitable to manufacture wind turbines in the United States and China, 'without a thought for the highly skilled workers that it leaves behind'. Turner said he understood the frustration of the workers who had occupied the factory the day before and was 'sympathetic to their concerns'. He argued that Vestas was leaving the workers 'high and dry' and with 'very poor' redundancy packages and no negotiation. He said it was 'totally unacceptable' that those who worked at the site for two years or more 'were entitled to only twice the statutory pay, while those who had been employed for less time would receive even less'. It reflected 'very poorly on a company as profitable as Vestas' (Turner 2009).

It also emerged that the government had offered Vestas some support, but to no avail. Ed Miliband argued that 'for months, we have worked with the company to understand what would be required to convert the factory to making onshore blades for the UK. The issue for Vestas was not subsidies, but how it could get enough orders' (Miliband 2009). Joan Ruddock was reported to have told workers that after extensive talks with Vestas management 'no matter what they offered, Vestas were not interested in keeping the factory open making wind turbine blades' (Perry 2009x; DECC 2009). The impression given was that the firm was only interested in developing green production where it could make the highest returns.

There was a tangible sense from the workers affected by the closure that the firm's management had misled them. Workers said Vestas had promised to re-equip the factory for the British market for onshore turbines, only to decide that there were better investment opportunities elsewhere. Then the firm said it would mothball the plant for two or three years until demand picked up – ignoring the fact that it was impossible to mothball skilled workers for such a time. Relations with the workforce were already strained. The firm had been guilty of safety breaches, which had damaged some workers' health (TUC 2009b). It was also perceived as having 'an anti-union management and a culture of bullying' (Milne 2009). This was compounded by the behaviour of Vestas managers during the occupation. They immediately threatened workers with dismissal rather than negotiate, refused to allow food in and then sacked the occupiers with a pizza delivery. Vestas was backed by the BWEA, which decided only after the occupation was almost over that the market for onshore wind turbines in the UK was 'too small to sustain a UK-based factory in the long term' (Harvey 2009).

Even after the occupation was finished, this misinformation and mistreatment continued. Engel told journalists that the company could review its decision to strip the 11 workers identified as participating in the sit-in of their redundancy benefits (Lewis and Fouché 2009). Despite rumours that the redundancy pay had been secured, in September Mike Godley told *VentnorBlog* that no payments had been made (Perry 2009w). A month after protests had ended, Vestas announced that its global profits from July to September had been £150 million, 70 per cent up on the previous year (BBC 2009). Ironically, five years on, Vestas announced it had chosen the Isle of Wight as its site to build the blades for the world's most powerful offshore wind turbine (*Telegraph* 2014). Vestas' behaviour on the Isle of Wight suggests that renewable capital is just as rapacious, profiteering and insular as the fossil fuel multinationals it has ambitions to replace. It also suggests that the neoliberal approach to climate politics, which relies on the goodwill of business agents, is not sufficient to ensure even the first tentative steps towards a low-carbon energy regime.

The Labour government and the limits of ecological modernisation

The Vestas factory occupation punctured the neoliberal and ecological modernisation discourse of the Labour government. Just before the closure was announced, Peter Mandelson announced that the UK was 'on the edge of a low-carbon industrial revolution' and promised that the government would pursue a 'more interventionist strategy supporting the growth industries of the future' (Grice 2009). The contradiction between government rhetoric and the reality of the factory closure continued throughout the summer. Also a week before the occupation, Prime Minister Gordon Brown described a vision of green revolution powering economic recovery, with 1.2 million people in the UK employed in the green sector 'producing energy-saving products, construction companies erecting renewable energy systems' within a decade (Brown 2009). On 15 July, Mandelson and Ed Miliband launched Labour's low-carbon transition plan, which estimated that the 880,000 workers already in the low-carbon sector would be joined by 400,000 more by 2015 (Vidal 2009). But the low-carbon job figures were found to be inflated by a bizarre array of products, from skylights to wooden pallets and noise insulation materials, just as the Vestas factory finished producing its last batch of blades (Pagnamenta 2009). It was against this political background that some workers at the plant took their decision to occupy it.

The government immediately came under pressure to intervene, most of all because the workers involved in the occupation and their supporters called for nationalisation from the beginning. At Westminster, Labour MP John McDonnell (2009) said:

> Vestas workers are occupying their factory, and it behoves this House to send our support to them. They are not only fighting for their jobs but are at the forefront of the campaign against climate change, and they deserve our support.

The occupying workers made it clear that if government intervention such as subsidies or direct orders were not sufficient, then the government should nationalise the plant so they could continue manufacturing wind turbines.

The Labour government's underlying policy paradox was well summed up by an exchange between Vestas supporters and Joan Ruddock at her constituency surgery on 7 August. Asked whether a feasibility study had been carried out to nationalise the factory, Ruddock was quoted stating:

> We live in a market economy, all the advanced economies think the same. The only economy that does not have a market is North Korea ... It's not appropriate! The government does not want to be producers of wind turbines, and we did not want to be bankers.
>
> (Morris 2009h)[6]

Ed Miliband took the same stance throughout the protests. Asked at Congress about nationalisation, he replied: 'I do not think government should be in the business of running wind turbine factories. I do not think that is what government is best at' (TUC 2009a: 126). Former director of Friends of the Earth Tony Juniper pointed out the problem with trying to deliver a low-carbon economic transformation based on neoliberal principles. The inconvenient truth was that 'aspirational targets and the market on their own cannot deliver'. Government intervention was also needed in the form of 'clear, significant and sustained financial incentives alongside regulatory action across all countries'. He wrote: 'Market mechanisms can certainly play their part but need to be backed up. Look at Denmark and Germany, where renewable power has rapidly expanded' (Juniper 2009).

The most ministers did was to make promises and offer smaller amounts of money for other projects. During the occupation, the government awarded £6 million to Vestas' offshore research and development division (Mathiason 2009). At a meeting with Isle of Wight councillors after the protests had ceased, Miliband promised government support for green jobs on the island, including the development of tidal energy in the Solent, and a scheme for 'rotawave' technology, and money to upgrade some of the available wharfage on the Medina River (Perry 2009o). Vestas worker Sean McDonagh, who had met Joan Ruddock, reported that the minister had said those who took part in the sit-in should not lose their redundancy benefits (Perry 2009x). Overall, the Vestas occupation demonstrated the limits of neoliberal and weak ecological modernisation, particularly in the context of infrastructure projects where state intervention is required.

Vestas: harbinger of a new red–green alliance?

The Vestas occupation was a critical test for the climate movement in the UK, which had begun to flourish. However, it would be a mistake to analyse these climate actors as one homogeneous block: the experience made it clear that very different types of environmentalism were present. Some actors rose to the challenge, while others proved unable to meet it. Environmental NGOs offered little more than nominal support to the Vestas workers during their struggle. After the closure was announced, Friends of the Earth supported the Unite union campaign to keep the plant open (Brooks 2009b). It created an online petition urging the government intervene. Local Friends of the Earth members were active around wind turbine applications and some took part in solidarity activity, but they did not play a leading role.

Greenpeace had an even lower profile. It put out press releases criticising the government's hypocrisy over its green plans when the closure was announced, and some local Greenpeace members supported solidarity activity. But the organisation was not a factor in the dispute. One Greenpeace member posting on *The Guardian*'s 'Comment is Free' website, lamented the lack of activity, pointing out that its UK executive director John Sauven is also the brother of Rob Sauven, Managing Director of Vestas Technology UK, which wasn't closed down and was given a government grant (LastUuhtii 2010). The Green Party was also at most a supportive bystander as the protests unfolded. Caroline Lucas, the Isle of Wight's Green Euro-MP, visited the protests and called for a workers' cooperative to be created (Perry 2009v). Martin Thomas spoke for many of the socialists involved who felt the party's response had been poor: 'The Green Party Trade Union Group turned up with a stall for a day or so, and a few individuals who happened to be members of the Green Party have come to the roundabout, but that is it' (Thomas 2009c).

By contrast, the radical environmentalists, particularly Climate Camp and related organisations such as Workers' Climate Action, Climate Rush and other direct action groups, played a very positive role. The Camp for Climate Action national gathering formed a Vestas solidarity working group before the occupation and offered practical support. More importantly, climate activists delivered solidarity in the form of sit-ins, trespasses, glue-ins and other forms of protest (SVB 2009d). Thomas articulated the close bonds of solidarity that developed between socialist and radical climate activists, praising climate camp and other non-violent direct action people who organised many of the successful actions, 'most spectacularly the occupation of the roof of the East Cowes Vestas factory from 4 to 14 August'. Many

Vestas workers active in the campaign recognised that prejudices about these activists were misplaced. He wrote that the 'courage, imagination, and skills' of these environmentalists made an 'irreplaceable contribution, helping to enlarge the workers' (and maybe some socialists') tactical ideas – and doing it with very few arrests' (Thomas 2009c). Similarly, supporters of the Campaign against Climate Change took an active part in solidarity work.

Was Vestas the harbinger of a new red–green alliance? Certainly some commentators thought so at the time of the occupation. *Guardian* journalist Terry Macalister (2009b) believed that a unique 'red and green' army of trade union and environmental campaigners had been mobilised to save from closure England's only major wind turbine manufacturing plant. He quoted Greenpeace, who said the Vestas dispute promised a 'historic change' from a situation where the labour movement and environment activists found themselves on different sides of the fence, with one wanting to shut down polluting industries and the other defending jobs. John Sauven, Greenpeace UK executive director, said 'historically there has been animosity between the two sides. If we can build this new alliance and break down those perceived barriers, then there are all sorts of exciting opportunities'.

Another *Guardian* journalist Rachel Williams argued that the protest was significant 'not just for the way in which it has seen environmental campaigners, socialist activists and trade unionists join forces', but also for the way in which 'members of a previously non-unionised workforce in the largely conservative island community have been mobilised in a way they never dreamed of' (Williams 2009a). Neal Lawson from the Compass pressure group hailed 'the passion of the protesting workers and the obvious synergy of economic and environmental interests', which helped make the campaign against the Vestas plant closure 'a cause célèbre for both the trade union and environmental movements this summer'. He believed 'an alliance of red and green politics would transform the landscape of Britain' (Lawson 2009).

Patrick Rolfe believed *The Guardian* view was mistaken. He argued that the action taken at the Vestas wind turbine plant demonstrated the emergence not of a red and green coalition but 'two social movements ... are inextricably linked'. The environmental activists realised that the only system capable of making the economic changes required to achieve sustainability is one of 'democratically controlled, social production'. In parallel, the socialist movement realised 'the imminence of environmental destruction' meant we cannot wait until 'the democratisation of production before we build a sustainable economy'. He thought the 'seeds of a new society – socially and environmentally sustainable – must be germinated in the rotting corpse of the old' (Rolfe 2009c).

Neale (2009) said Vestas had brought socialists, trade unionists and environmentalists together in a new way, he argued in retrospect that 'the labels are a bit misleading'. Many of those who took part were all three, though they were socialists first and foremost. But 'everyone who came to the camp outside the Vestas factory commented on how everyone was cooperating in a new way'. Nick Chaffey argued that Vestas had been a positive coming together of environmental and trade union campaigns. Yet 'some in the environmental movement do not see or understand the significance of mass struggle, the role of the working class and the trade unions, or the need for a political alternative to the market' (Chaffey 2010). Vestas was characterised by workers taking action for their own jobs but also for climate protection and renewable energy; the forces that coalesced around it were secondary to worker agency and socialist politics.

What was the significance of the Vestas occupation for working-class climate politics? According to a socialist activist, for two months it was 'the centre of three great battles: on jobs, on the environment, and on renovating the labour movement' (AWL 2009c). Climate activist Sophielle (2009) said it seemed at the time that Vestas was 'where history is being made in the converging struggles for workers' liberty and environmental sustainability', while Thomas (2009b) wrote that the Vestas workers appeared to have lit a fire 'as shall never be extinguished'. For climate politics, the issues were well captured by an unpublished letter to *The Guardian* by Vestas workers and their supporters. They stated that the decision to stop making wind turbine blades on the Isle of Wight undermined the government's promise of a 'green revolution', ushering in significantly more renewable energy production and more green jobs. Environmental and trade union campaigners need to decide whether to let job creation and the transition to renewable energy production 'rest on the short-term business decisions of private companies whose guiding principle is their bottom line'. Instead, 'we need to act as a public collectivity, in our collective interest, including, if necessary, taking over plants and industries that cannot or will not deliver the change we need' (Morris 2009l).

It was the active role played by workers in both formal and ad hoc organisations that distinguished Vestas as an innovative development in climate politics. The verdict was well captured by Crow, who said the workers had 'done more for the future of green energy and green jobs in the UK in two weeks than the government has done in 12 years' (Williams 2009b).

Conclusion

The Vestas occupation problematised the transition to a low-carbon economy, by bringing both the impact of climate change on workers into the equation, but also workers as active climate subjects. The occupation suggested that some of the workers had understood the climate significance of the work they did and fought a class struggle in the face of business intransigence and government indecision. Although workers were pulled in different directions, as anticipated by Hyman's (2001) triangular model, the occupation showed that sections of the labour movement, particularly class-conscious socialists and trade unionists, could successfully meld the defence of jobs with the need for climate protection.

The occupation further showed how the general interest of preventing dangerous climate change could be formed out of the interests of particular actors (especially workers) and particular organisations (notably trade unions). It was this synthesis, rather than merely an alliance of disparate forces, that made Vestas the potential harbinger of a new climate solidarity movement. In short, the Vestas occupation provides further evidence that workers and their trade unions have the potential to develop into swords of climate justice.

Notes

1 Nearly 400 blog posts were reviewed, the majority from the local *VentnorBlog* – now called On the Wight http://onthewight.com (accessed 27 November 2014). The rest came mainly from the *Save Vestas Blog*: http://savevestas.wordpress.com, which was set up by solidarity campaigners and from the AWL website: www.workersliberty.org. The other significant online source was *The Guardian* newspaper: www.guardian.co.uk. Its journalists wrote extensively about the Vestas dispute, though much of their reporting never made the print editions. Other useful material appeared on its 'Comment is Free' site. Blog and website posts are referenced in the same way as printed material (see Chapter 1, note 6). Where multiple posts occur on the same date, these are indicated in order they first appeared, e.g. 2009a, 2009b ...

2 Mark Smith, another of the Vestas occupiers, reported (Morris 2009o) that 'we were 17 originally in the occupation, which went down to six at the end'.

3 The first attempt to rally Vestas workers to trade union support came from Graham Petersen, the UCU environment officer who visited the island in early May and spoke to local trade unionists (pers. comm., 9 January 2012). He also wrote on the *VentnorBlog* (Perry 2009p) about the example of Visteon and offered to assist workers with unionisation.

4 A brief account of the role of WCA and the socialist climate activists appeared in *The Guardian*, which also published a number of letters by participants (Williams 2009a; Lewis 2009; Maltby 2009; Maltby *et al.* 2009a; 2009b; Rolfe 2009d). See also Foster (2009a).

5 The Isle of Wight facility was not the only manufacturing plant in the UK, despite many reports at the time. Vestas had owned a small manufacturing plant in Scotland, but sold it to Skycon before the occupation (Corrections, *The Guardian* 11 May 2009). The Scottish plant later went into administration (Webb 2011).

6 Vestas workers Mike Godley and Sean McDonagh, together with Frances O'Grady, Bob Crow, Jack Dromey and other senior union officials met with Joan Ruddock on 6 August, where the minister reiterated the government's stance that it had 'exhausted all options in its power to keep the site open' (DECC 2009: 1).

References

Alex (2009) 'Vestas Closure is an International Issue', *Save Vestas Blog*, 24 July.

Amicus (2004) 'Winds of Change for Scotland', press release, 30 November.

AWL (2009a) 'Vestas Campaign Steps Up', 17 July.

——(2009b) 'Demonstration Planned to Back Vestas Workers', www.workersliberty. org 20 July.

——(2009c) 'Vestas: The Centre of both Jobs and Environment Battles', *Solidarity*, 3/ 156, 30 July.

——(2009d) 'Vestas Workers and Supporters Speak Out', *Solidarity*, 3/156, 30 July.

——(2009e) 'Vestas Workers and Supporters Speak Out', *Solidarity*, 3/157, 20 August.

——(2009f) 'Vestas Workers Keep Up Blockade: Day of Solidarity 17 September' www.workersliberty.org, 8 September.

——(2009g) 'Vestas: Sparking the Struggle, Seeing It Through', *Solidarity*, 3/159, 24 September.

——(2009h) 'Ex-Vestas Workers Decide Trades Councils Drive', www.workersliberty.org, 11 October.

Baugh, C. *et al.* (2009) 'Miliband Should Act to Save Vestas', *The Guardian*, 4 August.

BBC (2009) 'Wind Turbine Maker's Profits Soar', 27 October.

Brooks, R. (2009a) 'Vestas: MP Andrew Turner Urges Action from Lord Mandelson', *VentnorBlog*, 3:56 pm Monday, 8 June.

——(2009b) 'Friends of the Earth Call to Save Vestas', *VentnorBlog*, 1:53 pm Wednesday, 8 July.

——(2009c) 'Vestas Sit-In: Activists Blockade Ed Miliband's Office', *VentnorBlog*, 2:37 pm Monday, 3 August.

——(2009d) 'Vestas Protest: Day of Action Events around the UK', *VentnorBlog*, 12:16 pm Thursday, 17 September.

Brown, G. (2009) 'Britain's Green Revolution Will Power Economic Recovery', *The Observer*, 12 July.

BWEA (2009) *Powering a Green Economy: Wind, Wave and Tidal's Contribution to Britain's Industrial Future*, 22 April. London: British Wind Energy Association.

Chaffey, N. (2010) 'Britain's Offshore Occupation', *Socialism Today*, 140, July–August.

Darlington, R. (2009) 'Organising, Militancy and Revitalisation: The Case of the RMT Union'. In G. Gall (ed.) *Union Revitalisation in Advanced Economies: Assessing the Contribution of Union Organising*. London: Routledge.

DECC (2009) Note of the Meeting with Joan Ruddock, dated 18 August 2009. Obtained by Freedom of Information request, 26 March 2012.

Dwyer, P. (2009) 'Vestas Workers Take on Climate Change Minister in Oxford', *Socialist Worker*, 2162 (online only), 1 August.

Evans, R. (2009) 'Vestas: the RMT and Unite', *Solidarity*, 3/156, 30 July.

Foster, C. (2009a) 'The Rules of Revolutionary Socialism', *Solidarity*, 3/156, 30 July.

——(2009b) '17 September Day of Action', *Solidarity*, 3/157, 20 August.

Gall, G. (2011) 'Contemporary Workplace Occupations in Britain: Motivations, Stimuli, Dynamics and Outcomes', *Employee Relations*, 33(6): 607–23.

Godley, M. and Morris, V. (2009) 'The Vestas Fight's Still On', *Morning Star*, 30 August.

Grice, A. (2009) 'Labour's Industrial Revolution', *The Independent*, 20 April.

Harvey, F. (2009) 'Wind Industry body Deals Vestas Blow', *Financial Times*, 2 August.

Hyman, R. (2001) *Understanding European Trade Unionism: Between Market, Class & Society*. London: Sage.

——(2010) *Social Dialogue and Industrial Relations During the Economic Crisis: Innovative Practices or Business as Usual?* Geneva: International Labour Office.

Juniper, T. (2009) 'Global Cleantech 100: Is the UK Government Up for the Challenge'? *The Guardian*, 9 September.

LastUuhtii (2010) 'Greenpeace "Shuts Down" Arctic Oil Rig', www.guardian.co.uk, 31 August.

Lawson, N. (2009) 'How Green Socialism Can Save the UK', www.guardian.co.uk, 30 August.

Lewis, P. (2009) 'Vestas in Court to End Factory Sit-In', www.guardian.co.uk, 29 July.

Lewis, P. and Fouché, G. (2009) 'Vestas Factory Closes Despite Campaign', *The Guardian*, 12 August.

Macalister, T. (2009a) 'Vestas Wind Turbines Prove Resilient Amid Economic Gloom', www.guardian.co.uk, 11 February.

——(2009b) 'Vestas Dispute: Red and Green Coalition Forms to Fight Wind Plant Closure', www.guardian.co.uk, 23 July.

Maltby, E (2009) 'Labour's Green Rhetoric is Hollow Unless it Acts Now to Protect Vestas', www.guardian.co.uk, 27 July.

Maltby, E. *et al.* (2009a) 'Industrial Effects on the Environment', *The Guardian*, 23 July.

——(2009b) 'Vestas Workers and WCA reply to *Guardian* Article: You Can't Leave Saving the Environment and Jobs to the Market', www.workersliberty.org, 14 August.

Marsh, G. (2001) 'The Windy Isles: New Opportunity for UK's Wind Industry?' *Refocus*, 2(6): 18–20.

——(2006) 'Building Momentum', *Refocus*, 7(6):52–55.

Mathiason, N. (2009) 'Government Grants Vestas £6m – But Factory Will Still Close', *The Guardian*, 28 July.

McDonnell, J. (2009) Hansard HC Deb 21 July 2009, vol. 496, col. 846.

Miliband, E. (2009) 'Why Vestas Closed Isle of Wight Plant', *The Guardian*, 24 July.

Milne, S. (2009) 'Even the Isle of Wight Wants Miliband to Buck the Market', *The Guardian*, 22 July.

Morris, V. (2009a) 'Occupying Korean Car Workers Greet Vestas Occupation!' *Save Vestas Blog*, 29 July.

——(2009b) 'A Vestas Worker Speaks About the Struggle', *Save Vestas Blog*, 30 July.

——(2009c) 'Message from Visteon Occupation Belfast Spokesperson', *Save Vestas Blog*, 30 July.

——(2009d) 'Fraternal Greetings from Lindsey Strike Committee', *Save Vestas Blog*, 30 July.

——(2009e) 'Occupationitis: Now Thomas Cook, Dublin Have Come Down with It', *Save Vestas Blog*, 31 July.

——(2009f) 'Warrington Protest – Keeping Up the Pressure on Vestas', *Save Vestas Blog*, 1 August.

——(2009g) 'Picket of DECC, 3 Whitehall Place Tonight', *Save Vestas Blog*, 6 August.

——(2009h) 'We Picket Joan Ruddock, Climate Change Minister, on Vestas Eviction Day', *Save Vestas Blog*, 7 August.

——(2009i) 'Striking Chilean Miners Send Support', *Save Vestas Blog*, 11 August.

——(2009j) 'Protest at the South East England Development Agency, 12/8/09', *Save Vestas Blog*, 13 August.

——(2009k) 'Brazilian Trade Union to Vestas Workers', *Save Vestas Blog*, 14 August.

——(2009l) 'Vestas Workers and WCA Reply to *Guardian* Report', *Save Vestas Blog*, 16 August.

——(2009m) 'Vestas Workers Solidarity Groups Around the Country', *Save Vestas Blog*, 21 August.

——(2009n) 'Workers' Climate Action at Climate Camp', *Save Vestas Blog*, 25 August.

——(2009o) 'Direct Action Will Be Needed. We Are Asking For Help with That – Mark Smith', *Save Vestas Blog*, 29 August.

Mulholland, H. (2009) 'TUC at a Glance', www.guardian.co.uk, 17 September.

Neale, J. (2009) 'Vestas Changed the Climate', *Socialist Review*, September.

——(ed.) (2010) *One Million Climate Jobs: Solving the Economic and Environmental Crises*. London: Campaign against Climate Change.

Norman, B. (2009) 'Save Jobs at Vestas Wind Turbine Plant', *The Socialist*, 587, 8 July.

Pagnamenta, R. (2009) 'Lord Mandelson's Claims of 880,000 "Green Jobs" in UK a Sham', *The Times*, 16 July.

Perry, S. [Sally] (2009a) 'Are Vestas Leaving the Isle of Wight? UPDATE 8', *VentnorBlog*, 9:40 am Tuesday, 28 April.

——(2009b) 'Vestas Staff Occupy Newport Offices: Breaking News: UPDATE 2', *VentnorBlog*, 9:17 pm Monday, 20 July.

——(2009c) 'Vestas Sit-In: Day 9 Report From Inside', *VentnorBlog*, 11:49 am Thursday, 30 July.

——(2009d) 'Vestas Sit-In: Day 10 Report from Inside: Redundancy Payments Postponed for all Staff', *VentnorBlog*, 2:57 pm Friday, 31 July.

——(2009e) 'Vestas Sit-In: Fish and Chips for Friday Update: More Photos', *VentnorBlog*, 9:51 pm Friday, 31 July.

——(2009f) 'Vestas Sit-In: Billy Bragg Dedicates Songs to Vestas Workers', *VentnorBlog*, 9:59 pm Friday, 31 July.

——(2009g) 'Vestas Sit-in: East Cowes Vestas Roof Occupied: UPDATED', *VentnorBlog*, 8:02 am Tuesday, 4 August.

——(2009h) 'Vestas Sit-In: Eviction Notice Granted by Court', *VentnorBlog*, 11:20 am Tuesday, 4 August.

——(2009i) 'Vestas Sit-In: Workers Leave in Dramatic Exit Updated', *VentnorBlog*, 12:43 pm Friday, 7 August.

——(2009j) 'Vestas Protesters Arrive at Andrew Turner's Office to Find It Closed', *VentnorBlog*, 1:27 pm Friday, 14 August.

——(2009k) 'Banner Held Outside Andrew Turner's Office', *VentnorBlog*, 2:36 pm Friday, 14 August.

——(2009l) 'Vestas Protest: Mike Godley Quashes Rumours of Campaign "Takeover"', *VentnorBlog*, 1:49 pm Tuesday, 18 August.

——(2009m) 'Vestas Protest: Marine Gate Blockade Moved by Police (photos) UPDATE 2', *VentnorBlog*, 11:28 am Tuesday, 22 September.

——(2009n) 'Vestas Protest: Still No Redundancy Payment for Sacked Workers', *VentnorBlog*, 12:31 pm Wednesday, 23 September.

——(2009o) 'Representative from Isle of Wight Meet Ed Miliband', *VentnorBlog*, 2:41 pm Thursday, 15 October.

Perry, S. [Simon] (2009p) 'Vestas Chief Talks on the Company's Future', *VentnorBlog*, 12:34 pm Tuesday, 28 April.

——(2009q) 'Vestas Sit-in: Update Interview with Those Inside', *VentnorBlog*, 3:07 pm Tuesday, 21 July.

——(2009r) 'Vestas Sit-in Told To Leave or Be Removed: Update', *VentnorBlog*, 5:01 pm Tuesday, 21 July.

——(2009s) 'Vestas Sit-in Day 2: Overnight Update', *VentnorBlog*, 9:11 am Wednesday, 22 July.

——(2009t) 'Vestas Sit-in: Wednesday Supporter Rally Photos', *VentnorBlog*, 2:14 pm Thursday, 23 July.

——(2009u) 'Vestas Sit-in: Bob Crow (RMT) Delivers a Rousing Speech (video)', *VentnorBlog*, 8:28 am Friday, 24 July.

——(2009v) 'Vestas Sit-in: Isle of Wight Green Euro-MP Proposes Rescue Plan', *VentnorBlog*, 5:36 pm Thursday, 30 July.

——(2009w) 'Vestas Sit-In: Police Informed Security Stopping Food "Breaches Human Rights"', *VentnorBlog*, 10:48 pm Friday, 31 July.

——(2009x) 'Joan Ruddock MP Says Vestas Sit-in Workers Should Get Their Redundancy', *VentnorBlog*, 5:34 pm Thursday, 6 August.

——(2009y) 'Vestas Protesters Climb Up Southampton Crane: Updated', *VentnorBlog*, 2:35 pm Tuesday, 15 September.

PCS (2009) 'Vestas Fight is Our Fight', press release, 14 August.

Press Association (2009) 'Climate Change Campaigners Stage Protest at Mandelson's Home', www.guardian.co.uk, 10 August.

RMT (2009a) 'RMT Pledges Full Support to Vestas Occupation – Bob Crow to Visit Factory Tomorrow', press release, 22 July.

——(2009b) 'RMT to Provide Legal Assistance to Vestas Workers as Union Demands Urgent Meetings with Ed Miliband and Company Bosses to Save the Factory', press release, 24 July.

——(2009c) 'Occupation Holds Back Vestas Factory Closure Date as Company Extends Consultation Period', press release, 31 July.

——(2009d) 'RMT Keeps Up Pressure on Vestas in Advance of Court Hearing', press release, 3 August.

——(2009e) 'RMT Accuses Vestas of Knocking Back Turbine Factory Rescue Deal', press release, 7 August.

——(2010) 'One Year After the Vestas Wind Turbines Occupation a New, Unionised Factory Rises from the Ashes', press release, 26 July.

Rawnsley, D. (2009) 'A Vestas Diary', www.workersliberty.org, 29 July.

——(2010) 'Workers Are the Power and Strength We Need', *Solidarity*, 3/165, 7 January.

Robinson, S. (2009) 'Protest at the Department of Energy and Climate Change', *Socialist Worker*, 2161 (online only), 25 July.

Rolfe, P. (2009a) 'Activists Spark Fight on Wind Turbine Closure', *Solidarity*, 3/154, 25 June.

——(2009b) 'Vestas Workers – Up for a Fight!' *Solidarity*, 3/155, 9 July.

——(2009c) 'We Will Build the Sustainable Society!' *Solidarity*, 3/156, 30 July.

——(2009d) *Space, Nature, and Society: Social Movement Struggles for Environmental Protection*. BA dissertation. University of Cambridge.

Ryland, E. (2010) 'Danish Wind Power Policy: Domestic and International Forces'. *Environmental Politics*, 19(1): 80–5.

Simms, A. (2009) 'No Green Shoots on Climate Change', www.guardian.co.uk, 1 May.

Sophielle (2009) 'An Inbox Full of Persuasion', *Save Vestas Blog*, 24 July.

SQWenergy (2008) *Today's Investment – Tomorrow's Asset: Skills and Employment in the Wind, Wave and Tidal sectors: Report to the British Wind Energy Association*, October 2008. Cambridge: SQW.

SVB (2009a) 'A Statement from a Vestas Worker', *Save Vestas Blog*, 12 July.

——(2009b) 'Success at Newport Mass Leafleting to Save Vestas', *Save Vestas Blog*, 18 July.

——(2009c) 'Protest at Prince's Visit Gets Message Across', *Save Vestas Blog*, 18 July.

——(2009d) 'Climate Camp Pledges Support to Vestas Workers', *Save Vestas Blog*, 20 July.

——(2009e) 'Solidarity in Trafalgar Square, Friday 31 July – Big Thanks to Gerry', *Save Vestas Blog*, 31 July.

——(2009f) 'The Picket line – Organisation', *Save Vestas Blog*, 2 August.

——(2009g) 'Brendan Barber letter to Ed Miliband', *Save Vestas Blog*, 3 August.

SWP (2009a) 'Wave of Solidarity for Action', *Socialist Worker*, 2162, 1 August.

——(2009b) 'Workers of the World Back the Struggle at Vestas', *Socialist Worker*, 2163, 8 August.

——(2009c) 'Day of Action Shows Growing Support for Vestas Workers', *Socialist Worker*, 2164 (online only), 15 August.

——(2009d) 'Vestas Solidarity Round-Up', *Socialist Worker*, 2165, 22 August.

——(2009e) 'Vestas Workers Interviewed: In the Eye of the Storm', *Socialist Worker*, 2166, 29 August.

Telegraph (2014) 'Blades for World's Most Powerful Offshore Wind Turbine To Be Built in UK', *The Telegraph*, 12 November.

Terry, I. (2009a) 'Vestas: "The Strength of Standing Together"', *Solidarity*, 3/158, 10 September.

——(2009b) 'How We Found the Confidence to Organise and Take Over Our Factory', *Socialist Review*, September.

Thomas, M. (2009a) 'How Vestas Workers Became a Power', *Solidarity*, 3/156, 30 July.

——(2009b) 'Vestas: Maintain and Extend the Pickets!', www.workersliberty.org, 7 August.

——. (2009c) 'Vestas: Organise, Debate, Unite in Action: Building the Broader Campaign', *Solidarity*, 3/157, 20 August.

TUC (2009a) *Congress Report 2009*. London: TUC.

——(2009b) 'Wind Firm Blows Thousands on Dermatitis', *Risks*, 412, 27 June.

——(2009c) 'TUC Calls for Government Help in Halting Vestas Factory Closure', press release, 31 July.

Turner, A. (2009) Hansard HC Deb 21 July 2009, vol 496, col 803.

TUSDAC (2001) Note of Policy Group Meeting (11th), 17 December.

——(2005a) *Greening the Workplace: a report by the TUSDAC unions. June 2005*. London: TUC.

——(2005b) *Environmental priorities for the third term – 1. Energy, union capacity and transport*, 30 June 2005. London: TUC.

——(2009a) Minutes of the TUSDAC Working Group Meeting, 9 July.

——(2009b) Minutes of the TUSDAC Policy Group Meeting, 13 July.

Unison (2009a) 'Branch Acts on Threatened Green Jobs', press release, 23 July.

——(2009b) 'Derby Members Back Vestas Workers', press release, 4 August.

Unite (2009a) 'Unite Seeks Government Intervention to Save England's Wind Turbine Plants', press release, 19 May.

——(2009b) *Unite's Briefing on the Campaign to Save the Vestas Wind Turbine Plants in England*, May 2009. London: Unite.

——(2009c) *Unite's Submission to the House of Commons' Environment Audit Committee Green Jobs Inquiry*, 4 June 2009. London: Unite.

——(2009d) '"It's Not Too Late to Save England's Last Wind Turbine Plants" says Unite', press release, 21 July.

——(2010) *Unite General Secretary Election – Candidates' Messages, October 2010*. London: Unite.

Vestas (2009) *Annual Report 2009*. Randers: Vestas Wind Systems A/S.

Vidal, J. (2008) 'UK Wind Farm Plans on Brink of Failure', *The Observer*, 19 October.

——(2009) 'Dawn of a Renewable Energy Era as Government Unveils Climate Plans', *The Guardian*, 15 July.

Walker, P. (2009) 'Protesters at Vestas Wind Systems Plant Fired by Food Parcel', *Guardian website*, 28 July.

Walker, T. (2009a) '600 Face Sack at Turbine Plant', *Socialist Worker*, 2159, 11 July.

——(2009b) 'Vestas: Fighting for Jobs and the Environment', *Socialist Worker*, 2160, 18 July.

Weaver, M. and Morris, S. (2009) 'Staff Occupy Isle of Wight Wind Turbine Plant in Protest against Closure', www.guardian.co.uk, 21 July.

Webb, T. (2009a) 'Closure of Turbine Factory Takes the Wind Out of Britain's Low-Carbon Sails', *The Guardian*, 29 April.

——(2009b) 'Vestas UK Chief Says Britain Must Speed Up Windfarm Construction', www.guardian.co.uk, 7 August.

——(2011) 'Wind Turbine Maker Skykon in Administration', *The Guardian*, 6 January.

Williams, R. (2009a) 'Vestas Wind Turbine Pickets Mount 21st Century-Style Protest', www.guardian.co.uk, 24 July.

——(2009b) 'Vestas Wins Court Order as Protest Spreads', www.guardian.co.uk, 4 August.

7 Climate and class

A missing link

Introduction

Climate change raises gargantuan questions about humanity's relationship with the planet. Climate is an important influence moulding human culture, while human society is now an agent affecting climate in ways unimaginable in previous epochs. Climate change is simultaneously interconnected with many other significant global inequalities. It is the result of interactions between the planetary ecosystem and international socioeconomic relations, and characterised by large uncertainties. Climate change denotes causes, effects and policies from global to local scales and as a result, requires international and interdependent solutions, without excluding unilateral action.

Newell and Paterson (2010: 7) pose the overarching research question within this field: what will determine whether, as a society, we can avoid the most dangerous aspects of climate change? This chapter addresses the question in light of mainstream approaches and the findings from trade union practices. It also returns to the specific questions posed in the introduction. The first section discusses whether workers organised in trade unions possess the interest and power to tackle dangerous climate change, and whether unionised workers can become strategic climate actors. The second section appraises the variable geometry of union climate politics in light of the UK trade union experience with climate change, and addresses whether trade unionism in the twenty-first century can succeed in reinventing itself as a social movement capable of tackling climate change. The third section discusses some of the implications of the book for climate politics, employment relations and trade unions.

Climate change and workers

The failure of current climate politics

By the second decade of the twenty-first century, the climate emergency had reached a new level. Greenhouse gas emissions from fossil fuel use were continuing to increase, with the 400ppm threshold exceeded. New forms of extreme energy from unconventional sources (such as fracking and tar sands) became more significant, with rising demand for coal, oil and gas. Despite numerous high-level gatherings, the promised transition to a low-carbon economy is not taking place, or at least not at a pace commensurate with the scale of the climate threat. No global agreement to reduce emissions has been signed, while multilateral efforts such as EU ETS are barely functioning. At the same time, fuel poverty increases. Technological fixes such as CCS are not deployed on the scale required, nor is renewable energy rolled out to the extent necessary. Without a drastic change of direction, the catastrophic prognoses of a 4°C rise in average global temperatures by the end of the century appear more likely.

The dominant approaches to climate change discussed in Chapter 2 have been unable to adequately answer the question of how society can avoid the most dangerous aspects of climate change. Neoliberal and ecological modernisation discourses neither do justice to the magnitude of climate change nor conceive of the scale of transformation necessary to tackle it. Neoliberal proponents believe markets are the answer, while ecological modernists look to technology and to the state for solutions. A range of powerful critiques suggest these mainstream framings do not adequately explain the social mechanisms that give rise to emissions. Further, the dominant discourses look to precisely the same social agents (capital and its states), which have caused climate change, to put it right. Their failings are evident from the continued growth in greenhouse gas emissions and the inability of businesses, nation states and international bodies to find the means to curb them. Some scholars point out that these framings do not adequately account for the unequal impacts of climate change and climate policy, particularly on workers. These failures suggest the search for an alternative approach, which could explain the social causes and impacts of climate change, while pointing to potential actors who could galvanise the movement to tackle it.

A different approach is needed, taking the evolving physical science of climate as its basis, but also one that uses insights from disciplines such as politics, sociology, geography, political economy and international relations. Normatively, such an approach to climate change would be socially grounded and explicitly political, avoiding the apparent technocratic neutrality of positivistic scientism that characterises neoliberal and ecological modernisation discourses. It would question existing power relations at different scales, challenge powerful vested interests and avoid rationalising business-as-usual. It would critically employ conceptions such as structure and agency to make sense of the context for social transformation and the potential forces that might carry this out. This book proposes a Marxist approach, with explicit emphasis on workers and their trade unions as crucial to this alternative conception.

Another climate politics is possible

The Marxist approach articulated in Chapter 2 rejects the dualistic framing of climate change in the hegemonic discourses. Instead labour is posited as the crucial nexus of nature and society. Climate change is an expression of what Smith (1984) called the 'production of nature' and results from the social relations of production of contemporary global capitalism. Climate change indicates deep-seated contradictions within this mode of production all the way down. An important strand of Marxist literature suggests that to alter the way the climate is changed, it is necessary to supersede the dominant social relations of production.

The relationship between class and climate is often disputed, even by writers sympathetic to organised labour. Class is best understood as the product of exploitation. Class-as-exploitation provides the most convincing conception of class, and one that is most useful for elaborating on the social-climate nexus. The process of class formation under capitalism begins with the extraction of surplus labour time through lengthening the working day, making work more intensive through the application of technology and through the reorganisation of the labour process. These processes connect workers' exploitation and ecological degradation and are extended here to include climate change. The commodification of labour power and the 'free gifts of nature' (including the atmosphere) are the parallel processes through which capital simultaneously exploits labour while imperilling the biosphere.

More concretely, some scholars suggest that workers and working-class communities are often most vulnerable to the impacts of environmental degradation (and climate change in particular), with the fewest individual resources to adapt to it. Similarly, extending this argument to climate change, workers and working-class communities already face the impacts of floods, storms, droughts and wildfires. Globally, workers are already experiencing water shortages, food price hikes and health impacts, and can expect these to worsen as global and local temperatures increase, sea levels rise and ecosystems are further disrupted. The impact of climate policy on workers as a specific social group has largely been neglected in climate discussion. Yet workers are often expected to pay for the costs of climate policies, whether through higher prices, increased taxes or the loss of employment.

Generally workers are represented as the passive victims of changes foisted on them from the outside (such as unemployment) or as backward-facing seekers of special privileges opposing necessary climate action. Often they are simply lumped together with employers as productivists. These representations ignore the possibility that climate impacts constitute good reasons for collective workers' climate action. An adequate conceptualisation of climate change would take the impacts on social inequalities and power into account. The actual lived experience of workers, the deep-seated structures that shape their lives and the expected impacts of future climate change, provide workers with a special, concrete interest in climate matters. Their location within the dominant social relations of production also provides workers with the collective capacity to affect the way climate change is tackled.

Workers and climate agency

The foregrounding of workers in actually-existing climate politics challenges the undifferentiated 'we' in questions about whether an heterogeneous 'society' can avoid the most dangerous aspects of climate change. Class divisions mean 'we' should not assume the same structures that gave rise to climate change in the first place will continue; more tersely, 'we' cannot rely on the same business and state actors who caused the problem to tackle it. Society itself is divided and riven asunder. This is what is wrong with efforts to promote climate capitalism. If capital and its states are the progenitors of climate change, then the worker-based approach challenges the role of capital and existing states as part of the solution. The interdependence of finance and other forms of capital means that no section of private business is considered to have sufficient interest in combating climate change. This is also likely to proscribe the latitude existing states have to take action on the issues. A fresh approach requires a critical distance from business actors and their supporters on climate matters. The ability of non-state actors such as NGOs, given their ties with capital and lack of autonomous political power, to tackle climate change at a deep structural level should be questioned. This does not imply a sectarian assault on climate activist campaigns. If climate NGOs want to tackle climate change, then they cannot rely on the philanthropy of capital, nor become satellites of its states. Politically, class criteria introduce a vital metric to clarify who are climate enemies and where climate allies can be found.

The approach promulgated here does privilege one particular social actor, namely, waged workers. The contention is that organised labour is the most advantageous starting point to develop a climate counter-power. Class organisations are collectivities that workers form in order to advance their class interests. These range from highly self-conscious organisations such as trade unions and political parties to much looser forms of social networks, caucuses and committees. These organisations, if they articulate workers' interests in class terms, are capable of cohering a powerful climate movement. The labour movement is a potential site where a global political vision on climate change can evolve, directly confronting existing socio-ecological relations and empowering a coherent alternative vision. Climate activists could make alliances and join coalitions with organised labour to form a working-class-based climate movement. This would be a social movement with workers' self-activity at its core.

It is possible to identify some important climate stirrings among trade unions internationally, which suggest workers have both the interest and the power to challenge the dominant climate politics, as well as the motivation and capacity to establish an alternative climate politics. Chapters 3 and 4 discuss the ways in which workers' interests are articulated in trade union climate politics, though class considerations are subordinate to ecological modernisation framings in official union discourse. Starting from a core interest in the employment implications of climate change, some trade unionists have gone further with the concept of 'just transition', questioning the distributional consequences of existing climate policy and perceiving workers as likely to lose out further in any market-led transition to a low-carbon economy. Radical thinkers identify existing property relations as responsible for these outcomes and advance democratic public ownership (or 'energy democracy') as part of the solution to tackling climate change. Similarly, challenges to the nature of work, the contemporary labour process and the purpose of current production raise, albeit embryonically, questions about the dominant social relations of production. These class framings indicate distinctive workers' interests on climate change, and provide good reasons to expect workers' collective action in climate politics.

Social agency concerns not only actors' reasons for action but also their capacity to respond. Chapters 5 and 6 examine distinctive forms of workers' action on climate change. Workplace union climate representation embraces a wide range of activities, from fairly low-level interventions for energy saving and recycling, to more ambitious elements of strategic planning and control. The involvement of trade union reps in workplace decision-making on climate matters, from the energy systems used in workplaces to transport arrangements for staff, suggest novel avenues for climate mitigation and adaptation. Given the importance of work relations in generating greenhouse gas emissions, workers have a vital role to play in embedding low-carbon practices in workplaces. Union reps already provide a glimpse of the enormous potential in this area of climate politics (LRD 2007; TUC 2009, 2012).

More radical mobilisation, including forms of industrial action and solidarity with workers taking collective action, is discussed in Chapter 6. The Vestas workers who occupied their workplace and their colleagues outside who supported them indicated a strong commitment to carbon-mitigating employment. Their response was more than simply disappointment with redundancy; rather, workers had taken seriously the low-carbon transition promised by the firm and the government. Similarly, the climate solidarity offered by other trade unionists, workplace reps and climate activists around Vestas was sufficiently powerful to rock both the employer and the government for many weeks and put climate politics at the centre of public discussion. The Vestas struggle was defeated, but it is unlikely to be the last occasion where workers take militant forms of collective action on climate matters. The occupation exhibited the unique if often latent power of organised labour to struggle for climate justice.

Trade unions, as organisations of waged workers, have a general ecological interest in preventing climate change, due to the interdependence of exploitation and climate degradation, and because of the impacts of climate change and climate policy on workers (including but not restricted to employment). More significantly, trade unions retain the capacity to affect substantial as well as smaller changes at various scales throughout the production process, through their own activities (including forms of industrial action), together with implementing measures agreed with employers. Recent UK union experience provides some evidence for these propositions. Organised workers are potentially strategic climate actors, whose capacities and interests to tackle climate change are generated by the social structures that shape other aspects of their lives.

It is pertinent to ask whether the trade union climate activity discussed in this research was limited to the temporal and spatial context of early twenty-first-century UK politics. Was it the strategically selective context of a globalising political economy experiencing uneven and combined development, the prospect of a successor to Kyoto and the Labour governments between 1997 and 2010, which explain why these forms of climate action flourished? While some UK trade unionists took advantage of the opportunities available during this period, they were neither tied to the Labour government's climate policies nor greatly assisted by them. Trade union representatives articulated their own versions of climate politics almost a decade before the Labour government came to office. Discourses such as just transition, originating in the North American labour movement and propagated through high-level international union channels, pre-dated Labour in power. Although significant developments took place between 1997 and 2010, union climate politics continued to flourish despite the economic downturn and changes of administration. The tenacity of union reps in the face of adversity is remarkable.

Similarly, forms of union climate action are not confined to the UK, developing in Europe, as well as in the United States, Australia and elsewhere across the globe (Vitols *et al.* 2011; Snell and Fairbrother 2011; Räthzel and Uzzell 2013). Climate politics began to be integrated into trade union internationalism during this period, weaving threads of climate solidarity that are likely to endure. Such internationalism does not rest simply on identical conditions or the superficial commonality of experience; rather, it presupposes a collective economic interest based on the universal interdependent exploitation of waged labour by capital. The changing structures of capitalism, particularly in its recent incarnation as neoliberal globalisation, drive trade unionists to consider international solidarity. Similarly, the unevenness of the workers' movement globally makes such solidarity necessary. Working-class internationalism also requires a common political vision and has to be actively organised, with union leaders and members open to learning lessons from distant struggles as well as those closer to home.

Trade unions and climate politics

Recent research discussed in Chapter 2 has begun to grapple with trade union intervention into the climate realm. Hyman (2001) attempts to capture the variable geometry of trade union ideology, which is fruitful for assessing the strengths and limitations of unions as climate actors. He argues that trade unions inevitably face in three directions: towards the market, society and class. Unions as climate actors are buffeted by competing pressures of the structures that define them and by other agents within these contexts. The trichotomy parallels three distinguishable conceptions of climate politics: neoliberalism, ecological modernisation and Marxism.

Other insights into the potential role of unions as climate actors can be gained from social movement unionism. This conception requires unions to lead not only their own members into climate action, but also to draw in their wake other workers, their communities and fellow dissenting actors. Labour geographers also offer some important insights into the challenges faced by unions as climate actors. While there is a positive emphasis on the need to 'bring workers back in', these critics warn that the uneven spatial terrain can constrain workers' action. Labour geography cautions against local boosterism, which accommodates with capital and states while masquerading as new labour internationalism. It highlights the dangers of economistic 'militant particularism' – taking assertive industrial action for conservative goals – for working-class ecology. Instead, a more transformative solidarity is necessary for climate change to become integral to the core mission of organised labour.

Hyman (2004) asked whether trade unionism in the twenty-first century can succeed by reinventing itself as a virtual social movement. By the end of the first decade of the twenty-first century, many union representatives in the UK had begun to engage with climate politics for the first time. Climate change became a more strategic policy priority for some union leaderships internationally. Some union representatives took the science of climate change and translated it into the politics of employment relations. They recast earlier concerns about government industrial strategy, fiscal policy and poverty-reduction in climate terms, giving added relevance to union political intervention. These union representatives emphasised the work dimension, both in terms of the causes of climate change and the consequences rising temperatures will bring, as a direct result of a changing climate and indirectly from government and employers' policies to mitigate and adapt to climate change. Climate politics became a trade union issue, while many unions and their representatives became actors in the embryonic climate movement.

The promise of climate solidarity is tempered by the extent to which some trade unions accommodate to the dominant ecological modernisation and neoliberal climate discourses. Although a minority of trade unionists, activists and some leaders did grasp the significance of climate change and did begin to act on it, trade unions have not sufficiently transformed themselves, their policies, structures and orientation, either to direct a comprehensive range of climate struggles or to hegemonise the nascent climate movement. The evidence suggests that most unions in the UK still have some distance to travel before becoming fully social movements dedicated to climate goals.

There is a danger of conflating workers' objective interests with their subjective motivations, and the risk of assuming that trade unions *per se* (in fact, their current leading representatives) articulate consistently the interests of their own particular members, never mind the general interests of workers. There is no mechanical relationship between workers, unions and class consciousness in the climate realm, as elsewhere. Beneath general-isations about workers and their organisations lies what Gramsci (1971) regarded as 'contradictory consciousness', a mixture of different ideological and material pressures, with framings ranging from more superficial common sense to quite profound appreciations.

Similarly, while there may be some advantages to examining the formal positions expressed by trade unions, it is understood that these are generally the views of the union leaders at particular conjunctures. These views are themselves subject to change in different conditions and indeed to challenge, not simply from other union bodies but also crucially within trade unions themselves, from other factions vying for leadership and indeed from other lower-level officials and ordinary members. To speak of 'workers' and of 'unions' as if they were a single entity is to oversimplify the matter. Trade unionism, like other social movements, involves collective action as well as individual choices, various networks and ultimately rich, often contradictory and varied debates. The top-down view will need to be supplemented with bottom-up approaches that capture the tensions and contradictions between and within collective organisations such as trade unions.

Class-based trade union climate action

This investigation of trade unions in recent decades has found a number of significant examples of a class-based and worker-focused climate politics. At least three prominent areas stand out. First, radical conceptions of just transition, climate jobs and energy democracy indicate the development of a class-based ideology, in which the interests of workers are articulated and climate change is framed in class terms. Similar embryonic considerations apply to some union stances on the public ownership of vital climate infra-structure such as the railways; the emphasis on socially useful production; and on distributional issues of winners and losers from climate policies. Second, forms of climate representation at work exhibit elements of sub-jective working-class formation and organisation. Third, union involvement in the Vestas occupation and other public demonstrations indicate distinctive forms of working-class mobilisation.

In Chapter 3, it was suggested that just transition is probably the most fertile union climate conception developed so far, synthesising the climate perspectives of organised labour and making a distinctive theoretical inter-vention into the complex world of climate politics. Just transition pro-blematises the idea of a low-carbon economy, by asserting the irreplaceable role of the workers who will bring it about. At this level, it draws into question the structure and content of the low-carbon terminus. Minimally, just transition poses unavoidable questions of who pays collectively and individually for this evolution and asks how society will equitably divide up the costs and benefits. In the stronger, more radical form originally envisaged by Mazzocchi, just transition could represent an effort to articulate specifically workers' interests in the process, taking a long-term strategic view of the trajectory of the world economy and the likely restructuring ahead, within which unions will need to represent members' interests.

However, the official union version of just transition internationally (and in the UK) largely boils down to some sort of government intervention to counteract the market. Despite some formal recognition of weaker versions of just transition at international and national levels, it is a long way from being implemented by any existing states. Critics rightly argue that unions need to make just transition more concrete, with a sharper focus on what exactly the low-carbon destination will look like. Just transition, even its more top-down, bureaucratic and partnership incarnations, is still a breach with neoliberal climate assumptions. But a just transition clause in any new climate agreements is only of value if it stimulates a real transition to a low-carbon economy – and therein lies the problem (Sweeney 2014). Just transition is also susceptible to co-option by the ecological modernisation discourse, as recognised by Labour politicians and encouraged by some trade union leaders.

Chapter 3 also discusses trade union conceptions of 'green jobs' – and more radically of 'climate jobs' – to capture the kind of decent work that workers expect in a low-carbon economy. For some trade unionists, green jobs extend beyond work that directly concerns climate protection, to embrace an amorphous variety of jobs. While the broadening of green jobs to include most existing work makes tactical sense in terms of universalising the necessary transformation of all employment relations, the lack of precise definition and blurriness at the edges weakens its utility. It requires additional clarity about socially useful and climatically sensitive work. Climate jobs are more narrowly defined, in terms of work that contributes to emissions reduction and adaptation, though this still encompasses a wide range of employment across energy and transport. However, the class element is brought out in two distinctive ways. First, these jobs would be direct, public sector jobs and explicitly subject to democratic oversight, not exposed to market pressures nor contracted out to the private sector. Second, workers in sectors affected by emissions reductions could seek alternative employment in this 'National Climate Service', thereby tackling the vexed issue of unemployment (Neale 2010). In this conception of climate jobs, workers would gain from the transition to a low-carbon economy.

Similar emphasis with class connotations is the demand for public ownership of vital climate infrastructure. Most visible in the UK is the appeal to renationalise the privatised railway system (and to a lesser extent the buses), as part of an integrated publicly-owned transport plan. The demand has a distinctive climate edge, given lower emissions from rail and bus transport compared with cars, lorries and aeroplanes. It is also considered a remedy for higher fares and for new investment, instead of profits drained off to shareholders and exorbitant management salaries. In the UK, although NUM and TUC leaders continue to demand the nationalisation of the remaining coal industry, union officials elsewhere in the energy sector and the TUC do not currently demand social ownership of electricity generation, nuclear or gas industries, despite comparable climate and other benefits from doing so. This reflects the political calculations of senior trade union officials, seeking to preserve their insider status. However, other activists, union members and more radical union leaders are more supportive of demands for public ownership.

There is some limited evidence of a revival of 'socially useful production' by some trade union activists, and what has been called 'energy democracy' within climate change discourse (Sweeney 2012). In the UK, this harks back to earlier discussions, particularly the Lucas Aerospace and other workers' plans, which understood socially useful work in terms of energy conservation, reducing waste and non-alienating labour. Although not fully developed in contemporary discussion and some way from earlier related discussions of workers' control of production, these embryonic ideas put workers at the centre of climate transitions and more profoundly challenge the assumptions made by the dominant discourses.

As we saw in Chapter 4, there is a significant emphasis in UK trade union publications on wider distributional issues of winners and losers from climate policies. On a national level, union leaders were prepared to challenge the windfall profits from the EU ETS and to demand that this revenue be spent tackling fuel poverty or on new climate infrastructure projects. Similarly, some workplace climate reps engaged with their employers over the distribution of gains from emissions reductions, in the form of bonuses for workers or to use revenue to improve job security. 'Cut carbon, not jobs' became more than merely a slogan during the economic downturn: where employers made financial gains from energy efficiency measures implemented by their employees, some union reps campaigned for this revenue to be used to benefit workers through maintaining employment levels or increasing wages.

Chapter 5 indicates further articulations of worker interest in climate matters, with trade union climate representation at work exhibiting important elements of class organisation. Some union reps became active climate subjects. This form of climate representation is unique, novel and dynamic. For climate politics, it provides a unique focus on worker representation and employee voice. There is significant evidence from the UK context that union reps could act as drivers in workplaces and communities to tackle climate change. The Green Workplaces projects provide substantial evidence that union reps could become strategic climate actors in the workplace and their wider communities. Union surveys discussed in Chapter 5 evidence several thousand union climate activists in public and private sector workplaces. This layer of union reps report a plethora of activities where carbon reduction at work took place at their instigation or at least (when the initiative came from management) with their active support. Significant reductions in workplace carbon emissions were accompanied by widespread worker participation, including specially-organised committees, conferences, forums and film shows. A handful of formal workplace agreements were signed between unions and employers. In other cases, workers and their representatives undertook training in climate awareness. More widely, these union carbon activists organise in networks, sometimes through their individual unions but also via unofficial campaigns. Although the role attracted some new faces, including younger members, women and black and minority ethnic workers, these representatives were still mainly drawn from the pool of existing, if somewhat reinvigorated union activists.

Chapter 6 highlights a third form of class-based activity, namely climate mobilisation. At the height of an economic downturn, the Vestas occupation was the most high-profile example and went furthest in challenging the dominant climate framings. Vestas workers' motivation had a more overtly climate dimension because some had been attracted to the plant out of the desire to produce green technologies for green energy, while others believed government rhetoric about the shift to a low-carbon economy. The direct action taken by workers in the face of redundancy, coupled with the show of solidarity they received from other workers and climate activists, pointed to a distinctive worker-based approach to progressing climate politics. The Vestas occupation was remarkable because it took place in a sector with little previous collective trade union organisation. While resistance may have appeared less likely when closure was announced, after encouragement from external activists and trade unionists, some workers at the plant were less constrained by union officialdom once they decided on a more radical course of action. Support from the RMT, acting more like a social movement union, provided an organisational skeleton after the occupation had begun.

Vestas workers did not receive a level of international or domestic solidarity sufficient to keep the plant open. However, the imaginative direct action that featured in the solidarity protests around the occupation was significant. Activists organised solidarity in dozens of places across Britain to support the Vestas workers. Although the campaign was unable to keep the plant open, it prevented closure for additional weeks and thereby secured better redundancy terms for most of those affected. The protests were significant beyond the plant and the locality, extending to the wider national climate debate. The protests also revealed deep-seated climate solidarity that transcended the particular local context of the dispute.

Finally, some union leaders have also been prepared to mobilise members to take action on climate change, both at work and with wider national campaigning organisations. The most spectacular example internationally was the 21 September 2014 mobilisations across the globe. In the UK, high points include The Wave and G20 demonstrations in 2009. Taking action on climate change went beyond largely passive financial support or signing postcards. Taking initiatives at work or in communities, whether it was organising a film show and discussion, putting on an exhibition, or more confrontational forms of direct action indicated that organised workers could chart a new climate path of their own volition. However, a working-class-based climate approach was never the dominant framing within UK unions during this period, with the exception of the Vestas occupation.

Between class and ecological modernisation

Ecological modernisation framings were highly prominent with global climate politics around the turn of the century and trade union bodies internationally reflected this discourse in their own articulations of climate politics. This research found similar themes in the UK context, where most trade union leaders and TUC representatives subscribe to ecological modernisation, rather than class-struggle climate politics. Ecological modernisation framing is evident in union submissions to UN climate negotiations. Globally, most unions support the Kyoto Protocol and back demands for emissions targets. They had some success in getting a minimal notion of just transition acknowledged within UNFCCC texts and eventually gaining a formal role within the COP climate process, though the failure at Copenhagen cauterised this recognition.

A strong orientation towards ecological modernisation was also evident within UK domestic politics. Union support for government climate policy was explicitly sought from the beginning of the Labour government, when Tony Blair invited union leaders to contribute to climate policy after Kyoto. With the establishment of the joint union–government body TUSDAC to oversee this collaboration, union leaders became significant players supporting the Labour government's climate policy. TUC officials supported the Stern Review and the Climate Change Act in ecological modernist terms, taking up both government mitigation targets and adaptation proposals. When the Labour government turned towards an active green industrial strategy after the onset of recession, TUC officials were among its most high-profile backers. This orientation towards an active, interventionist industry policy continued under the Coalition government.

Union leaders' support for the Labour government's climate policy was consistent, but it was not uncritical. For example, Unison backed the Friends of the Earth campaign for an 80 per cent emissions reduction target for 2050, going beyond the government's more cautious opening proposal of 60 per cent. TUC leaders asked the government to go further with fiscal proposals such as taxing energy companies. Emphasis on adaptation showed that they understood the need to make climate politics as much about immediate issues affecting workers in the present, rather than simply a matter of targets and restructuring for the future. This approach reflected certain criticisms of the dominant, top-down climate regime.

The partnership approach articulated by TUC officials fitted with the ecological modernisation discourse. This research found evidence of support for technological fixes and for social dialogue. A number of individual union and TUC leaders saw climate change as a vehicle for promoting their conception of partnership with government and employers, emphasising the 'non-adversarial' potential for collaboration around emissions reduction. Some participants in the Green Workplaces projects also saw relations as non-confrontational. While some employers clearly welcomed the opportunity to work with union reps for common environmental objectives, other managers saw the intervention of unions as at best an unhelpful distraction or worse as an unwanted encroachment onto their own sphere of decision-making. But union reps are not generally doing the bosses' or the government's work on climate matters. Indeed, they often have to struggle against the wishes of their employers and managers to gain a voice on climate questions at work.

The ecological modernisation approach is also evident with CCS, where TUC and energy union leaders promoted an explicitly technological fix with important potential for emissions abatement. The union framing of CCS should not be reduced simply to a sectional defence of existing jobs, though the potential for future jobs cannot be discounted. Rather, support for CCS is a pragmatic response to conditions in British industry and globally, with wider applicability to steel, ceramics and other energy-intensive industries affected by climate policy. Given the scale of coal reserves and the extent of global demand, the idea of 'leaving it in the ground' seemed to have little grip. Support for a technology that could limit emissions from fossil fuel energy and heavy industry is consistent with workers' climate interests and living standards at various scales. However, more concrete questions about new coal-fired power stations remain problematic, as long as the technology has not been scaled up and rolled out.

Between class and the market

While much of UK union framing of climate issues resides between class and ecological modernisation, there is also some evidence of accommodation to market approaches, reflecting some of the structural and ideological pressures on unions. This is consistent with international and other UK research. Most union leaders and TUC officials are critical supporters of the EU ETS, or at least did not actively oppose it. Although some union leaders were sceptical about emissions trading when it was first mooted in the early 1990s, they pragmatically came to support EU ETS once it took shape. In the context of climate change, some warn about carbon leakage, but often in protectionist and sectionalist terms identical to those of employers.

However, this accommodation to mainstream neoliberal climate policy is accompanied by some distinctive demands. TUC officials call for revenues raised by the sale of permits to be used for fuel poverty reduction, for a windfall tax on profits made from permit trading and for putting ETS on the bargaining agenda of workplace reps. As the scheme took shape, unions took a more critical stance, mainly because of the consequences for energy-intensive industries, where UK unions had a higher density of members. Union officials succeeded in getting recognition of the role of employee representation in the Carbon Reduction Commitment (CRC), even though it was originally a measure aimed solely at employers.

More controversially, as we saw in Chapter 4, the dominant union approach on aviation was outright support for a third runway at Heathrow. Although this was justified by the thin veneer of EU ETS, it was inconsistent with a thoroughgoing commitment to emissions reductions. Union officials have emphasised occupational and employment considerations on climate change since the late 1980s. This is reflected in the least climate-conscious positions taken on energy-intensive industries and on aviation. However, some other unions, including those with members in the aviation industry, recognise the contradiction and joined the opposition to airport expansion. Even within more market-orientated policy, union officials made efforts to incorporate workers' concerns, to widen worker representation and to open new fields of collective bargaining, such as with EU ETS and the CRC.

Implications

This book makes an original contribution to climate politics and employment relations in three significant respects. First, starting from Marxist conceptions of the production of nature and global political economy, it highlights the relationship between the exploitation of waged labour by capital and the parallel processes of climate degradation by capital. The mechanism identified is the form taken by the transformation of the labour process under capitalism, whereby the real subsumption of labour to capital (the production of relative surplus value through work intensification, reorganisation and mechanisation) simultaneously involves the utilisation of huge quantities of energy, the vast consumption of natural resources and immense waste. The process now involves the commodification of the climate itself – what is dubbed *the real subsumption of climate to capital* – and under capitalism leads to an irreparable rift in the metabolism between climate and society.

Second, the book foregrounds the class dimension, developing a conception of workers and their organisations under certain conditions as strategic climate actors, agents whose exploitation and resistance to it is in symmetry with their struggles for climate protection. Thus workers possess a deep-rooted interest in climate mitigation and adaptation, and through collective bodies such as trade unions (as well as other mass democratic associations) the capacity to tackle the perpetrators. The very structures that generate and reproduce waged labour also enable self-conscious workers to collectively tackle both the root of their exploitation and related ecological matters. This goes beyond the plausible conception of workers as hardest hit by both ecological events and environmental regulation.

Third, the book extends the variable geometry of trade unionism articulated by Hyman (2001) to ecological and climate matters, highlighting how individual trade unions and their representatives at various levels are subject to the simultaneous material and ideological pressures of the market, the state and class. This conception contributes to an explanation of the actual behaviour of trade union leaders, elected and appointed representatives as well as rank-and-file members when faced with climate questions. These insights, along with those of social movement unionism and labour geography, suggest a conception of climate-conscious and class-conscious trade unionism. The research found evidence for these claims in fresh and previous neglected data on recent UK trade union efforts to engage with climate change over the last generation.

The methodology employed in this research was chiefly the critical analysis of published and unpublished texts, speeches, briefing papers and submissions produced by elected trade union leaders and their full-time officials. The advantage of this method is to represent the arguments articulated by these key individuals and other representatives, often in their own words, and to express their interpretation of their organisation's interest in climate matters. Given the neglect of this data – especially in the UK context – such an approach adds considerably to our knowledge. However, it also has limitations: the research largely captures the evolution of official union discourses, rather than attempting to engage with the processes generating such discourses.

These sources were supplemented by the critical interpretation of some trade union survey data, alongside a small sample of interviews with trade union and government officials on just transition and the use of blog posts as additional written sources. The need for additional materials arose from recognition of the limitations of documentary sources, written deliberately for certain political audiences and which would not necessarily articulate clearly all the key issues under consideration. The surveys consist of detailed returns from a self-selected group of trade union reps, who are not necessarily representative of the whole population. However, qualitative data retrieved from open questions in these surveys provide important indications of trade union representatives' attitudes towards climate mitigation and adaptation, and the possibilities for affecting such change at work. In addition, some of the contradictions and tensions – for example, over car parking and the benefits of energy saving – between workers and their employers, and between different groups of employees, came to light through these surveys.

Further insight into the deeper meaning and understanding of climate change for these union representatives and wider layers of workers, whether members of unions or not, could have been garnered from conducting more semi-structured interviews. This method has been utilised internationally (Räthzel and Uzzell 2011) to understand and reconstruct high-level union framings, and in Britain for non-union climate champions (Lewis and Juravle 2010; Swaffield and Bell 2012). Although more high-level officials in the UK context could have been interviewed, it was felt that their views were already well represented in the documents they had authored or contributed to. Hearing the views and voices of wider layers of union representatives would shed further light on strategies to tackle climate change.

Implications for the field of climate politics

If the central question is how to avoid the most dangerous aspects of climate change, then mobilising workers, who possess the collective capacity, interest and organisation to tackle climate change, is a positive conclusion that follows from this research. What does a focus on organised labour bring to the climate politics field of study? This book demands investigation into the deep structures and mechanisms that generate climate change in the first place and into the impacts of climate change on actual social formations on the other. Labour stands at the nexus of these concerns. The focus on labour also provides an exceptional metric for climate politics, if it is to tackle the question in an equitable and socially just fashion. As such, class structures provide a crucial lens for understanding the limits of the dominant framings of climate change and the possible alternatives to them. But class also proscribes agency. Organised labour, based on waged work and integral to every major society within global capitalism, is a social actor with significant reasons to tackle climate change and the potential power to address the forces, processes and structures that cause it.

The Vestas dispute discussed in Chapter 6 was a significant indicator of the state of climate politics in the UK in the first decade of the twenty-first century. It showed how far various climate actors were able to deliver on promises to promote a low-carbon economy. The closure of the wind turbine manufacturing plant reflected particularly badly on its owners. The firm gave the impression it was only interested in developing green production where it could make the highest returns. The BWEA industry body (now RenewableUK) was a weak advocate for the emerging industry. The factory occupation was equally calamitous for the Labour government, which had prioritised the low-carbon restructuring of the British economy. Just before the plant closure was announced, ministers declared that the UK was on the verge of a low-carbon industrial revolution. The Vestas occupation was a critical test for climate campaigns in the UK, which had become more prominent as climate change rose up the political agenda. The established environmental NGOs offered little more than nominal support to the Vestas workers during their struggle. By contrast, some radical activists played a very positive role with climate solidarity.

The main original contribution of this investigation for the climate politics field of study is to bring organised labour back in as an essential climate agent. The book makes the case for trade unions as strategic climate actors, worthy of further research within the field of climate politics. It outlines a conception of workers' climate action. The strength of the research design is that it depicts new insights and important relationships. But these are early steps in the field, where there is only limited recognition in the literature of these emergent developments. One weakness is the tentative investigation of wider social relations of climate. Some systematic mechanisms by which capitalism generates carbon emissions are mapped, but require further exploration. A related point is that the likely forms taken by the climate rift for workers need to be elaborated, beyond general risks from floods, famine and other impacts. If a neoliberal climate transition is effectively underway, it is important to chart its direction and effects. If not, it is important to understand what this means for workers and working-class communities. Enunciating the contours of a socially just, low-carbon society and the scope of climate jobs also remain work in progress.

Implications for the employment relations discipline

The British trade union movement has taken some significant steps towards making climate change an integral part of its basic mission. Within the discipline of employment relations, the study of climate change has become a legitimate line of enquiry. Many union leaders, reps and members are cognisant of the importance of climate change and its impacts on workers. Sections of organised labour are beginning to articulate a vision of a just, low-carbon society – in other words to formulate their own independent, class-focused conception of climate change. Workers and trade unions have also started to wage climate struggles for such objectives. Union climate activists are building their own official and unofficial networks to prioritise climate matters within and beyond their unions. The economic downturn did not stymie union concerns with climate change; on the contrary some linked recovery with the green restructuring of the economy. Some union-backed projects were able to demonstrate how their workplace interventions were reflected in quantifiable emissions reductions. Of course, these were generally in better organised workplaces and in organisations where union activity was already well established. With union density down to only a quarter of workers in the UK, a strategy of union-driven carbon abatement would also require a significant revival in union organising in workplaces that currently have little or no union presence.

The Vestas occupation provides a useful barometer of the variable contours of union climate politics. Unite, which had a handful of members at the plant before the occupation, made token efforts to keep it open, before retrenching to welfare advice. By contrast, the RMT put national and local resources into the struggle, demonstrating the possibilities of social movement unionism and the virtues of climate solidarity. The TUC did not play a prominent role in the Vestas occupation, although Vestas certainly made an impact on its proceedings. Vestas was not the harbinger of a new red–green alliance. Most of those who led the solidarity were already part of organised labour and active in the climate movement. It was the integration of climate concerns with workers' action that defined the new synthesis. Vestas came to illustrate the vitality of worker-led direct action in pursuit of climate jobs and the potential for workers' climate action, mobilisation and power. As probably the most significant example of class struggle over climate matters yet seen in the UK, Vestas may herald the future shape of effective climate politics.

Most union leaders internationally (and in the UK) are ambivalent about their enemies and allies in the climate process and to an extent accommodate to the dominant climate politics. They do not articulate a consistently anti-capitalist discourse, whose political conclusions follow from the assessment of capitalist production as the root of climate change. They remained within the parameters of market and society suggested by Hyman (2001). At the other end of the spectrum, few trade unionists currently frame climate change in terms of the metabolic rift or production of nature. Political representation for workers also remains vexed, at best in mostly social democratic forms internationally. The Labour Party is the only mass, union-backed electoral vehicle in British politics, yet it is not (despite some occasional promises) currently committed to empowering trade union climate action.

This book demonstrates the continuing relevance of the employment relations discipline and the significance of work to the field of climate studies. The vitality of the discipline will be confirmed by the ability of researchers to engage with emerging fields of study such as climate change. The interest taken by unions in climate change provides further proof that employment relations cannot simply be reduced to jobs and pay, though of course both matter for climate politics and for their own sake. The employment relations discipline confronts questions of who bears the costs of the transition and who may lose. The challenge for the discipline is to theorise the involvement of workers and unions in climate politics. The book highlights the possibilities for extending theories such as Hyman's geometry and social movement unionism into the realm of climate politics. More significantly, it contributes to an emerging field, what Uzzell and Räthzel (2013) call 'environmental labour studies'. There are further research possibilities within the field of employment relations. There is scope to examine the perspectives of individual trade unions in particular states as well as comparative studies of unions in other countries, to obtain a more detailed picture of different union stances towards climate change. The profile and activities of workplace representatives on climate change also deserve thorough investigation. More widely, research is needed on workers' perceptions of climate change, how they frame it and what they are prepared to do about it.

Implications for trade unions

If the findings of this book are accepted, then a rather different strategy for most trade unions and union leaders ought to follow. Trade unionists in the

UK have much to learn from international union engagement with environmental matters. Trade union reps will need to understand climate change mitigation, securing agreements at different scales of the state and in workplaces. This means assessing the impacts for workers of climate change itself and on government climate policy. Minimally, it involves an active low-carbon industrial policy with climate jobs at its heart, and the vigorous pursuit of adaptation strategies (such as indoor workplace temperature), where tangible improvements could be won on immediate issues that animate workers. However, trade unionists would have to challenge the dominant neoliberal and ecological modernisation orthodoxies, which foreground employer and state action with little regard to workers. A more independent, class-focused approach would involve substantial rethinking on issues such as EU ETS and aviation. It includes a sharper opposition to escalating fossil fuel extraction and utilisation. Minimally, it means contesting the private ownership and control of energy and transport infrastructure – especially the lack of democratic oversight of these vital climate levers. Maximally, it means imbuing visions of emancipation with a climate dimension.

A premium for trade union climate action is global workers' solidarity, grasping opportunities to help some workers make progress on climate issues – but not at the expense of other fellow workers. The task of unions, wherever they are, is to recruit new members as well as retain existing members. Increasing union density is a prerequisite for renewed generalised workers' power, but focusing on strategically important climate-related sectors in energy (particularly renewables) and transport would help unions meet their climate and wider political goals. Politically, climate change demands that unions re-examine notions such as a 'balanced' energy policy, which was always a fudge to satisfy competing interests but can no longer be used as a fig-leaf for the fossil fuel sector. Internally, it means reinvigorating the democratic channels between and within trade unions, bringing the oxygen of debate to climate deliberations.

A class-based approach would take a more critical stance towards trade union relations with other actors. It would abandon the wishful thinking of partnership with unwilling employers and governments. Of course trade unionists at all levels would continue to engage with these actors in bargaining and policy formulation, but no longer on the basis of the polite fiction of notional common interests. Instead, union representatives would articulate workers' collective interests, making alliances with climate activists on shared goals such as eliminating fuel poverty and opposing extreme energy (such as fracking). Finally, trade unions should redouble their efforts to put union reps' climate activities on a statutory footing, with the right to time off for activities, facilities and training. There is evidence that union reps could be catalysts for climate action in workplaces and communities. The demand to unshackle the unions now has an added green dimension to it. Such rights will not be conceded without serious campaigning. But for the sake of the climate and for workers' interests, they are rights well worth fighting for.

Conclusion

The approach set out in this book goes to the heart of the social, political and economic processes that cause climate change; or to put it differently, it identifies key mechanisms that drive greenhouse gas emissions. The drive to create surplus value (mainly in the form of profits) is vital for explaining the uncontrolled and unrestricted use of fossil fuels. The real subsumption of labour to capital is paralleled by the real subsumption of climate to capital, intersecting at the point where energy-intensive technologies are substituted for living labour in the competitive drive for increased profits. The continued and expanding exploitation of waged labour coincides with the degradation of the climate. The common root is the self-expansion of capital, which provides workers with the structural interest for tackling climate change simultaneously with their own exploitation.

The causes of climate change are intrinsic to the basic contradictions driving capitalism. Capital will seek to commodify the 'free gifts of nature', including the atmosphere. But these efforts are likely to fail, since prices generally do not reflect an optimal ecological 'value' under conditions of capitalist production. The flaws of market mechanisms result from the process of commodification itself. Technological change under these conditions will not take place for social need or climate restoration, but only for profit. Class struggles take place around technologies, concerning who benefits and who pays for innovations.

Can capitalism effectively respond to climate change? If capitalism is ultimately the systemic cause of climate change, then the owners and managers of capital (and their government representatives) are unlikely to be able to resolve it. As long as fossil fuel capitalism remains profitable, capital will find markets for these energy sources and further greenhouse gas emissions will result. But the critique does not dismiss all efforts at reforming capitalism. Capitalist structures can be moulded and shaped, as movements for change at work, for the vote, feminism, anti-racism and the environment movement have shown historically. Structural changes will have to take place on a global scale, involving a rapid retooling of production and distribution systems, particularly agriculture, energy, transport and urban structure. These will only come about as a result of massive, democratic public intervention and widespread global and national regulation of the market-based regime. Transitional reforms could limit the power of capital and point towards more social, planned and democratic forms of climate governance. Previous social movements show that capital and its states invariably have to be forced, often against their immediate interests, to tackle issues of great magnitude such as climate change. There is considerable experience in the labour movement of constructing united fronts around transitional demands to effect small-scale palliatives as well as more radical transformations.

Ultimately, a Marxist approach suggests that a society based on collective, democratic control over publicly-owned resources, as well as significant changes to the labour process (including working time and workers' control), would provide more rational social relations of production for avoiding climate change. A socialist system of 'sustainable communism' is the most appropriate structure for restoring the social-climate metabolism. Such a system could only result from working-class self-emancipation. It has nothing in common with previous Stalinist states. While this 'utopian' goal remains valid, no existing state currently fulfils these criteria, for socialism or for sustainability. Class matters to climate change. The focus on working-class politics provides insight into the mechanisms behind the emissions that bring about climate change, the impacts it will have (along with the phalanx of climate policies) and a sharper focus on the agents to tackle it. Above all, the forces of organised labour, principally the trade unions, are becoming climate actors internationally. This is the promise of climate solidarity.

A working-class-based climate movement, centred on the revived power and organisation of the trade unions, could represent a glimmer of hope after recent disappointments. Workers are likely to be confronted by the effects of climate change and to struggle against them regardless of what their employers, the state or environmental NGOs do about it. Trade unions could play an irreplaceable role in bringing workers into climate politics and shaping the goals and strategies employed to tackle climate change. The challenges of climate change should not be underestimated. But it was precisely for epoch-making struggles that the labour movement came into being. The confluence of class and climate is now a burning necessity.

References

Gramsci, A. (1971) *Selections from the Prison Notebooks*. London: Lawrence and Wishart.
Hyman, R. (2001) *Understanding European Trade Unionism: Between Market, Class and Society*. London: Sage.
——(2004) 'The Future of Trade Unions'. In A. Verma and T. Kochan (eds) *Unions in the 21st Century: An International Perspective*. Basingstoke: Palgrave Macmillan.
Lewis, A. and Juravle, C. (2010) 'Morals, Markets and Sustainable Investments: a Qualitative Study of "Champions"', *Journal of Business Ethics*, 93(3): 483–94.
LRD (2007) *The Environment and Climate Change: A Guide for Union Reps*. London: LRD.
Neale, J. (ed.) (2010) *One Million Climate Jobs: Solving the Economic and Environmental Crises*. London: Campaign against Climate Change.
Newell, P. and Paterson, M. (2010) *Climate Capitalism: Global Warming and the Transformation of the Global Economy*. Cambridge: Cambridge University Press.
Räthzel, N. and Uzzell, D. (2011) 'Trade Unions and Climate Change: The Jobs versus Environment Dilemma', *Global Environmental Change*, 21(4): 1215–23.
——(eds) (2013) *Trade Unions in the Green Economy: Working for the Environment*. London: Routledge.
Smith, N. (1984) *Uneven Development*. 1st edn. Oxford: Blackwell.
Snell, D. and Fairbrother, P. (2011) 'Toward a Theory of Union Environmental Politics: Unions and Climate Action in Australia', *Labor Studies Journal*, 36(1): 83–103.

Swaffield, J. and Bell, D. (2012) 'Can "Climate Champions" Save the Planet? A Critical Reflection on Neoliberal Social Change', *Environmental Politics*, 21(2): 248–67.

Sweeney, S. (2012) *Resist, Reclaim, Restructure: Unions and the Struggle for Energy Democracy*. New York: Cornell Global Labor Institute.

——(2014) 'Climate Change and the Great Inaction: New Trade Union Perspectives', Working Paper No. 2. New York: Trade Unions for Energy Democracy.

TUC (2009) *Unions and Climate Change*. London: LRD.

——(2012) *Green Unions at Work*. London: LRD.

Uzzell, D. and Räthzel, N. (2013) 'Introducing a New Field: Environmental Labour Studies'. In N. Räthzel and D. Uzzell (eds) *Trade Unions in the Green Economy: Working for the Environment*. London: Routledge.

Vitols, K., Schütze, K., Mestre, A., Chavanet, S., Marquant, S., Poupard, J-F. and Jakubowski, A. (2011) *Industrial Relations and Sustainability: the Role of Social Partners in the Transition Towards a Green Economy*, European Foundation for the Improvement of Living and Working Conditions, 29 June 2011. Dublin: Eurofound.

Index